CREATIVE
CASTING

CREATIVE CASTING

JEWELRY · SILVERWARE · SCULPTURE

BY

SHARR CHOATE

EDITED BY BONNIE CECIL DE MAY

DRAWINGS BY THE AUTHOR

PHOTOGRAPHS BY THE AUTHOR
EXCEPT WHERE OTHERWISE NOTED

CROWN PUBLISHERS, INC., NEW YORK

To Earle

THE AUTHOR WISHES TO EXPRESS HER APPRECIation and acknowledge her indebtedness to Bonnie Cecil De May for her time-consuming work in editing the original manuscript and for her assistance in organizing and preparing the material for publication.

She also wishes to express gratitude to Hugh Leiper, F.G.A., managing editor of the *Lapidary Journal,* who foresaw the need for a book on casting from the response to a series of articles on casting written for his magazine by the author.

Gratitude is also expressed for the assistance of Billie and Joe Bernstein, professional photographic specialists, for their advice regarding the photography.

Express gratitude is extended to the following craftsmen and manufacturers for their contributions of articles for photography, photographs of finished articles, of equipment, and photographs of equipment and information regarding various techniques: E. A. Anderson, San Jose, Calif.; Louis B. Beardslee, Woodside, Calif.; Lou Binkley, San Jose, Calif.; Dr. Robert Coleman, San Jose, Calif.; Ray Churchill, Los Gatos, Calif.; Anne Donnelly, Redwood City, Calif.; Ted Hammond, San Carlos, Calif.; Earle Krentzin, Livonia, Mich.; John Leary, San Jose, Calif.; Stanley Lechtzin, Philadelphia, Pa.; Ernest Mahlke, Oneonta, N.Y.; Bart Mann, San Angelo, Tex.; Ruth Noble, Orinda, Calif.; Helen Pegram, San Diego, Calif.; Henry Rianda, San Jose, Calif.; Edna Sayre, Los Altos, Calif.; Jayne Smith, Santa Clara, Calif.; and the San Francisco Museum of Art (Henri Matisse Richard O'Hanlon).

Also to: Acri-lux Dental Manufacturing Company, Long Island City, N.Y.; Emesco Dental Manufacturing Company, New York, N.Y.; Handler Manufacturing Company, Garwood, N.J.; J. F. Jelenko and Company, New Rochelle, N.Y. (technical information and photographs); Jeweler's Aids Company, Laurelton, N.Y.; Nelson Vacuum Pump Corporation, Berkeley, Calif.; Alexander Saunders and Company, New York, N.Y.; Southwest Smelting and Refining Company, Dallas Tex. (all technical information and photographs in Chapter 18); Tescom Corporation, Minneapolis, Minn.; Torit Corporation, St. Paul, Minn. (technical information and photographs); Whip-Mix Corporation, Louisville, Ky. (technical information and photographs); and Wilkinson Company, Santa Monica, Calif. (technical information and photographs).

Published by Crown Publishers, Inc., 225 Park Avenue South, New York, New York 10003.

CROWN is a trademark of Crown Publishers, Inc.

Manufactured in the United States of America

Library of Congress Catalog Card Number: 66-26172

ISBN 0-517-56174-3

10 9 8 7 6 5 4 3 2 1

First Paperback Edition, 1986

LIST OF COLOR PLATES

BLACK AND WHITE PHOTO CREDITS

Numerals indicate figure numbers, except where page is indicated.

Acri-Lux Dental Manufacturing Company, *26*
Anderson, E. A., *191–92, 194–97*
Coleman, Dr. Robert, *16, 70*
Emerson, Dorothy Taylor (of Dr. Coleman articles), all of page 126
Emesco Dental Manufacturing Company, *106*
Handler Manufacturing Company, *230–32*
Jelenko, J. F., and Company, *100, 107, 115, 249*
Jeweler's Aids, *18, 240*
Krentzin, Earle, *132–33*
Lechtzin, Stanley, *131*
Mahlke, Ernest, all of page 135
Nelson Vacuum Pump Corporation, *89*
Rianda, Henry, all of page 127

Saunders, Alexander, and Company, *90, 98–99, 105, 109, 200*
San Francisco Museum of Art, all of pages 133 and 134
Southwest Smelting and Refining Company, *308–16*
Tescom Corporation, *121–22*
Torit Corporation, *78, 89, (right), 103, 122 (right), 302*
Whip-Mix Corporation, *80–81, 102, 108*
Wilkinson Company, *111–12*

All other photographs in color, black and white, and all illustrations not acknowledged above are by the author

Foreword

THOUGH CASTING IS ONE OF THE OLDEST ART crafts, only in recent years has the novice craftsman become interested in exploring the many possibilities it has to offer for expanding his activities into working with precious metals and creating more intricate and larger objects. It is to fill the need for definite information on the subject that this book has been written.

As the "lost wax" method is the most popular form of casting, because it gives the craftsman the greatest degree of accurate replacement of an original model, it has been treated in detail. However, sand and cuttlefish bone casting, limited to uncomplicated models, and hollow core casting, normally beyond the scope of the hobbyist craftsman because it is usually used for large objects, are included for those who care to experiment.

It has been taken for granted that anyone who takes up casting has had previous experience in silversmithing, because every casting emerging from a mold requires finishing or surface treatment of some kind. However, in Part Two, this phase of the work has been treated in detail as it applies to casting, though enameling, an art form in itself, has been covered only for use as accents on a casting surface. Further use of enameling is best explored in books that cover the many possibilities this craft has to offer.

Because nothing can take the place of experience in any art form, the author has, insofar as is possible through the medium of the printed word, tried to give the novice the benefit of her own experience by pointing out the pitfalls, how to avoid them, and how to correct mistakes.

The material is presented in the order in which the techniques detailed are applied. If the fundamentals outlined, which are the outcome of years of research by the dental profession, industrial casting engineers, and professional jewelry craftsmen, are carefully followed, satisfactory castings should result.

Introduction

CASTING IS ONE OF THE EARLIEST OF ALL metal-working methods. Prehistoric implements show a gradual progression from those crudely fashioned in stone to those cast in metal. One primitive casting method for making tools was to carve an impression of an ax-head into the flat surface of a stone slab. A funnel-like groove cut from the stone's edge directly to the hollow of the carved shape served as a sprue. The molten bronze or copper metals were poured into the mold through this groove. In some instances, a flat stone covering was placed over the carved area, which formed a contained mold. The Navajo Indians follow a similar procedure, carving designs in tufa (a fine-grained volcanic stone) to cast belt buckles, rings, pendants, and necklaces such as the famous design used in the Nezzah necklace with its hand-wrought squash-blossom links. Though the Navajos call this sand casting, it is not to be confused with sand castings that are made with foundry sand.

Eventually, casting progressed to the core method, in which the metal cast was just a skin thick enough to give strength. Knight's *American Mechanical Dictionary* lists bronze as one of the first metals used for casting in the cire perdue or lost-wax casting method as early as 2230 B.C. In the book of Isaiah (712 B.C.), mention is made of the calf cast in gold by Aaron, which was fashioned of molten metal and decorated with a graving tool. A bronze figure of Nero was cast by Zenodorus, a Greek craftsman, for the Colossus near the Temple of Venus in Rome. Museums now preserve some of the more famous productions of Lycippus and his Greek fellow-craftsmen, who were using the cire perdue method in the eighth century. Seville Cathedral in Spain has a candelabrum cast in 1562 by Bart Morel which remains as an outstanding example of this method of casting. The numerous figures and statuettes, the foliage and the delicate scrollwork were all cast in bronze.

Lost-wax castings can be produced by two different methods. An entire object is cast, or the object is cast in sections and then assembled. The latter method is called piece-casting or *Malaga à la Française*. In history books mention is made of piece molds and piece-casting as early as 328 B.C.

Today centrifugal casting, known also as lost-wax, cire perdue, disappearing model, and liquid forging, is the most widely used method of casting. The common method of centrifugal casting is by no means a modern process. The technique, which gives clarity in detail, was used by Benvenuto Cellini and others in the founding arts in the sixteenth century.

Centrifugal casting machines are mentioned as early as 1809 in English patent records. This method consisted of placing the molds upright on pivots or revolving bases. Centrifugal force carried the molten metal to all parts of the mold. In 1857 an American patent described wheel molds presumably used for railroad cars. As the metal was cast, the initial flow became the outer perimeter or tread of the wheel, and the second portion of molten metal became the body or hub of the wheel. Rapid rotation of the molds caused the metal to adhere to the walls as it solidified.

Centrifugal casting as it is now done is more aptly called centrifuge casting. True centrifugal casting is used primarily for articles with hollow cores (see Fig. 1a). It is identical to other lost-wax modeling and molding procedures, except that the mold is attached to a revolving shaft which rotates the entire mold on an angle. The molten metal enters the mold from a stationary crucible positioned above the rotating mold, and flows down into the pattern chamber, where it is forced centrifugally against the inner walls until it solidifies to the thickness desired for the finished hollow casting.

FIG. 1a

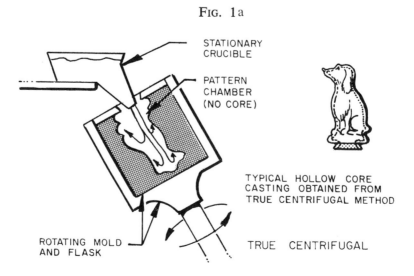

STATIONARY CRUCIBLE

PATTERN CHAMBER (NO CORE)

TYPICAL HOLLOW CORE CASTING OBTAINED FROM TRUE CENTRIFUGAL METHOD

ROTATING MOLD AND FLASK

TRUE CENTRIFUGAL

Semicentrifugal casting involves molds stacked in a rotating rack with a common sprue or funnel (see Fig. 1b). The molten metal enters the rotating molds from a stationary crucible positioned above the stack, and the centrifugal action pulls the metal into the outer areas of the mold, filling them first.

In centrifuge casting, which is the more common centrifugal casting method and the one detailed in this book, a single mold travels at the end of a rotating arm, and the metal enters the pattern chamber from the crucible, which rotates on the arm of the machine along with the mold (see Fig. 1c).

FIG. 1b

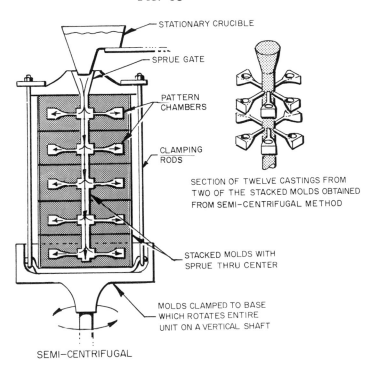

STATIONARY CRUCIBLE

SPRUE GATE

PATTERN CHAMBERS

CLAMPING RODS

SECTION OF TWELVE CASTINGS FROM TWO OF THE STACKED MOLDS OBTAINED FROM SEMI-CENTRIFUGAL METHOD

STACKED MOLDS WITH SPRUE THRU CENTER

MOLDS CLAMPED TO BASE WHICH ROTATES ENTIRE UNIT ON A VERTICAL SHAFT

SEMI-CENTRIFUGAL

FIG. 1c

CASTING METHODS USING CENTRIFUGAL FORCE

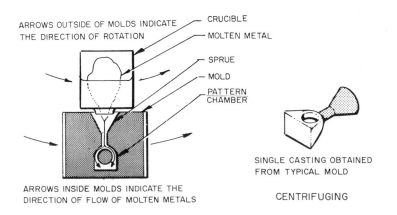

ARROWS OUTSIDE OF MOLDS INDICATE THE DIRECTION OF ROTATION

CRUCIBLE

MOLTEN METAL

SPRUE

MOLD

PATTERN CHAMBER

SINGLE CASTING OBTAINED FROM TYPICAL MOLD

ARROWS INSIDE MOLDS INDICATE THE DIRECTION OF FLOW OF MOLTEN METALS

CENTRIFUGING

In semicentrifugal and centrifuge casting, the molten metal is held in place by the centrifugal action until the metal solidifies. True centrifugal casting depends entirely on the rotation of the mold to hold the metal against the inner walls until it solidifies.

Molds can be made, in addition to the standard method detailed in this book, of green sand, or by using frozen mercury for models. The frozen-mercury model is dipped in a ceramic slurry until many coatings have built up around the model. When the ceramic covering is thick enough, the mercury is melted at any ordinary room temperature or at 32° F., after which the ceramic mold is fired (baked) to produce a mold which will withstand the shock of the impact of molten metal against its inner chamber walls. *Mercury fumes are extremely toxic and use of this element by inexperienced craftsmen is not advocated.*

The next step forward was compression casting machines which made possible a greater degree of refinement in articles cast by the lost-wax process. The upper portion of the machine is placed over the mold that holds the molten metal. As this is being done, a sufficient amount of air pressure is applied to the mold to force out the gases and allow the metal to flow into even the most intricate tracery of the pattern chamber. The thin gossamer of housefly, bumblebee or dragonfly wings, etc., can be cast in lacy strands of precious metal by using pressure casting machines.

Centrifugal casting per se remained a casting method for large objects until 1907, when Dr. Taggart, a dentist, introduced it to other dentists who experimented with the method, hoping to perfect cast inlays for teeth that would replace malleting flake gold into prepared cavities. A Dr. Campbell in Missouri used a Hoosier cowbell as a casting flask. A wire loop such as an extra long bucket bail was added to the bell, the clapper removed, and the model and its sprues embedded in the investment plaster. After the mold had been heated, the prepared metal in molten stage was poured into the sprue, and the bell swung first in pendulum style, then in a circular motion, to force the metal into all areas of the pattern chamber. This action resembled the old trick of swinging a bucket full of water over one's head in a circular motion.

In 1940 centrifugal casting methods were adopted for manufacturing jewelry and soon they became available to the nonprofessional craftsman. Prior to its use in the jewelry trade, vacuum action was combined with the investing procedures of mold making to produce an air-free mold, which was patented in 1935. Vacuum casting, combined with centrifugal casting, was also attempted in 1935, and patents on this method were finally issued in 1940–42. However, successful vacuum-centrifugal casting was not accomplished until 1948, by A. L. Engelhardt in California. Continuous improvements in all the various machines, including large production models employing the centrifugal casting method, continue to make this form of casting extremely popular and versatile for both the professional and the novice craftsman.

Sand casting, confined to uncomplicated objects because of mold construction, was developed in the fourteenth or fifteenth century, but was first mentioned in writing only after it came into prominent use in the sixteenth century. However, examination of very early Egyptian and Chinese articles finds evidence of sand casting.

Perhaps the most recent development is that used for making large panels. In addition to being cast with molten metal poured from a crucible, the panel is cast by spraying molten metal at 1,100° F. from a specially designed gun onto the surfaces until the desired thickness is obtained.

Part I

CASTING

CHAPTER 1

Design

DESIGN IS AN INTEGRAL PART OF THE ENTIRE casting process. It should take precedence over all the other aspects of the medium, but not at the expense of technique or craftsmanship.

Articles which can be fashioned by hand-wrought and beaten metal techniques or by forging should not be cast. Castings should be limited to objects that cannot be produced by any other process. Observation of work done by expert craftsmen will show that the casting medium is the only one possible when the design has intricate detail, when it is impossible to solder small pieces, and when the texture cannot be produced by any tool.

Though there are very few techniques for jewelry making that have not been used for several centuries, today the numerous precious metals available and the breaking away from the old principle that the material determines the design allows for greater variety in color, texture, and application. Of course, the inherent characteristics of the materials should always be used to the greatest advantage without divorcing utility from esthetic values.

All good design must have proper proportion, line, shape, mass, balance, rhythm, and emphasis—values that are required for all art forms.

The ultimate use of the article will determine the overall proportion and arrangement of masses and areas. The design, when divided into sections, should have one portion which stands out, not necessarily in size, but in form, color, and in the technique used. All portions must combine to give a feeling of unity, so that the secondary masses direct the viewer's attention to the main point of interest. Simple proportions such as 1:1 and 2:1 leave much to be desired. Proportions of 3:5 and 7:5 are more interesting (see Fig. 2).

A sense of unity is attained if one's eye can follow a curved horizontal or vertical line to another part without interruption. This can be determined by masking out, or by covering parts of a design with a sheet of paper and observing the remaining portion. If the design appears complete without the deleted area, the relationship of the proportions is not correct.

Straight lines, either vertical or horizontal, indicate quiescence; angular, curved, or jagged lines denote strain or agitation; curved lines indicate rhythm; converging or radiating lines emphasize the center of interest or focal point, thus unifying the complete design.

Jewelry designs should be based upon the

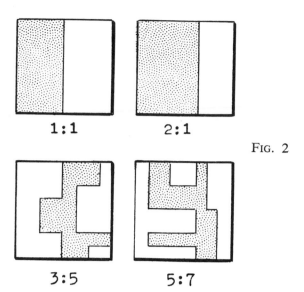

1:1 **2:1**

Fig. 2

3:5 **5:7**

Fig. 3

Fig. 4

best possible arrangement of geometric, non-objective, and abstract patterns, all of which can be embellished in many ways with gemstones, textures, and other surface treatment. Designs can be either simple or complicated, but there must always be a sense of order and coherence. Articles can be created to accent a particular stone, texture, or detail of the metal work, or to illustrate particular facets of one's avocation or the events of one's daily life. For example, one craftsman created a small design of his home and the path he takes to his work. Small gemstones placed in the textured metal represent his wife and children. The complete design includes those things important to him in his daily life around which his activities revolve.

In forms of nature one finds an inexhaustible source for design. Objects such as leaves, seedpods, small flower buds, insects, etc., burnt out in the replica casting method, form complete designs in themselves. These same objects also can be developed into fascinating abstract designs according to the craftsman's creativity (see Fig. 3).

Inspiration can come from going out into the garden, the fields, the woods, the beaches, and the river's edge to look at the ordinary things in nature. The eye can act as a camera taking in each detail. A 1–15x loupe or magnifying glass zoomed in on a leaf or seedpod will serve to show the diverse forms and textures that abound in nature.

Photographic prints enlarged several times and enlarged sections of negatives, project the pattern of a leaf vein, the flow of a line, the vigor of a curve, and the beauty of textured surfaces (see Figs. 4 and 5). Other sources for design can be found in photographic sections of a knothole in a weatherbeaten piece of driftwood or fence, the woodwork detail on an old house, and the play of shadows through iron grillwork.

Comparing a geranium leaf with the lacy spines of a carrot top, it can be seen that both contain useful facets for design interpretations. Compare also the following plant forms for design concepts: spruce cones, fir tree tips, beardtongue buds, magnolia seedpods, seeds of hercules club, leaf of an aracea, underside of a sage leaf, spadix of anthirium, squash tendrils, wild cucumber blossoms, young garlic shoots, empty pods of sweet alyssum, underside of a wild carrot bud, cornflower and sunflower buds, morning glory buds, cypress twig tips, cedar

FIG. 5

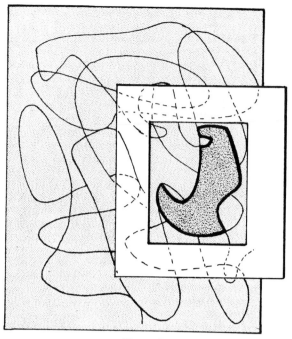

FIG. 6

Decorative pieces, of course, need not be confined to interpretations of nature. Attractive nonobjective designs can be found in simple doodles. Filling a sheet of paper with freely drawn intertwining lines and shading various areas with different values of gray combined with black and white brings out a nonobjective design which can be clearly defined by outlining (see Fig. 6).

A dark-colored length of string dropped easily on a sheet of light-colored paper will form itself into an interesting nonobjective pattern that can be traced. Soft lead, annealed copper, or brass wire, bent or twisted into pleasing shapes, will also give no end of ideas for original designs. An advantage of the latter is that wire bending allows for altering the design without losing the original idea (see Figs. 7 and 8).

Symmetrical designs can be developed from any design sketch, whether geometric, abstract, or nonobjective, simply by standing a mirror on edge and observing what develops as the mirror is moved fanlike across the design. When a pleasing design appears, a line is drawn across the paper along the edge of the mirror to mark the center. The complete design can then be traced on a piece of tracing paper (see Fig. 9).

FIG. 8

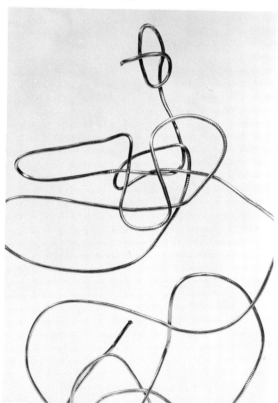

bark peels, carnation leaves, ginkgo leaves, begonia buds, skin of prickly pear, cantaloupe rind, sunflower kernels, passion flowers, and so on.

Often the inexperienced artist can produce a wealth of material for design more readily usable than those sketched by a trained artist who is able to record in minute detail almost as much as the camera records on film.

Abstract designs, such as unusual and humorous interpretations of dogs, cats, butterflies, deer, insects, and mice, can be developed into fresh contemporary design ideas. Such objects, however, should be kept free of excessive detail or overworking of the design.

FIG. 7

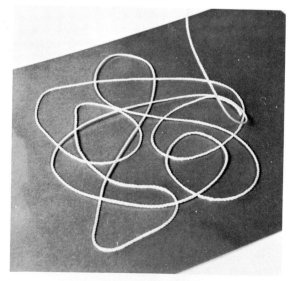

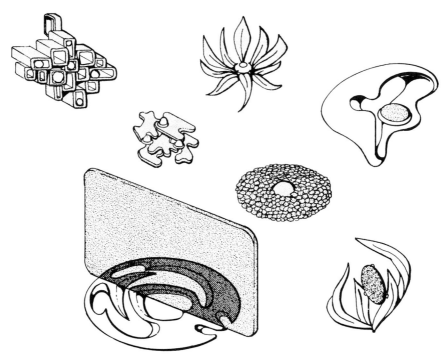

FIG. 9

Small crystal specimens purchased from mineral suppliers are often used as the nuclei for designs which attract and hold the viewer's attention; for example, small amethyst crystal clusters suspended in open areas of a design, small round or square wax wires radiating from a central base under a specimen with corresponding natural crystals, and small wulfenite crystals nestled in blades of wax that have been constructed to resemble the specimen itself (see Fig. 10).

When using gemstone materials, keep in mind that gemstones need subordinate areas of texture, form, or color to direct attention to the stone, which should always be the focal point of interest. Faceted stones, because of their brilliance, need very little surrounding area to emphasize their beauty (see Fig. 11).

Though a craftsman uses many of the mechanical means described here in developing and planning designs, his artistry lies in choosing the right one for his purpose. To create stimulating and interesting designs takes more than the perusal of rules and precepts. Observation of what the best artists have done, and adapting and expanding ideas thus garnered are necessary to broaden one's knowledge and critical ability. As in all art forms, techniques, though mastered to perfection, will not alone produce sound designs.

FIG. 10

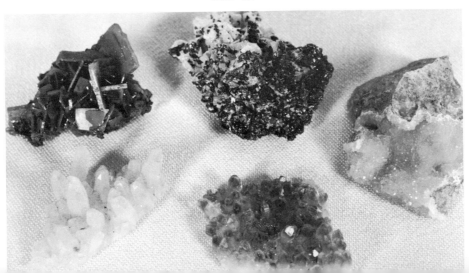

Fig. 11

Fig. 12   Tumbled Stones

Fig. 13   Cabochon Gemstones

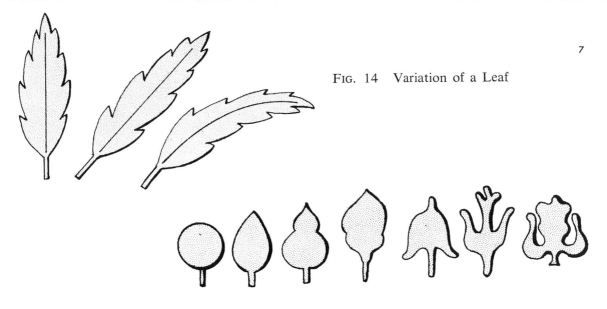

Fig. 14   Variation of a Leaf

Fig. 15   Variation of a Leaf

Fig. 16   Design development of a withered apple
            (by Dr. Robert Coleman)

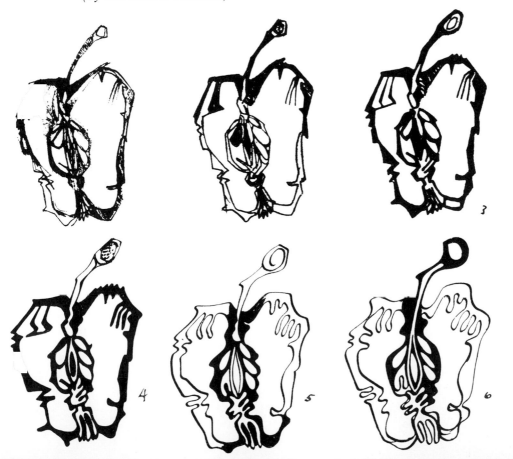

CHAPTER 2

Tools and Materials

THE TOOLS REQUIRED BY THE CASTING CRAFTS-man include many of those used in other branches of metalwork. Some special tools can be improvised from standard items or custom made to exactness, according to the ingenuity and manual dexterity of the craftsman, but large items such as furnaces, presses, casting machines, and vacuum pumps must be purchased from suppliers of jewelry equipment. Manufacturers offer machinery and equipment time-tested and proven efficient by long use in the jewelry trade and the dental profession.

The intricacies of adapting calibrating registers for weight, temperatures, pressures, and rotational speeds to equipment makes it inadvisable for anyone to attempt to build such specialized apparatus himself. Home-built devices usually result in only moderately satisfactory castings or complete failures.

Some of the tools listed are not necessary for the beginner but are included here because of their value in solving technical problems that sometimes arise. Many listed were originally developed by craftsmen when a determined search for a specific tool proved futile. Information on such special tools has been gathered from shop talk, correspondence, technique demonstrations, and personal experience. The usefulness of each tool varies with the dexterity of the person using it; therefore, several similar tools are listed.

The tools are grouped under the headings of the various techniques so that some are listed more than once. For example, the first group lists tools and equipment that are absolutely necessary. The second group lists adjuncts which, though not required to perform the technique steps, make some procedures easier or permit the craftsman to expand his knowledge of casting and related metalworking techniques into the realm of the professional. The third category lists production tools used only by financially affluent casting enthusiasts working toward professional status, by production shops, and by recreational, school, and other group endeavors. These are mentioned only because of their relationship to the casting techniques.

TOOLS AND MATERIALS
FOR LOST-WAX CASTING

Wax Models

Basic:
1. Wire gauge
2. Carvers, scrapers, spatulas (hoe, hatchet, pointed, or puddle-type blades or tips)
3. Precision carving knife or scalpel
4. Alcohol lamp, Bunsen burner, or household candles
5. Eyedropper
6. Glass slab 3″ × 5″ × 1″
7. Ring mandrel
8. Ring size set
9. Small paint brushes
10. Soldering stand (tripod with wire grid)
11. Porcelain wax pots
12. Infrared lamp
13. Container for cooling wax
14. Jeweler's saw frame and blades
15. Sandpaper
16. Large sewing needle in dowel wood
17. Door knob, trailer dome set in dental plaster or plaster of Paris
18. Wax-press
19. Thermometer
20. Hand drill and assorted drill bits
21. Files with large single cuts (rasp or curved-tooth)
22. Hypodermic syringe
23. Small bench vise
24. Small metal snips
25. Trimming scissors
26. Orangewood sticks
27. Blowtorch

Adjunct:
1. Electric spatula, commercial or home-made
2. Electric wax pot
3. Dapping-die block and punches
4. Chasing tools
5. Bench stakes
6. Lead blocks

Production:
1. Small lathe for turning wax sections
2. Commercial wax ring masters
3. Die-sep
4. Commercial acrylics
5. Glass slab lubricant
6. Floral clay, plastic-tacking material, wallpaper cleaner

7. Household foil or bearing shims
8. Sticky wax

Replicas

Basic:
1. Same basics as listed for regular wax models
2. Killing and relaxing jars
3. Plastic and metal sprue pins

Adjunct:
1. Electric spatula
2. Electric wax pot

Materials:
1. Found objects
2. Sandarac varnish
3. Heavy-duty plastic spray (non-soluble in water)
4. Commercial fixing solution to preserve replicas
5. Relaxing additives
6. Absorbent paper towels
7. 70% isopropyl alcohol
8. Carbon tetrachloride
9. Ethyl acetate
10. Sodium cyanide
11. Cardboard
12. Rubber scrap
13. Plaster of Paris
14. Small cloth bag
15. Dry sawdust
16. Wide adhesive tape
17. Phenol (carbolic acid)
18. Emulsion-type glue (Elmer's, Wilhold, etc.)
19. Acetone

Spruing

Basic:
1. Spatulas
2. Metal crucible formers
   Large and small—1½″ to 3½″ diameter
3. Rubber sprue bases
   Small, medium, and large—1⅜″ to 3½″ diameter
4. Casting rings in four sizes:
   1½″ high × 1¼″ diameter 50 gram capacity
   1⁹⁄₁₆″ high × 1¾″ diameter 100 gram capacity
   2″ high × 2½″ diameter 225 gram capacity
   2¼″ high × 3½″ diameter 450 gram capacity

5. Larger flasks to 7″ high and 4″ diameter (used in larger machines)
6. Graduate cylinder, calibrated .0 to .250CC
7. Twisted wire dip stick
8. Plastic and metal sprue pins
9. 6″ metal rule

Adjunct:
1. Triple beam scale
2. Electric spatula
3. Electric wax pot

Materials:
1. Wax (wires, sheet, strip, rod)
2. White vaseline
3. Sticky wax
4. Thin lubricant (lightweight oil)

Investing

Basic:
1. Investment proportioner
2. Large graduate cylinder
3. ¾″-wide plastic or metal spatula
4. Large and small rubber plaster bowls
5. Measuring scoops
6. Bench knife
7. Scissors
8. Vibrating machine
9. Large container for water immersion
10. Casting rings and flasks (used in spruing)
11. 6″ square of sheet metal
12. Airtight container or humidor
13. Wire-mesh screen for large castings
14. Metal sheet casing for large castings
15. Large mixing pail for large castings
16. Needle-nosed pliers
17. Drip-spout water bottle

Adjuncts:
1. Mechanical spatulator
2. Triple beam scale
3. Vacuum investor
4. Vacuum spatulator

Materials:
1. Asbestos strips 1½″ to 3″ wide
2. Alcohol
3. Debubbleizers—wetting agents
4. Investment plaster

Burn-out

Basic:
1. Burnout furnace
2. Refractory trays

3. Refractory trivets
4. Temperature pellets
5. Casting machine–spring activated (cradles, balances, large and small tongs and crucibles)
6. Asbestos gloves or mitts
7. Casting shield or wash tub
8. Small clock

Adjunct:
1. Portable pyrometer
2. Vacuum-centrifugal combined casting machine
3. Pressure casting machine
4. Hand-caster

Production:
1. Electro-thermostatic controlled centrifugal casting machine
2. Machine-operated production casting machine
3. Large kiln or furnace for burn-out of large castings

Casting

Basic:
1. Torches or blowpipes using either oxygas, compressed air and gas, or oxyacetylene
2. Small scrub brush
3. Tooth brush
4. Dental scalers, picks, explorers
5. Small plastic-tipped or quartz-tipped tongs
6. Hot plate
7. Glass-stoppered bottles
8. Metal shears
9. Stirring rod
10. Stirring tongs
11. Charcoal blocks
12. Metal preparation crucibles of graphite, sand, magnesia, clay, alumina, zirconium

Adjunct:
1. Electric metal-melting pot
2. Sand-blast machine
3. Foundry tongs for large castings
4. Clay crucibles for large castings
5. Wire mesh for large castings
6. Vertical lift tongs for large castings
7. Shank ring for large castings
8. Blow torch
9. Bench shears
10. Electric pickle pot

Production:
1. Large sand-blasting machine
2. Ultrasonic cleaner
3. Gas-fired melting furnace

Materials:
1. Reducing flux
2. Asbestos strips 1″ wide
3. Asbestos gaskets and pads
4. Sulfuric acid
5. Casting metals
6. Commercial pickling solutions
7. Sparex no. 2 pickle compound
8. Nitric acid
9. Hydrofluoric acid in polyethylene bottles
10. Hydrochloric acid in glass bottles
11. Ordinary sand for pit for large casting molds

Hollow Core Casting

Basic:
1. Mixing container or pail
2. Spatulas—paddles
3. Pliers
4. Shaving brush
5. Regular paint brushes
6. Molding board
7. Carving knife
8. Torch
9. Scratch awl
10. Dental explorer instrument
11. Mold tray
12. Large crucibles
13. Tongs
14. Shank ring
15. Metal skimmer
16. Roller
17. Water measure

Materials:
1. Iron, aluminum, or copper wire (8 to 10 gauge)
2. Wood blocks, wedges
3. Investment plaster or dental model plaster
4. Table salt, stale beer, ammonia
5. Wax
6. Clay
7. Liquid wax
8. Strip metal
9. Shim metal
10. Reinforcing fabric—glass fiber (tissue, mat, woven, and woven tape)
11. Dusting talc
12. Reinforcing iron or wire
13. Rope, webbing, strong string, or steel strapping
14. Shellac
15. Liquid soap
16. Casting metal
17. Rubber mold materials
18. Mold frames
19. Core nails (chaplets)
20. Pickling solutions

21. Coloring materials:
ammonium chloride
copper sulfate
copper acetate
ammonium sulfide
sodium chloride
acetic acid
barium sulfide
potassium sulfide
hydrosulfide of potash

Cold Casting

Basic: Same tools as for Hollow Core

Materials:
1. Metals ground to fine powder
Bronze   100 to 300 mesh
Copper   100 to 300 mesh
Gold and brass   300 mesh
Lead   100 to 200 mesh
Nickel silver   100 mesh
Aluminum   200 mesh
Silver   200 mesh
2. Resins and hardeners
3. Mixing containers
4. Glass fiber fabric, rods, plastic rods

Finishing

Basic:
1. Side or end cutting pliers
2. Hacksaw
3. Jeweler's saw
4. Benchpin and stake
5. Ring clamp
6. Bench vise
7. Hand vise
8. Two sets needle files (one for gold only)
9. Standard files 6″ to 8″ long (flat, round, half-round, mill —smooth and second cut)
10. Swiss pattern files, 6½″ long (nos. 5, 7, 11, 15—"0" and 2 cut)
11. Ring size set
12. Ring mandrel
13. Rawhide mallet
14. Small pein hammer
15. Dowel wood
16. Flat wood strips
17. Garnet paper
18. Emery paper (various grits)
19. Hog and nylon bristle brush wheels
20. Wire bristle brush wheels (brass, steel, monel)
21. Tapered arbors
22. Jacobs chuck attachment
23. Polishing lathe (1750 to 3500 rpm)

24. Center punch
25. Scriber
26. Drill and drill bits (assorted)
27. Small chuck on 3/32″ mandrel
28. Sanding string
29. Buffs, tapered cones
    (felt, muslin, cotton, leather, emery)
30. Die-sinker's riffler files

Materials:
1. Tripoli
2. Pumice
3. Whiting
4. Chrome and tin oxide powders
5. White diamond rouge
6. Red, green, white rouge
7. Carborundum grits
8. Vaseline
9. Boxwood (or mahogany-maple) saw dust

Adjunct:
1. Flexible shaft and handpiece
2. Dental engine and handpiece
3. Assorted stones, burs (carbide and diamond), wheels, buffs, saws to fit handpieces
4. Scratch wheels

Production:
1. Large polishing lathe
2. Vacuum dust collectors
3. Drill press
4. Air-turbine drill
5. Large bench stakes
6. Large bench shears
7. Planishing, sinking, and raising hammers

Annealing, Soldering, Pickling

Basic:
1. Pickling tongs
   (copper, wood, plastic-tipped, quartz-tipped)
2. Pickling pan
3. Soldering stand
4. Wire grid
5. Charcoal blocks
6. Magnesite block
7. Asbestos sheet
8. Fire bricks
9. Quenching container
10. Glass graduate
11. Glass stirring rod
12. Glass-ground stoppered bottles
13. Bunsen burner
14. Torch and assorted tips
15. Iron binding wire
16. Hollow scraper
17. Tweezers, plain and locking
18. Solder snips
19. Solder push rod

20. Third-hand soldering aid
21. Carbon ring mandrel
22. Flux brushes

Adjunct:
1. Electric pickling pot

Materials:
1. Flux (commercial)
2. Boric acid
3. Borax
4. Wood alcohol
5. Antiflux (commercial)
6. Yellow ochre
7. Pickling acids (nitric, sulfuric, hydrochloric, hydrofluoric)
8. Sodium bichromate
9. Solders
   Silver—hard
      hard no. 1, medium, easy, soft
   Gold—10K hard, 18K easy
      14K hard, 18K easy
      18K medium, 18K hard

Gemstone Setting

Basic: In addition to other finishing tools:
1. Curved, flat, and rocking burnisher
2. Beading tools
3. Millgrain tools
4. Diamond-setting burs
5. Wire gauge
6. Stone-setting pliers
7. Round-nosed pliers
8. Flat-nosed pliers
9. Chain or sniped-nosed pliers
10. Ring-bending pliers
11. Bezel mandrel
12. Gem pusher
13. Carborundum stone
14. Round or pointed graver and handle
15. Loupe

Adjunct:
1. Bracelet mandrel
2. Dapping-die block and punches
3. Wire draw-plate and tongs
4. Screwplates and taps for small ear-wires
5. Tap and die set (.076″ [1.94 mm] to .022″ [0.056 mm])

Production:
1. Rolling mill
2. Gem-faceting and lapidary equipment

Materials:
1. Gemstones, various shapes
2. Pearls

3. Woods
4. Wire—gold, silver
(round, flat, square, half-round, bezel)
5. Tubing—silver
6. Findings—ear-clips, ear-screws, cuff-link swivels, tie-tacks, pin-backs (brooches), bola slides, pendant loops, bails, jump rings, chains, clasps, cords
7. Dopping wax
8. Asbestos strips
9. Cement or epoxy
10. Gum tragacanth
11. Isopropyl alcohol
12. Soldering investment
13. Sticky wax
14. Glass slab

Surface Decoration

Basic:
1. Burnishing tool
2. Scratch wire wheel brushes
3. Matting tools
4. Copper and stainless steel dipping wires
5. Small paint brushes
6. Cotton-tipped sticks
7. Chasing tools, assorted
8. Pitch block or box and pitch
9. Chasing hammer
10. Gravers (line, plain, round, flat, onglette)
11. Graver handles
12. Graver sharpener
13. India stone
14. Arkansas stone
15. Leather strop
16. Jeweler's sandbag
17. Alcohol lamp
18. Buffing and polishing wheels and buffs

Adjunct:
1. Same as for finishing

Production:
1. Sand blast machine
2. Engraver's block

Materials:
1. Glycerine
2. Beeswax
3. Detergents
4. Liquid soap
5. Bright dip and pickling solutions (some constituents have been listed in rough finishing section)
6. Commercial oxidizing solutions
7. Potassium sulfide
8. Copper sulfate
9. Iron oxide solution
10. Ammonium chloride
11. Calcium chloride
12. Copper sulfate
13. Lead acetate
14. Acetic acid
15. Ammonia
16. Thin oil
17. Chinese white

Production
Material:
1. Blasting sand

Plating

Basic:
1. Boiling pan
2. Steam cleaner
3. Hot plate
4. Plating solution containers (Pyrex or glass)
5. Copper and platinum dipping wires
6. Self-locking tweezers
7. Plating machine
8. Wires and alligator clips
9. Thermometer

Materials:
1. Commercial stripping solution
2. Commercial plating solutions
3. Anodes (gold, silver, copper, nickel, rhodium, platinum, steel)
4. Distilled water
5. Detergent
6. Ammonia
7. Sulfuric acid
8. Sodium bicarbonate
9. Isopropyl alcohol
10. Masking lacquer
11. Wax pencils
12. Acetone

Enameling

Basic:
1. Small enameling kiln or furnace
2. Supports—trivets (metal and ceramic)
3. Kitchen tongs
4. Crucible tongs
5. Spatulas (large and small)
6. Enamel containers
7. Porcelain mortar and pestle
8. Glass stirring rod
9. Scriber
10. Wire pusher-spreader
11. Screen (100 mesh), baskets, shaker-top bottles
12. Small brushes
13. Fire bricks
14. Glass fiber brush
15. Buffing and polishing equipment

16. Gravers

Production: 1. Large enameling furnace

Materials: 1. Enamels (colors)
in grit, powder, wires, chunks
2. Transparent enamel
3. Copper sheet
4. Stainless steel sheet
5. Antiflux
6. Masking tape
7. Gum tragacanth
8. Wood alcohol
9. Pine and lavender oil
10. Blotter paper
11. Asbestos strip and sheet
12. Pumice

Adjunct
Materials: 1. Metal foils

Rubber Molds

Silicones, Cold Mold, and Hot Pour Compounds

Basic: 1. Disposable paper pallets
2. Sharp knife
3. Plastic or metal spatulas, ¼″
to ¾″ wide
4. Aluminum or wooden alignment pins
5. Dental flask or mold
6. Stationary or breakaway mold
frames
7. Double boiler
8. Bench vise
9. Hinged mold boards
10. "C" clamps

Adjunct: 1. Hydraulic wax injector

Production: 1. Large mixing bowls
2. Drill press
3. Pressure wax injector
4. Vacuum investor

Materials: 1. RTV synthetic rubber compounds
2. Cold mold rubber compounds
3. Hot pour rubber compounds
4. Rubber compound thinner
5. Mold parting or separating
agents
6. Wax
7. Talc, dusting powder
8. Petrolatum
9. Liquid soap
10. Acetone
11. Pie tin

12. Rubber bands
13. Heavy-duty oil
14. Reinforcement fabric
15. Dusting-powder dispensers with
long, tapering nozzles
16. Low-fusing alloys
17. Crack sealant
18. Dental plaster

Vulcanized Rubber Molds

Basic: 1. 2-part metal mold frame
2. Metal sprue and crucible pin
3. Sharp knife
4. Mold plates
5. "C" clamps
6. Bench vise
7. Electric vulcanizing press

Production: 1. Thermostatically-controlled
vulcanizing press

Materials: 1. Natural uncured rubber in ⅛″
sheets
2. Wax
3. Paraffin
4. Talc
5. Separating agents
6. Rubber bands
7. Low-fusing alloys
8. Dental plaster
9. Copper sheet (30 gauge)

Sand Casting

Basic: 1. 2-part metal frame or casting
flask
2. Carving knife
3. Round and half-round wood
mandrels
4. Wood sprue pins and base
5. Core tubing and pusher
6. Ram
7. Strike-off iron
8. Coarse and fine mesh screen
tray (or tea strainer)
9. Wooden or plastic spoon
10. Molding boards
11. Rubber bulb syringe
12. Steel wire or darning needles
13. Crucible
14. Tongs
15. Goggles

Adjunct: 1. Bellows
2. Larger casting frames or flasks
3. Large mandrels
4. Sprues
5. Cores

Materials: 1. Models
2. Sand
3. Shellac and varnish
4. Parting powder (talc, graphite, lycopodium)
5. Tufa stone or pumice blocks
6. Charcoal blocks
7. Binding wire
8. Acid dip

7. Crucible
8. Crucible tongs
9. Bench vise
10. Brushes
11. Goggles
12. Tray
13. Rubber bulb syringe
14. Sandpaper
15. Binding wire
16. Charcoal block

Cuttlefish Casting

Basic: 1. Coping or jeweler's saw
2. Tray
3. Sharp knife
4. Tapered wood alignment pins or wires
5. Tweezers
6. Cabinet, rasp, or vixen file

Materials: 1. Models
2. Cuttlefish bone
3. Common sand
4. Castor oil
5. Hard flux solution
6. Borax
7. Sodium silicate

CHAPTER 3

Wax Models

A MODEL IS A THREE-DIMENSIONAL OBJECT which, when encased in investment plaster, is eliminated by extreme heat to form a pattern chamber or mold for the entry of molten metal.

Models are preferably made of wax formulated to combine plasticity with stability so that a minimum of residue is left in the pattern chamber after the wax is eliminated during the burn-out. Models of other materials, such as wood and plastic, can be used, but they are less desirable because they leave an ash residue which contaminates the casting and pits the surface.

Wax characteristics

Wax is offered commercially in varying hardnesses, shapes, and colors. Color is strictly the whim of the manufacturer. A blue wax of one brand may be identical in cohesive and manipulative qualities to a green or pink wax from another manufacturer. The varying hardnesses allow the material to be bent, twisted, kneaded, sawed, drilled, filed, hammered, turned on a metal- or a wood-working lathe, and sculptured by almost any tool.

Waxes are made of viscous fluids, resins, and fillers. The viscous fluids in the formulae come from a variety of waxes, among them, highly purified white beeswax, carnauba, candelilla wax (these two from palm trees) and synthetics such as montan wax. Carnauba and montan wax with a high melting point and candelilla with a lower melting point all help to effect a glossy surface. Other waxes included in the formulae are ceresin and ozenite (earth waxes mined from old shale beds), which are added to give plasticity. To aid in congealing the mass, a small amount of paraffin is added.

The resins, of natural origin ranging from tree saps to animal exudates, include damar, balsam, kauri copal, shellac, and rosin. As modifying agents, resins add smoothness and luster to the surface of the model. Fillers for bulk are talc, starch, chalk, soapstone, pumice, barytes, and wood flour.

Solid aerosol added to the wax in small amounts (less than 5% of volume) aids in removing wax patterns from rubber molds. Hard waxes can be softened to prevent cracking and flaking by adding small amounts of polyethylene bits (less than 5% of volume) to the mixture. Gum damar used in small amounts makes the wax smoother for molding, and also prevents flaking and cracking. Ceresin, similar to paraffin in appearance, is harder, yet more plastic, and is often used in place of paraffin.

Purchase of small amounts of wax constituents is difficult and discouraged by wholesalers. Paraffin and beeswax are available, but the

FIG. 17

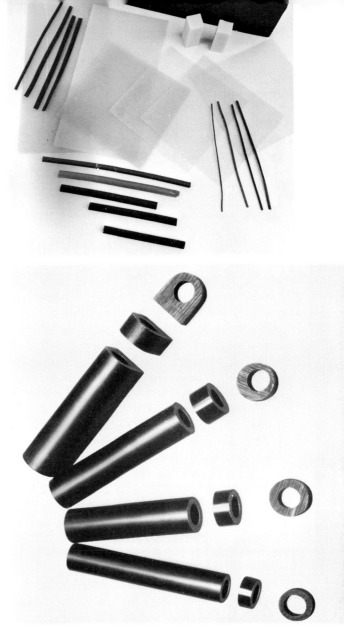

additives and relative ingredients are not easily obtained.

When wax is warmed or manipulated, the solid particles slide over one another, and the oils and fats act as lubricants. Crystallization occurs as the wax cools, and rigidity, provided by the resins, increases. Thin sheets of wax in gauged thicknesses are mostly beeswax with a small percentage of resins and oils. Neither beeswax nor plain paraffin should be used. The former is impure and leaves a residue during burn-out, and the latter is soggy when warm and flaky when cold. It is wise to try different kinds and brands of commercial waxes until you are completely familiar with their characteristics before blending several different waxes with the expectation of getting better results in specific instances. Waxes of animal extraction should be avoided, as they tend to separate in the compounds when heated.

Experiments with home formulae should be tested by placing a small amount of the wax mixture in a clean covered crucible and burning the wax away. If little or no residue is evident, the mixture is satisfactory. Dental specifications require that the melted wax must not leave a solid residue of more than .1% of the original weight of the model when vaporized at 932°F. Excessive ash residue in the pattern chamber after wax elimination will pit and discolor the casting.

Choosing the wax

FIG. 18

FIG. 19

The plasticity of wax allows freedom of handling which is not possible in other rigid materials. The shape and hardness of wax best suited for the specific design should be selected (see Figs. 17 and 18). It should then be determined whether the mass is to be decreased, increased, or merely arranged to form the design. Smaller designs and those with much detail are best constructed by means of wax build-up using wax wires and melted wax applied with a heated spatula. Large objects are easily molded directly from a sufficient block or sheet of wax which can be heated, sawed, filed, drilled, or turned on a wood-working lathe. Finer details can then be worked in with carving knives, scrapers, and heated spatulas (see Fig. 19).

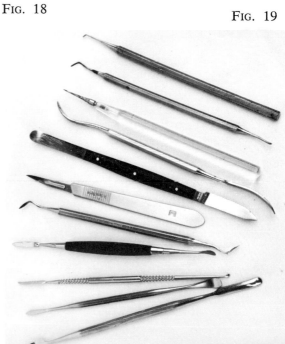

Heating the wax

Initial forming should be made with higher melting-point waxes. The flame of an alcohol lamp or a Bunsen burner is best for molding the wax in different ways. When these are being used, eye strain can be reduced if a metal back-drop painted with flat black paint is employed. A 3″-wide flange is bent to a 90° angle on one end of a strip of sheet metal 4″ wide by 15″ long. The metal is painted, and the lamp or burner is set on the flange (see Figs. 20 and 21). Ordinary household candles can also be used to heat the wax and the smaller tools. Pass the wax through the flame quickly, taking care not to volatilize it or melt it directly in the flame. Wax may also be held near an infrared lamp to allow it to be bent, twisted, and domed easily. It may be immersed in warm water maintained at a maximum temperature of 139°F. When the wax becomes too soft to mold, it must be immersed in water to return it to working consistency. Extremely cold water or continual dipping in any water breaks down some of the lower-melting constituents of the wax, causing internal stress, and the material may become crumbly while being molded or during the subsequent casting steps.

Temperature of the water used in molding the wax pattern should be maintained at 68°–74°F. The differential in room-temperature water is too great, for it varies from 38°–95°F., according to geographical location and the season of the year. The room, water, wax, and flame temperature norms should always be maintained at a minimum degree of variance.

Clean tools essential

Carving tools, scrapers, spatulas, water, and other tools and materials should be kept absolutely clean (narrow bands of colored tape wrapped around favorite tools or those used most frequently make them easy to identify on the work table). The build-up of excess wax on the carving tools is removed by wiping with a clean cloth. An occasional buffing and polishing makes all tools work better. Wax solvent or any ordinary painter's turpentine, which successfully dissolves and removes wax from bench tops, tools, and melting pots, is readily available at any supply house to aid in keeping one's work area as clean as possible.

FIG. 20

FIG. 21

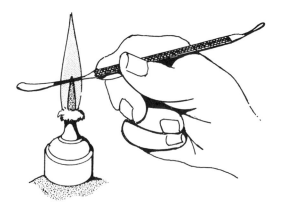

FIG. 22

Wax build-up

Tools are passed through the flame or held in the flame for short moments to heat them. Heat is applied to the shank of the tool, *not* at the tip or working surface, which would not only coat the working surface but also take the temper out of the metal in a very short time (see Fig. 22). The heated tool is touched to the wax supply until the tool is loaded with wax; it is then passed a second time through the flame to retain the heat and to transfer the wax to the model mass. The tool is reheated to mold, smooth over the transferred wax, and bring more material to the model mass.

Tools that have been held in the flame improperly so that the temper has been removed can be retempered or hardened by heating the tool tip of working area to a light straw color, which is approximately 430°F., and then quenching it in a light oil or cool water. Steel not quenched after heating but allowed to cool slowly will anneal or soften.

Excess wax is removed from the mass by heating the tool, wiping it clean, returning it to the flame for heat, and then applying the heated tool to the area where wax removal is desired. Wax is then wiped off of the tool with a clean cloth and the procedure repeated.

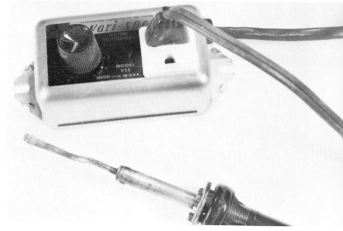

FIG. 23

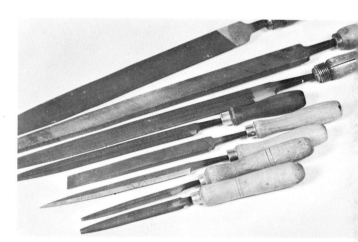

FIG. 24

Electric spatulas

Electric spatulas are ideal for use in molding the wax. They are available commercially with an assortment of tips. The spatula is thermostatically controlled so that the desired heat for the tip can be dialed.

An electric spatula can be constructed by converting a small electric soldering iron such as is used in the electronic industry. An iron with a replaceable tip, preferably one with a set screw, should be used. A short length of 8 gauge copper wire is cut and inserted in the opening. The protruding end is flattened to spatula shape and the end filed round. The iron is plugged into a small power rheostat, available in hobby shops or wherever home workshop equipment is sold (see Fig. 23). To obtain the desired heat, turn the control knob and test the heated spatula on a chunk of wax until the optimum heat level is reached.

The heated spatula is applied directly to the wax supply, carried to the model mass, and molded or worked as desired. Excess wax is removed from the model simply by wiping the tip of the spatula with a clean cloth and again applying it to the model.

Other basic tools

Larger masses of wax can be formed by using the following basic tools: a standard machinist's hacksaw; a jeweler's saw frame with a No. 4 blade; drills similar to those used in woodworking power drills; files of single, rasp, or curved-tooth cuts which do not clog as easily as regular metal-working files (see Fig. 24). Sandpaper with heavier grits which does not clog quickly is also used to form and smooth over larger models.

To carry wax to the model dip a small paint brush such as artists use in melted wax and apply it to the model. Wax is melted in small porcelain ladles or pots placed on a soldering tripod and heated with the alcohol lamp or Bunsen burner (see Fig., 25). Electric wax pots with thermostatic controls are also used to melt the wax and to maintain it at a constant working temperature (see Fig. 26). The ladle can be carried directly to the model and wax poured into larger areas if needed.

FIG. 25

FIG. 26

Small amounts of wax may be carried to the model on a large needle inserted into a short length of wood doweling or on a No. 23 sickle explorer (see Fig. 27). Ordinary eyedroppers are also often used to carry molten wax to the model. The eyedropper, two-thirds full of melted wax, is rotated quickly in the flame to keep the wax melted and then applied to the desired area of the model (see Fig. 28). A hypodermic syringe without the needle is an excellent tool for forcing molten wax into porous or inaccessible areas. The syringe is filled with wax and heated in the same manner used for the eyedropper (see Fig. 29).

Construction on a glass slab

Models can be constructed on a glass slab which has been thinly coated with a fine grade lubricant to allow easy removal of the wax construction without breakage or distortion (see Fig. 30). Use only enough oil to accomplish this removal, because an excessive amount prevents the wax from staying in position.

Gemstones, if part of the design, can be placed on the slab and positioned with floral clay or plastic-tacking material exactly as they are to appear in the final casting; the wax can then be built up around them. Wallpaper cleaner in the form of a pink putty-like material which is kneaded in the hands can also be used as a support for the gemstones (see Fig. 31). After this phase of the construction is completed, the small prongs or coronets should be bent back to permit removal of the stone so that the wax model can be removed easily from the glass slab with a large spatula.

Construction on a ring mandrel

Models are constructed on a ring mandrel just as they are on the glass slab. The mounting section of a ring can be built on the glass slab and then transferred to the ring mandrel for the addition of the ring shank, or the entire ring may be constructed on the mandrel. Preformed wax wires or flat wax strips are used for ring shanks.

A thin film of lubricant or very thin foil applied to the mandrel can be used to permit easy removal of the wax pattern. Smooth household foil works well, but finer thicknesses that

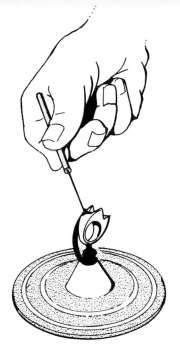

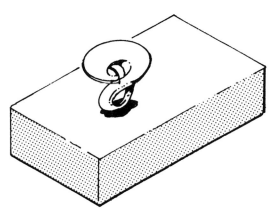

FIG. 30

FIG. 27

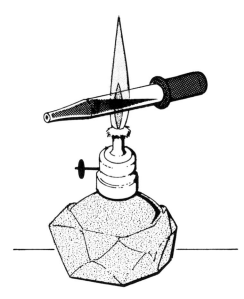

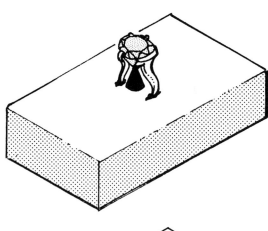

FIG. 28

FIG. 29

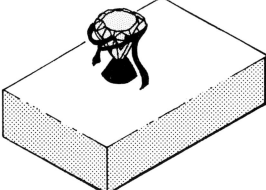

FIG. 31

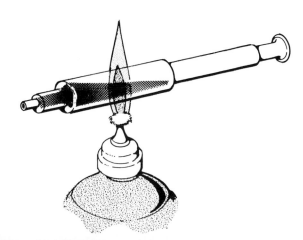

FIG. 32

FIG. 33

FIG. 34 Construction of a ring on carbon soldering mandrel

FIG. 35 Ring sizer and wire gauge

are sold in auto supply stores for bearing shims work better (see Fig. 32). The ring should be constructed one size smaller than desired. (Dimensional changes that occur during casting are approximately a minimal 1%. Shrinkage occurs in the investment and is irrelevant in jewelry casting.) In this way the ring will be a perfect fit after filing, sanding, buffing, and polishing have been completed on the inner surface of the ring shank. The ring mandrel is placed in a small bench vise to hold it in working position (see Fig. 33). It is not limited to construction of rings, but is used as a small base for other types of wax construction.

A simple ring mandrel can be constructed by determining the correct ring size and selecting a small plastic vial (such as coin holders or pill bottles) slightly larger than the ring size and filling it with dental plaster, casting investment, or plaster of Paris. A short section of ¼″ drill rod is inserted into one end for a shaft (see Fig. 36).

When the plaster has hardened, the plastic vial is broken away and the shaft extension inserted in a lathe chuck or drill chuck. A piece of sandpaper held between thumb and forefinger is used to sand the cylinder down to the desired ring size as the model rotates in the chuck. The plaster mandrel should be covered with thin foil to aid in removing the model after completion.

Rings, bracelets, and necklace links can also be made on a simple ring mandrel using half-round wax wire. A plastic vial marked with lines at intervals of 90° around the periphery of the vial and perpendicular to the vial length aids in positioning the wires correctly (see Fig. 37). The mandrel can be constructed initially in a smaller plastic vial or, if there is not one available, a discarded larger size could be sanded down to the desired size. Only a very thin film of oil is necessary to remove the finished wax model from a plastic vial.

Construction on found objects

Bench-stakes, doorknobs, and chrome-plated trailer-hitch domes positioned upright in blocks of dental plaster or plaster of Paris make excellent support bases which are useful in

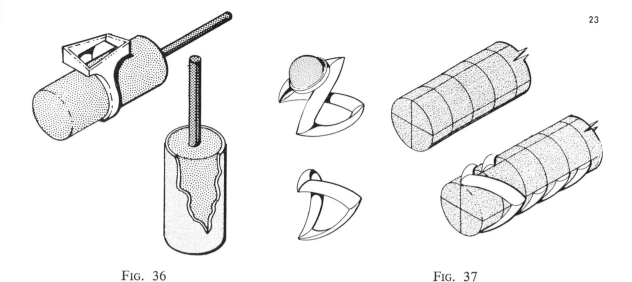

FIG. 36   FIG. 37

constructing objects on a curved surface. Curved wax forms are not easily constructed on a glass slab or ring mandrel. These bases also require a thin film of lubricant to aid in removal of the completed wax pattern or model (see Fig. 38).

Improvising noncommercial wax shapes

Desired thicknesses of wax sheet which are not commercially available can be made by coating a small cylinder with a thin film of lubricant, filling the vial with cold water, and dipping the vial quickly into hot melted wax. The thickness of wax depends upon the number of times the vial is dipped. When the desired thickness is obtained, the wax drippings are cut from the bottom of the vial with a warm knife.

The warm knife is used to slit the wax the length of the cylinder. The wax section can then be placed in warm water so that it can be flattened, shaped, or adapted to any desired form (see Fig. 39).

Wax wire shapes are produced by using a commercial wax-press. The press consists of a small cylinder internally threaded to match a threaded plunger. The cylinder is filled with a large wax rod and dipped in hot water so that when the threaded plunger is turned it forces the wax out through a preselected tip into a moving platform. Though the press is supplied with eight assorted tips, only one type and size of wire can be produced at a time (see Fig. 40).

A similar press may be constructed of brass or aluminum. Interchangeable discs with per-

FIG. 38   FIG. 39

forations for different wax wire shapes are placed in the bottom of the cylinder. Both the cylinder and the piston or plunger have handles which, when pressed together, force the molten wax through the perforations into a tall container of water to prevent the wax wire from sticking. The wax is heated in the cylinder by dipping it in a container of hot water (see Fig. 41).

Lead blocks with surface impressions are used to die-cast elements too small to be constructed of wax by hand (see Fig. 42). These include beads, half-domes, small leaves, acorns, rosebuds, teardrops, and other small objects. The wax models can be cast with a low-fusing alloy, and rubber molds made from these castings to produce additional identical wax patterns. The model is coated with a "die-sep" (separating agent for metal parts), and the molten lead is poured over it into a boxed frame. When the models are parted from the lead, a mold negative remains to form the small wax parts.

Inclusion of rough gemstone material in models

Tumbled stones or thin slices of unpolished gem material such as small azurite nodules or crystal-lined geodes of other minerals pressed down into a sheet of wax make attractive models for castings (see Fig. 43). The material is arranged into a design, outlined onto a piece of paper, removed, and a sheet of wax (20 gauge, thin enough to see through) is placed over the drawing. Thus, an exact impression of the material can easily be made in the outlined positions. The outer edges of the wax sheet are trimmed as desired, and the edges rolled or tapered off. Small prongs of 20–22 gauge wax wire in an upright position are added around the periphery of the impressions to hold the gem material when it is replaced. The needle and dowel wood tool is heated and used to make a hole in the wax sheet just large enough to insert the short wax wire prongs (see Figs. 44 and 45). When the casting is completed, these prongs are filed to the proper length and bent down over the edge of the gem material. This method of making prongs is much simpler than drilling holes in a finished casting.

With this technique of model making, drusy quartz or drusy chrysocolla, amethyst, pyrite crystals, and other small crystal formations in their natural state can be made into exotic creations of jewelry. The backing of the wax model beneath the gem material is lightened by melting holes in it with the heated spatula. This reduces the metal requirement and the weight of the casting (see Fig. 46).

Uncommon commercial wax shapes

In addition to the standard wax shapes of sheets, blocks, wires, and rods, wax is commercially available in larger extruded shapes.

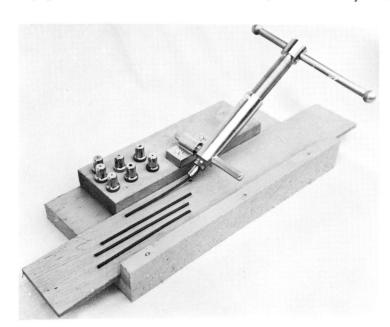

FIG. 40

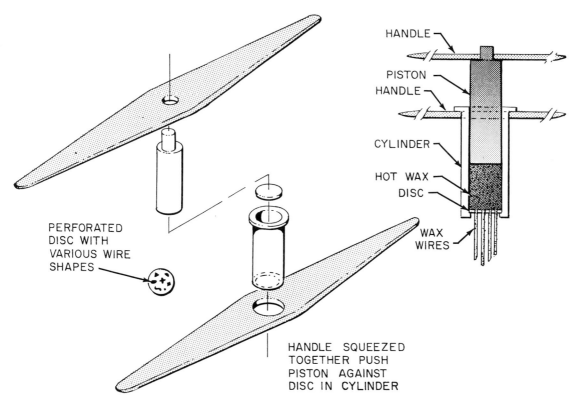

HANDLE

PISTON
HANDLE

CYLINDER

HOT WAX
DISC

WAX
WIRES

PERFORATED
DISC WITH
VARIOUS WIRE
SHAPES

HANDLE SQUEEZED
TOGETHER PUSH
PISTON AGAINST
DISC IN CYLINDER

FIG. 41

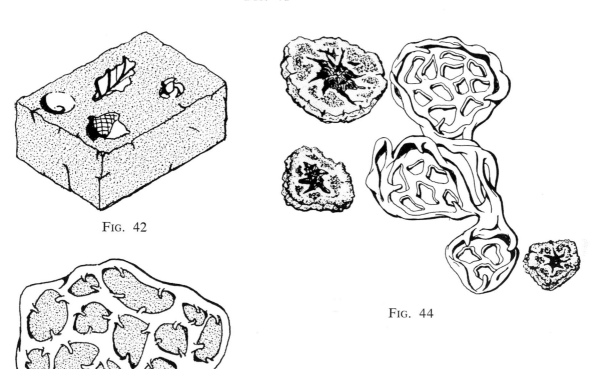

FIG. 42

FIG. 44

FIG. 43

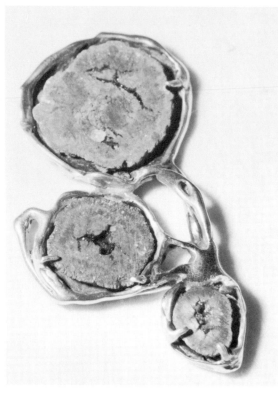

FIG. 45

FIG. 46

Wax ring models, partially formed and to be completed by the craftsman, are also available in sixty different designs (see Fig. 47). These ring masters can be altered with any of the regular wax molding tools to form original creations. Any breaks or cracks must be mended with a heated spatula.

Free forms or accidentals

Models called accidentals are made by slowly dropping small amounts of melted wax into a container of ice water. These can be cast in the forms they take when dropped into the water or, if desired, reworked with the carving tools before casting. Small wax wires for prongs can be added to accommodate gemstones if required by the design (see Fig. 48).

Two-part castings of one or more metals

Wax models, or sections of a design, can be constructed where a casting of two different metals is desired. Sections of castings can be constructed in wax, carried to the rough casting stage, and either finished or used as a base and support for another wax model. The first cast section is sprued with the second wax section, invested, and cast. Naturally, the first metal cast must be the higher-temperature metal. Before spruing it with the second wax section, the metal and the wax are temporarily separated, and the metal surfaces that mate with the wax are coated with soldering flux. The wax pattern is then reattached. In this way, the secondary, contrasting metal section will adhere to the first cast section. If a good "join" is not accomplished in the dual casting process, the two sections, after removal of the sprue wires, are soldered together. This two-metal casting technique is especially effective with flowers.

Gemstones cast with wax model

Gemstones can be imbedded in the wax pattern, remaining there during the entire casting process. Thus, gemstones can be cast into a cage-type pendant without the difficulty of adding the gemstone after casting is completed. This technique requires experimentation before success can be assured. It is said that stones of at least 6½ on the MOHS scale of hardness can be used for this process and emerge successfully in the cast article. However, a stone with the hardness of 8 should be used, though hardness alone will not ensure success. Genuine gemstone materials may have inclusions, fractures, or soft spots which will cause the stone to check, shatter, or change color upon contact with the molten metal. A small section of the material to be used in the casting, such as a tumbled stone or a rough chip, should be selected. The stone is imbedded in wax and put through the complete casting process. This determines which materials are unaffected by the prolonged heat of wax elimination and the shock of molten metal during the casting step (see Appendix for gemstone hardness).

Finishing the model

When the model is completely constructed and the surfaces are smoothed as much as possible with the metal instruments, a smoother surface can be achieved by swiftly passing the model through the flame. It requires a little practice to be able to smooth the model in the flame without melting, distorting, or unfastening any wax joints. The best method is to cover an orangewood stick or tapered length of wood doweling with a piece of clean used silk and burnish the surfaces to the desired smoothness. The same effect can be accomplished by painting the surfaces with eucalyptol applied with a cotton-tipped applicator. Small areas are coated, one at a time, then flushed with acetone before the next area is coated. Eucalyptol dissolves the wax during polishing, and the acetone stops the action, leaving a smooth, dry finish. Hard-to-get-to areas of wax models can be reached by threading a narrow length of satin ribbon through the draws. One end of the ribbon is held in a small bench vise and the other held by hand. The ribbon is saturated with eucalyptol and the model is slid along it. Each stroke burnishes the model. The model is then slipped off the ribbon and dipped in acetone, which cuts the action of the eucalyptol. All the surfaces must be checked for cracks made during bending or twisting of the model form and those found must be filled in with wax or they will be reproduced in the casting.

FIG. 47

FIG. 48

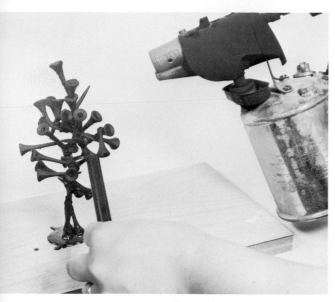

FIG. 49

Commercially prepared acrylic materials are useful in repair construction of models. The liquid, applied with a brush, dries quickly, hardens as part of the model, and burns out cleanly in the wax elimination step.

Wax models are also constructed in rubber molds made from previous castings or other models. Large castings made with the lost-wax method are produced without a casting machine. The large wax models are constructed of heavy-duty wax. Large carving knives and other tools create the desired form and surface textures. A blowtorch is used to smooth over areas (see Fig. 49).

Because every detail of the wax model will be reproduced in the casting, the model must be as perfect in detail, shape, and finish as possible.

CHAPTER 4

Replicas

REPLICA CASTINGS CAN BE MADE FROM ANY material that can be burnt out in the furnace and leave a pattern chamber free of ash residue. This includes the following objects in plant, marine, reptile, and insect life: leaves, twigs, bark sections, seedpods, cones, flower blossoms or buds, crabs, seahorses, starfish, snails, octopi, lizards, horned toads, spiders, bees, beetles, grasshoppers, and scorpions. In addition, many household objects, such as matches, Styrofoam, macaroni shapes, nutmeats, cigarette butts, etc., can be used (see Figs. 50, 51, 52, and 53).

Preparation of the replica model

Each object requires individual spruing steps. Insects and marine life, killed by being dipped in denatured alcohol, can be invested immediately after capture, also flowers and leaves that wilt immediately after being cut. These objects can be brushed with, or dipped in, sandarac varnish, or they can be sprayed with clear plastic or heavy-duty hair-spray. Without alter-

ing the surface detail, these coatings add rigidity to the object for support during the spruing and investment, and they attract the investment, making it easier to apply.

After the excess coating is shaken off, the object is placed on a sheet of thin wax (usually 28–32 gauge) which serves as a platform upon which to position the object for spruing and investing (see Fig. 54). This platform also acts as a support for the tiny antennae of insects and bugs. The object must be checked for weak or extremely thin spots, and these areas strengthened with wax from the underside or from any area that will not normally be visible in the finished casting.

Leg and wing joints, leaf and stem junctures, and seedpod stems also require additional wax for support. The wax is applied with the heated wax-filled eyedropper, or preferably with a long needle inserted into a section of doweling that will form a handle. The small drop of wax that can be carried on a needle is just the right amount needed to strengthen such fragile and delicate parts (see Fig. 54).

FIG. 50

FIG. 51

FIG. 52

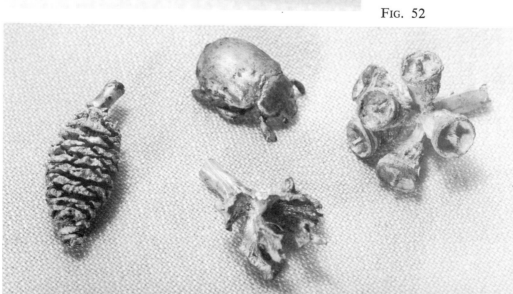

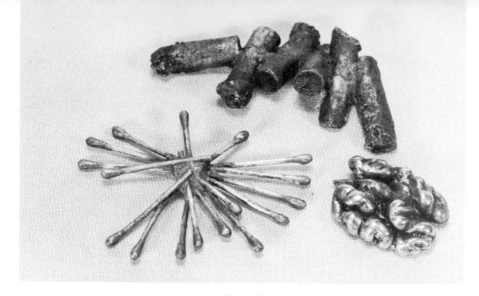

FIG. 53

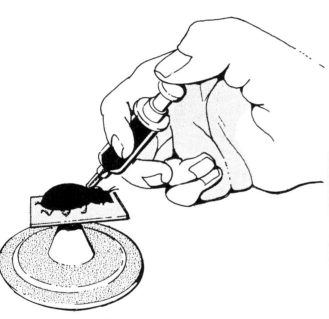

FIG. 54

FIG. 55

Wax is also applied to the undersides of leaves and flower petals with a paint brush to preserve as much of the detail as possible (see Fig. 55). The underside of insect wings can also strengthened with the wax, but may, in addition, need the support of sprue wires. The sprue wires not only support the extensions but also supply molten metal to thin areas before the metal cools, thus closing off the flow of additionally needed metal during the casting process.

Spruing porous objects

Objects of plastic, Styrofoam, cardboard (such as matches), paste forms (such as macaroni), potato chips, popcorn, etc., require a sufficient coating of spray or varnish to seal the porous material and give rigidity during investment.

A nonwatersoluble spray or coating is necessary here, or the water in the investment mix will cause the model to lose rigidity and form and collapse before the investment has set up.

Commercially prepared acrylic materials, available in liquid form for the same purpose, can be brushed onto the fragile and delicate portions of the model. This liquid quickly hardens without changing the surface textures, and it will burn out as quickly and as cleanly as the rest of the model.

Capture and preservation of replica objects

Various methods of preserving models can be employed. The variety of objects in desired sizes may be difficult to obtain, especially in urban areas or certain sections of the country where pesticides are used continually. Many

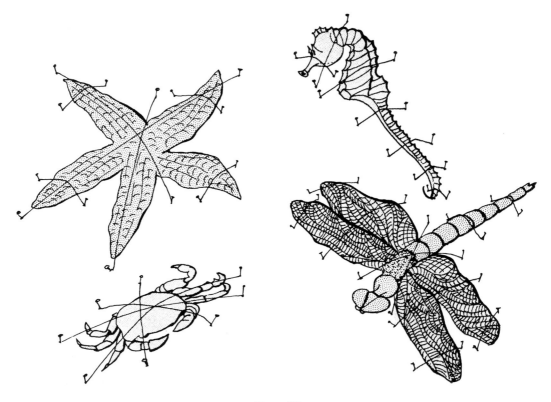

Fig. 56

species are protected by state fish and game de-
partment laws that either limit the number
that can be collected or prohibit all collecting
without a license. Pacific coast tide pools are
excellent collecting areas for small marine creatures, many of which contract when captured
and need to be relaxed by drugs before being
killed. In fact, they often contract so tightly
that preserving fluid does not reach the inner
parts and they cannot be sprued for investment, being still alive.

Marine creatures are collected and placed in
a container of natural habitat water from the
collecting area and refrigerated until they have
relaxed and expanded back to their normal
shape, after which they are killed by being partially frozen. One of the following additives
only—2% chloral hydrate, 70% ethanol, clove
oil, or menthol crystals—is mixed with the
habitat water for quicker relaxation. The specimen, if it does not react when prodded slightly,
is ready for a fixing or preserving solution. Wet
specimens are preserved for later spruing in a
container of 10% formalin mixed with the
habitat water. Commercial fixing or preserving
solutions are offered by manufacturers special-
izing in resins for plastic-embedment of objects.

The specimen being prepared for spruing is
removed from the preserving solution and
placed on an absorbent paper towel to drain.
It is then put into a container of acetone and
removed to another absorbent towel. The specimen is then handled immediately for the spruing steps. Specimens such as starfish, crabs, and
seahorses that can be dry-preserved are spread
on a sheet of Styrofoam plastic and fastened
down with string or small pins (see Fig. 56).

Insects usually do not contract and can be
killed instantly by being dropped into a jar
filled with 70% isopropyl alcohol. The dead
specimen can be removed and sprued immediately or stored in a covered container for future
spruing and investment. Larger specimens such
as tarantulas, scorpions, spiders, large beetles,
horned lizards, and chameleons can be handled
much easier if refrigerated to a state of tem-
porary hibernation. This avoids the possibility
of the specimen damaging itself through panic
when it is dropped into a killing jar.

Killing and relaxing jars

A killing jar that immobilizes and kills insects quickly is made from a wide-mouthed jar
with a screw-type cover (see Fig. 57). Various
chemicals, readily available at your local phar-
macy or scientific supply store, are used in the
killing jar. Killing agents such as carbon tetrachloride, ethyl acetate, and sodium cyanide are
all extremely poisonous and toxic and must be
handled carefully. Avoid contact and inhala-
tion. When working with toxic chemicals, pre-
cautions should always be taken to protect
children and uninformed persons.

If carbon tetrachloride is to be the killing
agent, the jar is filled with approximately ½
cup of rubber scraps, such as old jar rings or
pieces of inner tube. These are saturated with
the chemical and the excess liquid poured off.
A thin cardboard disc, cut to fit snugly inside
the jar and down over the saturated rubber
scraps, acts as a platform for the captured
animals or insects. Chemicals last a long time
in a tightly closed container before recharging
with the same chemical is necessary.

Ethyl acetate requires a base of plaster of
Paris in the jar bottom approximately ½"
thick. When this thin mix has set, the jar is
put into an oven at low heat to dry thoroughly.
The hardened plaster of Paris is completely
saturated with the chemical and the excess

FIG. 57

chemical is poured off into the original container. Recharging the jar is accomplished by redrying the plaster of Paris in the low-heat oven and adding the chemical as in the initial step.

Sodium cyanide used for a killing agent is added to the jar and covered with a ¼ " layer of dry sawdust. A ½ " layer of plaster of Paris is poured over the sawdust and allowed to set with the jar open. When the plaster has hardened, the lid is screwed on tightly and a label marked "poison" is applied to the bottle. The lower portion of the jar should be wrapped with wide adhesive tape to prevent the poison from scattering if the jar is broken. When the jar has lost its potency, it should be disposed of in an incinerator and a new jar made.

Wide-mouthed jars with screw-type covers are also used to relax animals and insects that dry hard and brittle (see Fig. 57). The jar is filled with a ½ " layer of sand. This is saturated with water to which a few drops of phenol (carbolic acid) is added to prevent mold from forming on the specimens. The sand is covered with a thin cardboard disc, cut to fit snugly inside the jar. Specimens should be kept in the relaxing jar not longer than one to three days, or they will decay. The jars should always be kept in a cool, dry place so that they will not sweat inside. Insects and animals should never be stored for later use in a container unless they have been previously placed in the killing jar, because parasites will devour them in a short time.

Insects may be placed in flexible plastic containers and frozen for delayed spruing, but must be relaxed and immediately sprued after thawing before they decay. Insects put through the killing and relaxing process may be mounted as shown in the illustration and stored for future use in casting (see Fig. 58).

Objects with a high water content, such as marine objects, should be preserved and sprued wet. The normal water in the live animal evaporates when the specimen is dried and sprued, and a collapse of the specimen becomes evident. The water content can be replaced with any material that will burn out clean in the furnace by inserting a hypodermic syringe, filled with the material, through any vent in the object (see Fig. 59). The water in the objects

will generate a considerable amount of steam in the mold during burn-out, so the venting sprue steps should be carefully followed (see Chapter 5).

Spruing flowers and leaves

Flowers, leaves, etc., may be frozen and submerged in a flask filled with the investment mix without being mounted on a crucible former (see Fig. 88); however, fragile sections and weak junctures should be strengthened with wax before freezing to eliminate the difficulty of applying warm wax to a frozen object. The article is placed in a shallow box or other container filled with sand, plastic chips, or table salt, and the material pushed up under the petals to position them correctly as they freeze. Small stems attached to the flower are usually too small to carry the molten metal to all areas of the mold in the casting process before solidifying begins. Such stems should be enlarged and strengthened with melted wax, and their shape preserved as much as possible.

An alternate method is to add a sufficient number of auxiliary sprues to carry the metal to the mold extensions. The main wax sprue should be attached to the flower before freezing and the petals adjusted frequently as the article freezes. When properly frozen, it can be removed from the freezing compartment, debubbleized, painted with creamy investment, and submerged gently into the investment-filled flask.

Flowers can be immersed in ice water for several hours to make the petals crisp, and then sprued and invested. The invested flask is placed in an airtight container or humidor and stored for several days before the firing and eliminating of the original flower. This produces a casting with undistorted detail. Distortion is apt to occur in thin sections if burned out too soon after investing. Flowers coated with the creamy investment should be allowed to dry slightly so that they are rigid enough to maintain their form when the investment is poured into the flask and around the painted models.

Seedpods and other dry materials can be found in all flower shops where dry arrangements are sold. Marine life in fixing solutions

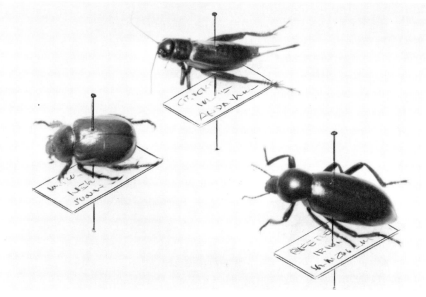

FIG. 58

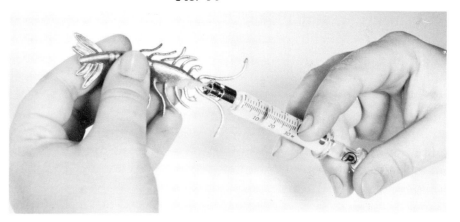

FIG. 59

are available in hobby and craft shops or science equipment supply houses. Shells do not burn out easily; they should be reproduced in a rubber mold and the resultant wax models invested and cast in metal. Dry replicas such as pods and cones need only to be dipped in acetone before wax or debubbleizer is applied.

Spruing edible objects

Nutmeats can be used as casting objects simply by spruing, debubbleizing, and investing (see Chapters 5 and 6). The finish is identical with the original surface. Salami ends sliced from dry salami rolls emerge with interesting effects. The salami, being quite greasy, attracts

small globules of water on the surface during investment, which enhances the surface of the cast article by producing a striated texture covered with tiny balls of metal. Plastic or metal sprue pins coated with wax are used as sprues and supports during investing.

Paste or macaroni-type products are available in a variety of shapes, such as, regular spaghetti strings, bow ties, shells, numbers, letters, twisted strips, and cartwheels (see Fig. 50). Materials of this type require a spray-coating of plastic applied with an aerosol can or a brush-on coating of an emulsion-type glue (Elmer's glue-all, Wilhold, etc.) thinned with water to a paint consistency. Conservative use of water for thinning is necessary, however, as additional moisture softens the paste object so that its rigidity is excessively decreased. Both types of coatings must be allowed to dry thoroughly before the next step. The debubbleizer readily adheres to the prepared dry surface and the investment coating can be easily applied.

Spruing found objects

Book matches torn from their cover and placed askew on a small disc of sheet wax make interesting cast objects (see Fig. 53). These, too, must be coated with plastic spray or the thinned glue coating because when painted onto an uncoated model the investment immediately wets the naked cardboard. The matches are fastened together with either quick-drying glue or wax.

Cigarette butts can also be cast in metal with similar preparation (see Fig. 53). Cigarette sections should be selected that do not have charcoal filters, because these do not always burn out in the elimination step. The pieces are arranged so that a thin plastic rod can be skewered through them for support. The cigarette fibers are filled with melted wax applied with a heated wax-filled eyedropper (see Chapter 3) or a hypodermic syringe used without the terminating slender needle.

Plastic objects can be used to make excellent models which are either eliminated in the burn-out step or used as models for silicone molds. Styrofoam shapes or objects can also be used and are easily formed into models. After being sawed into approximately the required shape, the Styrofoam is smoothed by rubbing one piece against another. This material being porous, it is necessary to fill the core or cells with glue or molten wax, applied with the eyedropper or the hypodermic syringe. Vibrating investment around an unprepared model of Styrofoam leaves only the tiny cell walls, which are not strong enough to carry the metal to all parts of the foam, even if they should withstand the vibration during the investment. Only the inner core is filled with wax, so that the surface texture is not altered.

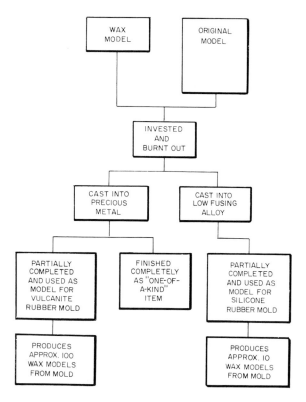

FIG. 60   Flow Chart of Casting Steps

CHAPTER 5

Spruing

Sprues are the wax wires used to support the wax model in correct casting position as it is encased in a fresh investment plaster mix. When eliminated in the wax burn-out, sprues leave passageways or tunnels through which the melted wax escapes from the mold, so that the molten metal can enter the pattern chamber of the casting flask. Smaller sprues serve as auxiliary passageways for the flow of metal to the hard-to-get-to areas. They also serve as escape valves for the venting of air and gases formed by the molten metal as it enters the mold (see Fig. 61).

Spruing is more important to casting than is generally realized by the craftsman. The principles are basically simple. Though there are other factors apt to produce undesirable results, neglecting sprues in this step of the process leads to many poor and incomplete castings.

Sprue sizes and lengths

Sprue sizes are determined largely by the size and bulk of the model. The main sprue should be as large (in a cross section) as the bulkiest part of the casting. If two or more bulky sections of the casting are separated by thinner areas, a sprue is required for each of the bulky areas (see Fig. 61). Some large castings may prohibit exceedingly large sprues, therefore, the same purpose is accomplished by adding auxiliary sprues to thinner outer sections of the wax model as far as possible from the main sprue. As the molten metal passes through the sprues or passageways, some of it collects on the walls, and "freezing" or solidifying begins. If the sprue is too small, it will freeze before sufficient metal has reached all of the outer convolutions of the pattern chamber, thus producing an incomplete or porous casting (see Fig. 61). Large sprues aid the flow of the molten metal that first strikes the walls of the pattern chamber. These walls become the skin or surface of the casting. Additional molten metal pouring into the chamber fills in the rest of the mold and freezes the excess metal that remains in the main sprue or crucible. This excess metal is called a button (see Fig. 61).

Spruing to the base of the model is not absolutely necessary unless the original texture or surface of the model is to be retained. Such articles as flowers, leaves, and insects must normally be sprued to the underside in areas that will not be visible on the completed casting (see Fig. 62).

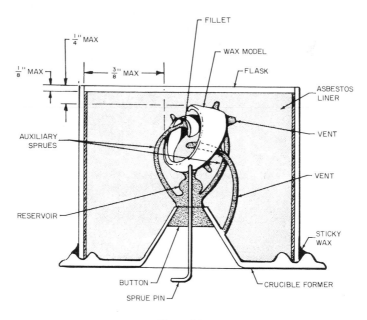

$$\text{FIG. 61}$$

Attaching sprues

The main sprue is attached directly to the tilted wax model with the heated spatula. The model should be attached on an angle, so that when molten metal flows through the sprue, it will not hit the wall of the pattern chamber directly, but rather with a glancing blow. The wax rod is flared to a fillet where it meets the model (see Fig. 61). This permits the flow of metal in all directions inside the mold with a minimum amount of turbulence.

FIG. 62

FIG. 63   Sprued insect

Sprues should be smooth and equal on all sides, and either straight or continuously curved without any right angles. Tapered sprues act like nozzles and spray the mold with a molten mass that freezes before the cavity is completely filled. Lumpy sprues produce rough inner surfaces and create turbulence in the stream of hot metal. During spruing, care must be taken so that no portion of the model is melted, otherwise additional wax build-up will be necessary. The model and sprues must be firmly attached to keep them from breaking away or vibrating loose during the investment steps.

Sprues are firmly and easily attached with sticky wax to the model. A small amount of sticky wax is placed on the area of the model where the sprue is to be attached, and the sprue is inserted into it (see Fig. 61). This works especially well on flowers and insects.

Mounting the model on a sprue base

At this point, it must be determined whether or not a sprue base can be used, and if so, what type and size (see Fig. 65). Standard centrifugal casting machines and centrifugal machines combined with vacuum force have crucibles to melt the metal before it is forced into the mold by the action of the machine. In both methods the sprue base is often incorrectly referred to as a crucible former, in spite of the fact that its main purpose is to form a sprue (opening or gate) in the end of the mold.

Metal sprue bases have a center cone rising 1¼″ from the base. The base and its cone act as a support for the wax model as it is being encased in the wet investment.

Rubber sprue bases are used for investing models that are to be cast with combined vacuum and centrifugal force. The rubber base has a steep-walled center cone to hold the model during the investment steps. A better vacuum is obtained in casting if the diameter of the cone is reduced. The rubber sprue bases have a lip around the base, and the casting flask snaps into this to make a seal which prevents leakage of the wet investment.

Mounting the model on a crucible former

Pressure casting machines require a rubber base to hold the model during investment. This base

FIG. 64   Single sprued model

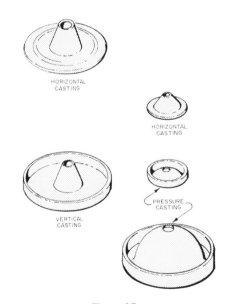

FIG. 65

forms a crucible (not just an opening or sprue as in the two forementioned methods) in which the metal is melted in the end of the mold. The cone is slightly shallower than the other cones, but not so shallow as to be flat-bottomed. Extremely shallow crucibles permit some metal to remain in the crucible instead of entering the pattern chamber, thus producing an incomplete casting. Deep-walled crucibles do not permit all of the metal to be heated to the molten stage at one time; therefore, some of the metal flows into the pattern chamber before pressure is applied, thus producing equally unsatisfactory results.

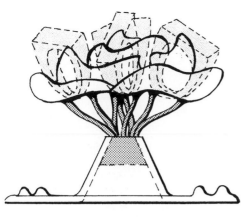

FIG. 66

FIG. 67

The crucible must be cleaned of all impurities, as these will not burn out and may contaminate the mold. All old investment must be removed from the crucible former or rubber sprue base. The bases or formers are then coated with a film of lightweight oil or white vaseline to aid in the removal of subsequent investment. Heating a metal tool and forcing it through the opening in the cone alters the rubber sprue bases so that they accommodate larger wax sprue wires or combinations of several small wax wires. Holes may be made in the cone walls to permit insertion of wax wires for venting. The sprue, consisting of several wax wires, is fastened to the base by molten wax poured around it at the opening. The ends of the wires can then be spread and attached to critical areas of the wax model. When multiple castings are to be made in one casting flask, each sprue wire is attached to a separate model (see Fig. 66).

Main sprues should be no shorter than ¼". Shorter sprues speed the flow of the metal too quickly into the mold, creating a backsplash. The same sprues should not be longer than ⅜" (see Fig. 61). Longer sprues slow the entry of the molten metal into the mold, so that freezing of the metal occurs before it reaches all areas of the mold. The longer sprues also deter the venting of air and gases from the pattern chamber. All joints between sprues should be flared and have smooth rounded corners or fillets with no right angles. Replica articles should be placed as close to the crucible as possible with the length of the main sprue held to a minimum.

A casting flask, also called a ring, is placed over the sprued model and onto the flat surface of the crucible. The distance between the model and the inner wall of the casting flask must be a minimum of ⅜" (see Fig. 61). The flask is removed and placed on the same surface as the crucible former; then a straight edge or scale is placed across the top of the casting flask and above the sprued model (see Fig. 67). Whatever the depth of the flask, both large and small models must be sprued to the crucible former so that they can be covered with exactly ¼" of investment. In other words, the flask does not have to be filled to the top with investment (see Fig. 61). A longer journey through a heavier layer of investment prevents the venting of air and gases. If the distance between the top of the model and the rim of the flask is less than ¼", the sprued model will have to be invested without a crucible former. (Models sprued for pressure castings should be covered with ½" of investment at the top to prevent the force of the vacuum from pulling the investment out of the flask.)

Other sprues are added as needed to carry the molten metal to the bulkier parts of the model (see Fig. 61). For very large castings, a reservoir can be added to the main sprue to maintain a molten mass close to the model. This can be drawn on for additional metal to fill the pattern chamber. The reservoir should not be separated from the model by more than ⅛". The short connecting sprue between the model and the reservoir can be larger than the balance of the main sprue.

Spruing basket or tree castings

Simultaneous casting of two or more wax models on a single crucible former with a common main sprue is called a "basket" or "tree" casting (see Fig. 68). The number of castings to be sprued in this manner is determined by the metal capacity of the casting crucible. It is better to cast fewer models at one time than to use the crucible to its capacity, because spillage and loss of molten metal may occur. Models made in a rubber mold are cleaned of all traces of talc, after which they are attached to the main sprue (like branches on a tree) or around the periphery of a small wax disc. A minimum space of ⅛" must be maintained between the models. Small models may need auxiliary sprues at strategic or critical points to ensure the flow of metal to all areas of the pattern chamber.

Spruing the vents

In addition to providing sprues large enough to supply all the needed metal to the mold, an important factor in casting is eliminating all the air and gases radiating from the mold (see Fig. 61). As the metal enters the mold, whether by gravitation, centrifugal force, or pressure, the model must be prepared to allow for the least possible resistance to the escape of gases. The air cushion in a mold does not build up a vacuum. If it did, casting processes with the molten metal in a crucible directly over the sprue opening would be impossible. A vacuum pulls the metal into the mold, whereas an air block restricts the flow of metal. The mold must be vented sufficiently to allow the air and gases to escape.

Small-size castings do not require vents, be-cause the air and gases escape through the investment. Medium-size castings can vent into the investment with the aid of short outer vents, usually constructed of 18 gauge wax wire ³⁄₁₆" long (see Fig. 61). Large-size castings require venting to the atmosphere outside the flask; these vents are also constructed of 18 gauge wax wire (see Fig. 61). The wax wire vent is placed on the main section of the model as far from the main sprue as possible, and is brought around in a curve and attached to the metal crucible former above the area that will be flushed with molten metal as the metal enters the main sprue. This allows the escape of air and gases into the crucible area. Pinholes in completed castings result when inadequate evacuation of gases impedes the flow of molten metal to all the areas of the mold before solidifying begins.

Inner vents are also used on medium and large castings. One or more vents of 16 gauge wax wire are placed at the juncture of the main sprue and the model. These vents are the last to fill with metal and act as extra reservoirs during the shrinking process of the molten metal to a solid mass. Vents should not be placed at strategic spots on the wax model and carried to the top of the investment ring, because such venting is usually local and of little value. Proper venting is effective if one end of the wax vent wire is attached to the sloping wall of the crucible former and run to a critical area (usually a draw or undercut), the other end left unattached (see Fig. 61). Thus, gases leave the cavity ahead of the flow of the molten metal, and are forced a short distance through the mold to meet the vent. By attaching the vent to the crucible, the spilling of molten metal from the mold is eliminated.

FIG. 68

Auxiliary sprues

Auxiliary sprues, in addition to being necessary to carry molten metal to thin outer areas of the mold, are needed to supply molten metal to any area below the juncture of the main sprue and the model (see Fig. 61). Flat patterns should be sprued on an angle rather than in a horizontal position.

Plastic sprue pins

Plastic sprue pins, used in place of metal sprue pins, which are nothing more than ordinary steel piano wire, should not be left in the sprued pattern to be eliminated during the wax burn-out. They should be removed from the main sprue after the spruing procedure is completed, just as the metal sprue pins are removed. The plastic pin, with a higher melting point than the wax model, expands in the sprue tunnel and moves around like a cork in a bottle until the heat reduces it to a liquid or flowing state (see Fig. 61). This expansion ruffles the interior walls of the sprue and leaves a powdery residue of investment which can contaminate a casting with resultant surface porosity. Coinciding with the action of the plastic pin, boiling wax, unable to escape, boils in the mold, causing rough surfaces on the inner convolutions of the pattern chamber.

Sprued models without crucible formers

Wax models too large to be used with a crucible former can be sprued by inserting a steel sprue pin in a section of sprue wire (equal in diameter to the thickest section of the wax model). The sprue is positioned upright on the glass slab or some other working surface. The auxiliary and

Fig. 70

venting wax sprue wires are added in the same manner as those attached to a model that has been sprued on a crucible former. Venting sprues returned to the imaginary crucible cone are temporarily attached to the glass slab or working surface (see Figs. 69 and 70). The casting flask should be positioned over the sprued model to check edge and height distances so necessary in both spruing techniques.

Spruing odd-sized models

Odd-sized models that do not fit any casting flask can be cast by bending ordinary tin cans to fit the wax model so that side and height distances can be maintained (see Fig. 71). However, particular attention must be given to the main sprue to see that it is centered in the flask and that the direction of the flow of the molten metal through the main sprue remains parallel with the flask wall. This type of flask, usable for one casting only and then discarded, requires some adjustment in the casting machine to center the sprue opening directly in front of the casting crucible accurately (see Chapter 8).

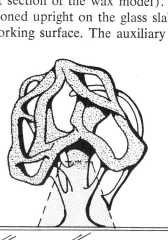

Fig. 69

FIG. 71

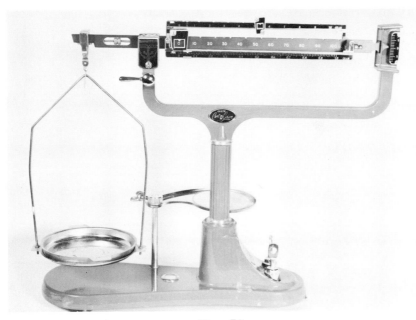

FIG. 72

Spruing models for pressure casting

Wax models sprued for casting under pressure should not have sprue wires larger than 14 gauge. If, because of bulk, a sprue larger than 14 gauge is called for, smaller sprues are substituted. Larger sprues will permit the flow of some of the molten metal into the mold before all of it is ready to enter.

The preceding systems of spruing ensure placement of the model or pattern in the center of the casting flask for even expansion of the investment to dispel trapped air and gases, and to assist the proper feedback of molten metal from the inner vent to the casting during the shrinking and cooling process.

Determining metal requirements

It is necessary to determine the amount of metal needed to replace the wax model and its sprues, including a small reserve. This is very important to ensure a successful casting. Filling the casting crucible on the casting machine with all of the metal that it will hold or guessing the amount needed is poor technique, to say the least. An inadequate amount of metal, or the molten metal sloshing out of the crucible as the casting arm is released—thus wasting the metal as well as causing possible injury to the operator if he is not properly shielded from the molten metal—usually results in an incomplete casting.

Weight determination of required metals (see Appendix for metal alloy content) is accomplished by weighing the casting crucible former normally used in one's shop and preserving this information for reference. The standard metal crucible former weighs approximately 2¾ ounces, depending on whether it is plain brass or chrome-plated; however, some small difference in weight exists between different makes of formers. The smaller formers, either metal or rubber, should be weighed by the craftsman, since no absolutes can be given.

The entire sprued model must be weighed on the crucible former on a triple beam scale (household scales are not accurate enough nor graduated small enough) (see Fig. 72). The weight is deducted from the previously determined crucible former weight. The remaining sum (weight of wax model with sprues) is multiplied by the specific gravity of the metal (see Appendix). This gives the amount of metal necessary to complete the casting. An easy method of determining a specific gravity factor or multiple is weighing a like amount of wax and metal. Silver uses a multiple of 10.46. This is determined by weighing a 1 inch × 1 inch square of 14 gauge wax sheet and then weighing an identical square of 14 gauge sterling silver, which is 10.46 times the weight of the wax. This method can be used to determine other wax/metal ratios not found on a specific gravity chart. If all the wax is weighed, no additional metal need be added for vent and sprue allowances. Molten metal occupies more space than metal in a solid state. A solid metal, in its effort to occupy the same space, requires reserve metal, or it resorts to porosity in order to fill the pattern chamber.

The alternate method of determining wax/metal ratios is to remove the sprued model from the crucible former and immerse it in a graduate cylinder two-thirds full of water (see Figs. 73 and 74). When the water level is observed, a double layer will appear on the surface. This is a meniscus (or curved upper surface of a liquid column), which forms when the containing walls are wetted by the liquid. The level of the water is noted at the underside of this surface. The wax model, or original pattern, is immersed on a small wire, looped to hold it so that it will not float. The rise in the water level is then noted, and the model removed.

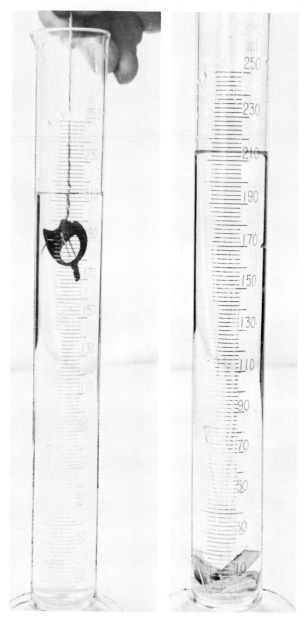

FIG. 73   FIG. 74

Sufficient metal is added to raise the water to the identical level made when the wax model was immersed. If only the wax model is immersed, 25% more metal must be added for vent, sprue, and reservoir allowances. This immersion method is fairly accurate and acceptable for ordinary models, but larger models do not fit well in the available graduate cylinders. Large lost-wax castings are sprued in the same manner as the smaller wax models; however, the standard blowtorch, or small butane torch, is used to heat the wax and attach the sprues and vents. The model is then weighed to determine metal requirements.

CHAPTER 6

Investing

INVESTING IS ENCASING A SPRUED MODEL IN A casting flask that is filled with a refractory material (mixed with water to specified water/powder ratios) called investment plaster. The plaster is vibrated down around the model to eliminate air entrapment in the bulk of the mold. The invested flask is allowed to stand for a sufficient setting time before being placed in the burn-out furnace. After the burn-out, the investment mold, which produces all the detail, is the only impression remaining of the original model.

Lining the flask

The casting flask is lined with asbestos strips 1½" to 3" wide (see Figs. 75 and 76). As the flask and investment do not expand equally, the asbestos lining paper acts as a cushion, allowing the investment to breathe and expand freely. The paper also aids in removing the old investment from the flask after casting has been completed.

The asbestos paper strip is measured by wrapping the flask with the paper and then cutting it to the required length. The edge of the strip is trimmed so that it is ⅛" narrower than the casting flask. This permits the investment to

adhere to the casting flask so that the mold will stay in place when it is placed on end in the burn-out furnace. It will also eliminate the possibility of the mold moving away from the casting crucible when centrifugal force is applied during the casting steps.

Flasks for pressure castings should be prepared in the same way. Asbestos liners allowed to come to the rim of the flask would permit the mold to breathe too freely so that there would be no pressure in the pattern chamber and the metal would not enter the cavity properly.

After the asbestos strip is measured, it is placed inside the flask with a ⅜" overlap, patted into place with the fingers, and "tacked" with a small amount of wax. This holds the paper in place as it is being moistened and during the vibration step. The paper should be wet, but not sloshy, as this would add more water to the investment mix than is needed. The lined flask is dipped quickly in a container of water and set aside to drain. It can also be moistened with a spray bottle or by holding it under the faucet and allowing the water to drip, *not flow*, over it. *Do not* touch the paper with the fingers after it is wet, as this compresses the paper and reduces the cushioning effect.

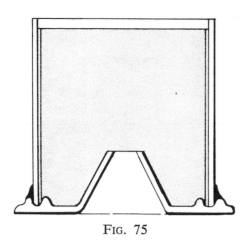

FIG. 75

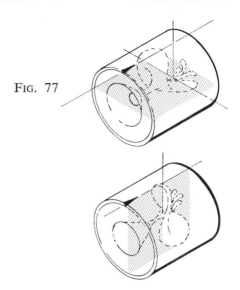

FIG. 77

FIG. 76

Ring notching for balance

To ensure that molten metal will reach all areas of the mold, the casting flask should be notched with a file on the outside at the rim. When investing a flask to be used on a horizontal casting machine, the notched flask, sealed with wax on the crucible former to prevent the leakage of material, is placed with the notch away from the operator so that the thin or intricate areas of the wax model will be to the right and the heavier areas to the left (see Fig. 77). When a flask is being invested for use on a vertical casting machine, the notched flask is also placed away from the operator, but the thin or intricate areas of the wax model are placed on the side directly opposite the notch, and the heavier areas on the same side of the flask as the notch. When the flask is placed in the casting machine cradle, it must always be positioned with the notch upright. (See Fig. 77.)

When the casting machine is released to initiate the centrifugal action, the molten metal flows to the side of the casting flask opposite to the direction of the machine spin. In this way small, thin, or intricate areas receive the first onslaught of molten metal when it is at its greatest point of fluidity.

Cleaning the model

Before investing, the model must be absolutely clean, so that the investment will adhere to the wax surface. Bubbles or rough spots on the casting indicate that air bubbles were entrapped on a dirty model at the time of investing. The model is cleaned with a cotton-tipped applicator dipped in a one-to-one mixture of hydrogen peroxide and tincture of green soap. The cleaner is rinsed off in room-temperature water and the model allowed to dry. Models must be perfectly dry when investing because any moisture dilutes the investment and causes air bubbles. Alcohol may be used to reduce surface tension on the model when this restricts complete adherence of the investment to the model.

Commercial debubbleizers reduce surface tension and aid in complete adherence of the investment without air bubbles. These solutions are painted onto the model, the excess solution blown gently away, and the model dried. Superfluous amounts of debubbleizer left on the model will attack the cristobalite and other investment constituents, so that the casting emerges with rough surfaces.

Although wax models when invested should be perfectly dry to eliminate the possibility of entrapped air bubbles on the model surface, a model after debubbleizing can be dipped in a solution of equal parts of liquid soap and water before investing. This produces a high luster on the casting surface.

Weighing and mixing the investment

The principal ingredient of casting investments is hemihydrates of gypsum amounting to 25–40% of the mix. The balance consists of coloring and modifying agents of silica (SiO_2) or silicon dioxide. Silica is a refractory that resists heating, but at high temperatures forms a mass into which the molten metals are flung. The gypsum acts as a binder, holding the other ingredients together and providing rigidity. The four allotropic forms of silica used in casting investments are quartz, quartz sand, trydimite, and cristobalite.

Cristobalite in its pure form is used as an investment material without other additives. It is a high-temperature mineral of volcanic nature often considered to be the result of lightning striking certain minerals. It is associated with trydimite and is made artificially by heating silica to temperatures of 2680°–3040°F. When the silica cools the cristobalite remains. (Cristobalite was named for the area in Mexico where it was first discovered [about 1868], Cerro San Cristobal, Pachuca.)

In addition to the modifying agents already mentioned, several reducing agents are added to the casting investments. These agents, either powdered copper or carbon, produce, during casting, a reducing (oxide-free) effect in the mold.

.Expansion of the silica, coupled with the expansion of the gypsum, compensates for the contraction of the wax pattern and/or any shrinkage of the metal during its solidifying in the mold. Expansion and shrinkage of molds and models is a critical problem only where definite tolerances are required, however; the shrinkage and expansion percentages (less than 1.6%) are immaterial to the craftsman. For casting, one investment is not recommended over another.

Investment should be purchased in small amounts of 5 to 25 pounds, unless numerous castings are planned for completion in a short period of time. Investment hydrates with age,

so that the resultant loss of strength increases the susceptibility of the mold to cracks and roughness in the pattern chamber. Because of this hydration, it is not possible to weigh the investment for the proper water/powder ratio accurately.

To fill the various sizes of casting flasks adequately, definite amounts of investment powder are required, as follows:

1½″ high × 1¼″ (out. dia.)   50 grs. powd.
1⁹⁄₁₆″ high × 1¾″ (out. dia.) 100 grs. powd.
2″ high × 2½″ (out. dia.) 225 grs. powd.
2¼″ high × 3½″ (out. dia.) 450 grs. powd.

A cubic centimeter of water weighs 1 gram; however, measuring the water in a graduate cylinder using cubic centimeters is the simplest method of determining water quantities. Water temperature should be maintained at 68°–74°F. (see Chapter 3).

Investment is weighed accurately on a triple beam scale that has gram calibrations (see Fig. 72). Some dietetic scales are calibrated thus, but household scales (calibrated in ¼ ounces) are too inaccurate for precise measuring requirements. To eliminate guesswork, a small scale called an investment proportioner can also be used to obtain the correct amounts of water and investment (see Fig. 78). The counterweight is adjustable to 40, 50, and 60 grams. The graduate used with the scale is calibrated from 0 to 25 cc. The investment cup has pivot points to keep it perpendicular in all positions. An eyedropper is used to control the water measurement. Most investment manufacturers recommend a water and powder ratio of 15 cc. of water to each 50 grams of powder.

Increasing the water to 17 cc. per 50 grams of powder gives a percentage of water to be used as a wetting agent for the mixing bowls and tools and does not affect the investment mix. Add the extra water to the mix measurements rather than prewetting the bowl, spatula, and mechanical mixer. When mixing, always add the powder to the water a little at a time (see Fig. 82). Care must be taken not to spill any of the water or powder, for they have been carefully measured and any change in the water/powder ratio would result in an unsatisfactory mold.

A smoother mix with fewer air bubbles (common to hand spatulation) can be produced by a mechanical spatulator which is hand-cranked

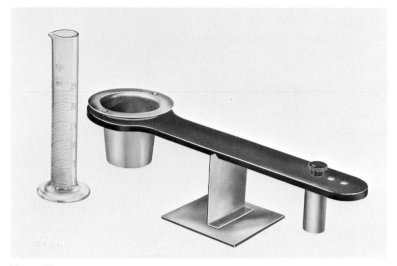

FIG. 78

FIG. 79

FIG. 80

FIG. 81

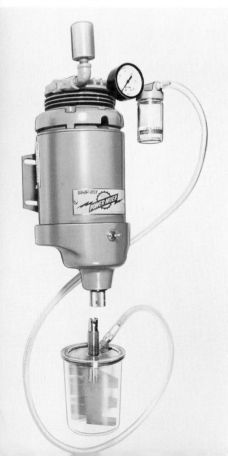

or turned by a crank attached to a wall bracket (see Fig. 79). The mix is spatulated for 30 seconds to 1 minute or according to recommendations for obtaining a homogeneous mix. If a mechanical spatulator is not available, the rubber plaster mixing bowl may be held in one hand, which rests on a mechanical vibrator, while spatulating continues with the other hand (see Fig. 79). Vacuum mechanical spatulators combine spatulation, vacuum, and vibration. They yield the best mix and maintain expansion and distortion tolerances in critically accurate castings, but such tolerances are not necessary for ordinary centrifugal jewelry casting (see Figs. 80 and 81).

Painting the model

A creamy consistency of investment mix is spatulated by combining a ratio of 22 cc. of water to 50 grams of powder. The cleaned model, coated with alcohol, is held in one hand. The other hand, resting on the mechanical vibrator, applies the creamy investment mix to the model, using a fine camel-hair brush as an applicator (see Fig. 83). In order to eliminate any entrapped air bubbles on the model or in the investment, the investment is pushed ahead of the brush and into all the undercuts, crevices, and intricate details of the model so that every surface is coated. The model must be checked for air bubbles continuously as it is coated. After the first coating is applied, but before it dries, the excess is gently blown away and a second coating applied as an added precaution against any air bubbles that may still exist. A thin dusting of dry investment on the model can be applied here to prevent the creamy mix from vibrating away when the heavier mix is added.

Filling the ring or flask

When the model has been sufficiently coated, the flask is immediately placed on the crucible former, which must be carefully checked to make sure that it is centered. Sticky wax may be used around the outside base of the flask to seal the joint between the flask and the crucible former during the vibrating steps (see Fig. 75).

The combined flask and crucible former is held in one hand, which rests on the mechanical vibrator at an angle so that the heavier invest-

ment mix can be poured down the inside wall of the flask to permit the investment to come up and encapsulate the model, thus preventing formation of air bubbles (see Fig. 84). The balance of the mix, added to the flask with the spatula, should be pushed ahead of the spatula for the same reason. The flask is filled to a predetermined depth, so that the investment covers the topmost part of the model by no more than ¼". The flask should not be filled to overflowing, as this would restrict venting of gases from the mold. After the flask is filled to the correct depth, it is held by the thumbs and forefingers of both hands, with the forefingers resting on the vibrator (see Fig. 85). The fingers act as a cushion during the vibration, which ensures that the model remains attached to the main sprue and crucible former. Excessive vibration causes the investment to move away from the model, thus loosening the sprues and vents. In this event, the pattern might partly break away from the sprue and the void fill with water, so that rough spots would appear on the casting.

To induce the desired vibration without a mechanical vibrator, the flask can be placed on a board and the underside tapped lightly with a small mallet. Vibration should always be continued until bubbles no longer come to the surface of the investment-filled flask.

A substitute vibrating machine can be made from a small bench motor and a section of hardwood 4" long and 1½" square. The corners are cut off a square section of wood to make an octagonal shape. A hole is partly drilled into one end, so that the hardwood block can be pressed snugly onto the shaft of the motor. The invested flask is placed on one end of a board 6" wide by 16" long. The opposite end of the board is placed over the rotating octagonal hardwood block so that the corners of the block strike the underside of the board, inducing the flask to vibrate. By moving the flask on the board toward the motor you increase the vibration.

Vibration of the investment as it is spatulated and vibration as it is poured into the flask eliminate most air bubbles. They also eliminate the need for a creamy investment coating.

Investing large models without crucible former

Large wax models (because of their bulk or

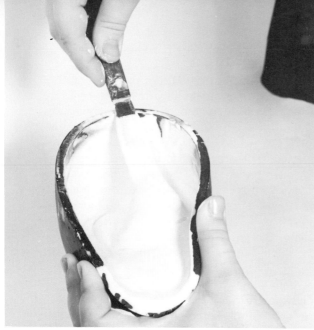

FIG. 83

FIG. 84

FIG. 82   INVESTING

shape) and multiple wax models sprued together for a one-casting operation cannot be sprued on a crucible former. They are invested by placing the asbestos-lined flask on a small square of sheet metal and holding the flask in position with sticky wax, or by placing the flask on a glass slab covered with a paper towel.

The sprued model with its auxiliary and venting sprues is carefully removed from the glass slab. The model is cleaned, wetted with the alcohol, and painted with the creamy investment mix to eliminate entrapped air on the surfaces of the wax model. The coating is gently blown off, and the second coat applied, a mechanical vibrator and a small artist's brush being used to work the investment mix into all the areas and surfaces of the pattern. The sprued model is set aside until the heavier investment mix is correctly spatulated and poured into the casting flask.

The sprued patterns are held upside down by the main sprue and gently settled down into the filled flask. Care must be taken not to create air voids. The minimum distance of ¼″ between the top of the model and the upper edge of the flask must be maintained. The main sprue is held with the thumb and forefinger, while the other fingers and the other hand hold the filled flask on the vibrator to eliminate excess water and air. Small auxiliary sprues or venting sprues which will vent into the crucible must be adjusted into position before the mix sets up.

After the investment has set up, the bench knife is used to carve a funnel-shaped crucible, similar to one formed when a crucible former is used (see FIG. 86). The crucible is flushed with running water to eliminate any investment particles (see FIG. 87).

Investing flowers without sprue base

Large flowers painted with creamy investment are invested by filling the flask with the mix and gently easing the flower down into the mix, while at the same time centering the stem. The stem is held upright, and when the investment has set up, the crucible is carved around the protruding stem (see FIG. 88).

Vacuum investing

An air-free investment, which is always preferred, is possible when all air and gases are

withdrawn from the investment as it is spatulated and after it is poured into the casting flask. Air entrapments cannot be eliminated entirely by vibration.

Vacuum is space exhausted to a high degree by an air pump so that the space measures a density lower than atmospheric pressure. To remove the air effectively, a negative mercury pressure of 27″ to 29″ at sea level is necessary. Vacuum investing units are equipped with gauges capable of registering such pressures (see Figs. 89 and 90).

FIG. 87

FIG. 85

FIG. 86

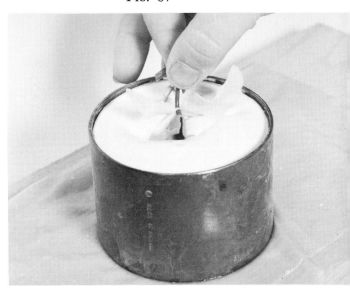

FIG. 88

Vacuum test

Adequate vacuum for investing can be determined easily by placing a container one-third full of water (68°F.) under the bell jar on the vacuum pump. When the pump is turned on, adequate vacuum is produced if the water bubbles or "boils" within 30 seconds. When this is evident, the reading on the pressure gauge should be noted for future use. This reading is used when vacuum investing subsequent flasks instead of the stated gauge reading given in the manufacturer's instruction sheet. It requires 28.5″ vacuum to evacuate air adequately from investment and 29.2″ to induce the "boiling" action of the water in the container.

FIG. 89

FIG. 90

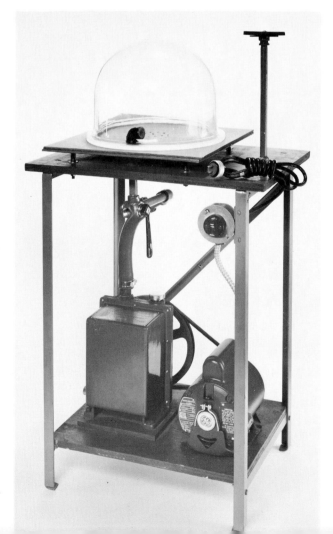

Water and powder ratios

Any type of investment can be used with the vacuum method. The asbestos liner in the casting flask and the painting of the model with creamy investment can be omitted. Pure cristobalite mixed with water (68°–74°F.) in the proportion of 21 to 23 cc. of water to 50 grams of powder produces an ideal mix. Other investments should be mixed with a ratio of 16 to 17 cc. of water to 50 grams of investment; however, a more viscous mix will retain air bubbles, even when the vacuum method is used.

Removal of air

Though vacuum investing reduces the porosity of the investment, often not all the air is removed by this method. On the wax model, flat or concave surfaces that are facing in an opposite direction from the air evacuator will entrap air bubbles. To eliminate this, the pattern should be sprued on an angle or in a tilted position (see Fig. 91). In this way, water vapor bubbles slithering across the surface of the wax model as they rise to the top of the invested flask will carry any clinging air bubbles along with them.

A collar of masking tape placed around the outer surface of the flask and extending about 1″ above the rim will prevent spillage or over-

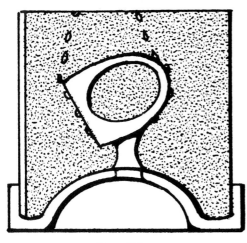

FIG. 91

flow of the investment as it expands under vacuum (see Fig. 92). The vacuum is released just as soon as the air is evacuated from the mix. If the mix is allowed to boil, it will create air bubbles around the wax model as the vacuum draws oxygen out of the water. Bubbling or boiling of the mix should not be permitted for longer than 10 seconds. The vacuum must then be reduced and air allowed to enter to compress the water vapor bubbles. This atmospheric pressure forces the investment into close contact with the model, thus producing a dense investment.

Cleaning the flask

The top of the flask opposite the crucible opening must be surfaced off with a spatula or bench knife so that the investment is level with the flask rim (see Fig. 86). This ensures a snug fit when the flask is placed against the backing plate on the casting machine. It is absolutely necessary to provide a good vacuum when the vacuum casting method is used.

Removal of crucible former

Set-up time for the invested flask varies from 7 to 15 minutes, depending upon the amount of water used in the mix. The crucible former is heated slightly over the alcohol lamp or Bunsen burner flame and rotated to release it at the juncture point of the cone and the main sprue. The plastic or steel sprue pins are removed by heating them and then grasping them with needle-nosed pliers (see Fig. 93).

Excess investment is removed from the outer surfaces of the flask. If it has run over the rim, it is pared off with a bench knife until level. The crucible is smoothed with the bench knife and flushed with running water to remove any particles of loose investment that might be adhering to the crucible walls (see Fig. 87). Otherwise, these could be carried into the pattern chamber by the molten metal. The flask is then placed on the work table and allowed to set for 45 minutes to 1 hour, or until the surface of the investment takes on a smooth plastic appearance.

Small amounts of investment (such as required for a ring mold) in the smaller casting flask can be induced to set up quicker than usual if the spatula is dipped in nitric or hydrochloric acid at the beginning of spatulation of the mix.

Investing extra-large models

Very large wax models are surface-treated before investing in the same manner as the smaller wax models. The sprued model is placed in the center of a molding board or on a smooth flat surface and temporarily attached to it in an upright position. A wire mesh screen (commonly called ½" rabbit wire) is formed into a cylin-

FIG. 93

FIG. 92

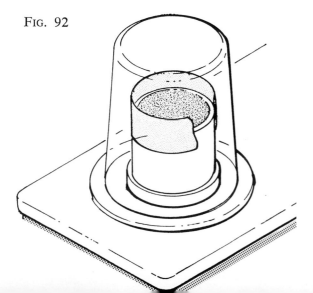

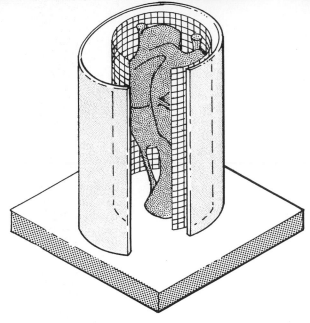

FIG. 94

der and stood on end so that it encircles the wax model (see Fig. 94). A metal cylinder, either a large can without top or bottom and slit length-wise, or a sheet of metal rolled into a cylindrical shape and fastened with heavy wire, is placed around the screen-enclosed wax model (see Fig. 95). Clay is packed around the lower rim to seal off the flow of the wet investment mix when it is poured into the container.

The investment is mixed with an electric mixer, or with a paddle placed in a drill press chuck, rotating at a reduced speed. The model

FIG. 95

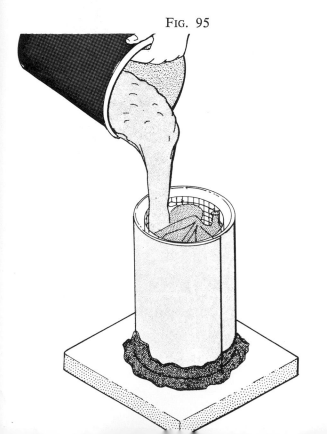

is painted with a creamy investment, and the investment is poured into the metal casing until the model is completely covered by approximately 1″ of investment.

When the mix has set up, the wire is loosened and the metal casing is peeled off the invested form. After the cylinder is removed, the mold is removed from the molding board, the crucible is carved, and the mold is carried to the kiln for wax elimination.

Delayed burn-out of invested flask

After investing, if the mold must be set aside before the casting steps are completed, the flask must be wrapped in a damp towel to simulate humid atmosphere. For longer periods, the flask could also be placed on a damp towel in an air-tight container, such as a humidor or a glass jar with a ground glass stopper which is available in wide-mouth sizes (see Fig. 96).

A mold, including those containing insects or flowers, that has been placed in a humidor or any other airtight container, can be kept for at least a week before burn-out and still produce a successful casting insofar as this phase is concerned.

Wax elimination should be completed only when the mold is ready to cast. No attempt should be made to burn-out a dry mold in the burn-out furnace. The mold will crack if burn-out is followed by a time lapse in which it is not protected in a humid atmosphere. The cracks expand as the mold is reheated to accept the molten metal, and the casting emerges with fins and feathers of the metal that have been forced into the cracks. The water that remains in the invested flask after vibration is necessary to conduct the heat evenly in the flask as the burn-out is completed.

It should always be kept in mind that success with one technique and brand of investment does not ensure success with others.

FIG. 96

Burn-out

CORRECT BURN-OUT ELIMINATES ALL WAX from the model and all moisture from the mold, thereby leaving a pattern chamber in the investment. It burns away any carbon residue of the wax remaining in the pattern chamber which would produce discolored castings. It also heats the mold and flask to the temperature necessary to receive the molten metal when casting takes place. The burn-out step is very important and must be done carefully.

Wax elimination

Burn-out of wax should never be done over a direct flame, because one area of the mold and investment heats while the other areas remain at a lower temperature. This causes a breakdown in the investment and results in an incomplete wax burn-out.

Burn-out furnaces

Gas or electric furnaces are used for wax elimination (see Figs. 97, 98, and 99). Gas furnaces require vents for the gas and wax fumes. Electric furnaces need only vent wax fumes, which is usually accomplished around the door openings. An exhaust fan mounted in the wall above the burn-out furnace and exiting to atmospheric pressure will aid in evacuating the pungent fumes from the work area. Electric furnaces offered by the dental trade are ideal for the craftsman. Gas furnaces with the necessary venting are used primarily for production work. Some oxidation of the investment occurs with electric furnaces because the venting is accomplished around the furnace door, but this is immaterial to the craftsman, for it does not affect the mold other than to alter the surface microscopically. Use of enameling kilns is discouraged unless they are professional models designed for use in wax elimination.

Pyrometers for the visual control of heat on furnaces are necessary, even though visual observation of the heated casting flask usually determines when the wax has been completely eliminated from the mold. Those without pyrometers require hit-or-miss calculations of heat temperatures, which is a frequent factor in unsuccessful castings. Small pellets, a combined preparation of metal oxides offered commercially, are used to check pyrometer readings if doubt exists regarding accuracy of the gauge (see Fig. 100). The small pellets, compounded to melt at almost any desired temperature up to $2000°F.$, are placed in the furnace on a strip of asbestos on top of the invested flask. The pellets blend and flow when their specified melting temperature is reached during the burn-out of a mold.

FIG. 97

FIG. 99

FIG. 100

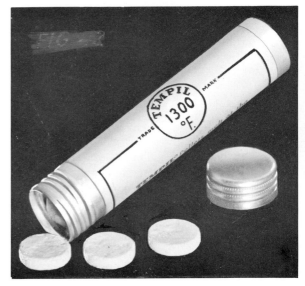

FIG. 98

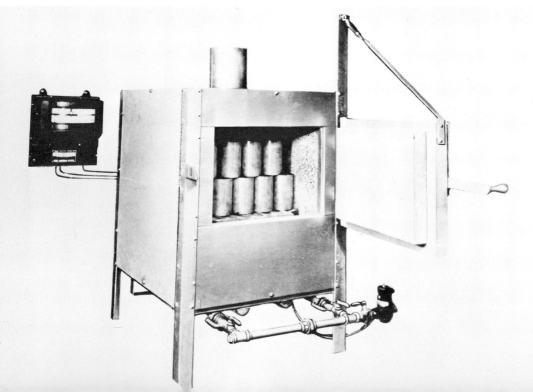

Rheostatic temperature controls are pre-ferred. Thermostats are also an adjunct of burn-out furnaces, but are usually available only on more expensive models (see Fig. 97). Thermo-static temperature controls provide a set tem-perature that does not exceed allowable limits, thus enabling the craftsman to leave the flask in the furnace for several hours, even over night.

Furnaces with exposed heating elements, which produce high heat spots that are apt to cause distorted castings, should not be used. A furnace with a muffle that separates the heating element from the mold distributes the heat evenly.

Small refractory trays are used in furnaces to retain the molten wax as it flows from the mold, which is always placed sprue-hole-down in the center and to the rear of the furnace (see Fig. 101). Prolonged use of a furnace without this tray will eventually damage the heating element under the furnace floor.

In addition to the refractory tray, small triv-ets of refractory material are used to elevate the casting from the tray slightly, in order to allow a free flow of air under the mold. The oxygen entering into the mold mixes with the carbon residue, forming a gas which vents out through the sprue opening. The process of the reduction of carbon residue in the mold can easily be understood by observing a piece of charcoal (which is carbon) as it is brought up to red heat with a blowtorch. When the torch is re-moved there is very little decrease in the volume of the charcoal, but when the flame is left on it, the charcoal disappears completely.

A small dual thermal temperature furnace is available which can heat an invested mold to 900°F. in 20 to 30 minutes and maintain that heat (see Fig. 102). The alternate temperature for the higher heating of molds is 1200°F., which is obtained in 35 to 40 minutes. The furnace does not have a pyrometer, dials, or gauges, because the heat is provided automati-cally once the heat switch has been placed in one of two possible positions. The automatic heat ceiling prevents unwanted overheating of the molds.

FIG. 101

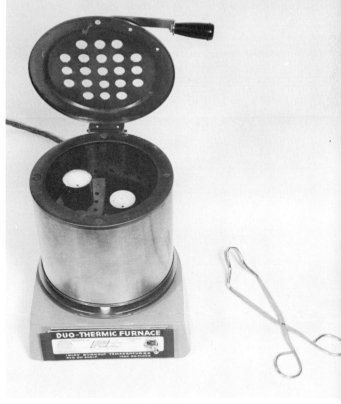

FIG. 102

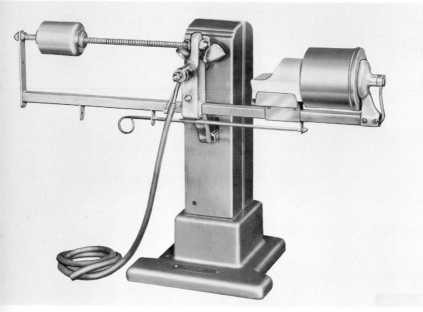

FIG. 103

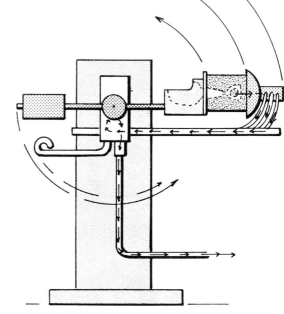

FIG. 104   Schematic of
vacuum-centrifugal casting machine

FIG. 105

Selection of the casting machine

It is wise to invest in the best and largest machine available that one can afford; however, the casting results achieved by craftsmen cannot be solely attributed to the machine used. The casting machine used is secondary to the skill used on the basic technique steps.

Machines are spring-activated, motorized, or electricity-actuated automatically, and operate at speeds of 500 to 1200 rpm (see Figs. 103, 105, and 106). The spring-activated models are more economical and better suited for all-around use by the craftsman. The arm extensions can be equipped with the extra counterbalances that are needed for larger castings, or they can be interchanged with arms that have longer extensions. Broken-arm machines are preferred and recommended over stabile-arm machines. The casting arm "breaks" to prevent the spill of molten metal out of the casting crucible before the cross-arm develops enough speed to exert centrifugal force. Stabile-arm machines require casting crucibles with a high protective wall on one side to prevent the sloshing out of the molten metal at the onslaught of the centrifugal action.

Straight pressure casting machines that force the metal down into the mold by air pressure produce the finest castings; but they are too expensive for most craftsmen (see Fig. 108).

With either the vacuum-centrifuge or air pressure casting machines, the thin silky gossamer of a bumblebee or horsefly wing can be reproduced in a lacy net of precious metal.

Production casting machines are capable of handling large flasks in which multiple wax patterns may be sprued in layers or ladders.

Electrically-activated automatic casting machines which heat the metal in the casting crucible are excellent but expensive (see Fig. 107). The temperature is indicated on the panel and, when the metal is within 50° of casting temperature, the burned-out mold is placed in the machine. The temperature of the molten metal rises, and when it reaches the required casting temperature the machine is released and the metal is centrifugally cast.

Vertically-mounted machines do not require protective shields as do the horizontal machines, but they should always be balanced ac-

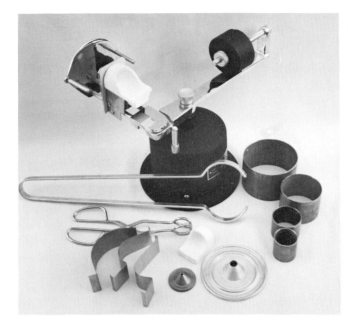

FIG. 106

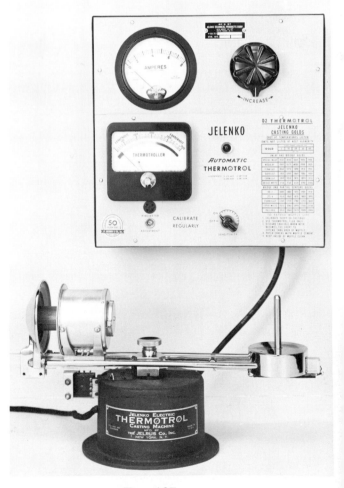

FIG. 107

cording to the manufacturer's instructions. Operation of casting machines that have not been leveled on a work bench will counteract the purpose of the centrifugal action. Counterbalances are important also. A level machine with improperly positioned counterbalances will affect the casting action. Horizontal machines can be mounted on a work bench utilizing a removable protective metal shield; however, a better method is to mount the machine in a metal washtub or a large drum bolted to a rigid and sturdy shelf placed under a bench that has a covered hinged top (see Fig. 110). The counter top can be utilized when the casting machine is not being used, if space is at a premium. This is an ideal mounting for short-statured people, for molten metal seldom flies up out of the casting area. It is also much easier when heating the metal just prior to casting to hold the torch in a downward position rather than straight forward. It is also easier to lift the arms and torch upward as the machine is released instead

of pulling them back and away.

A hand-operated pressure casting machine recently developed is available for casting articles in the lost-wax process (see Fig. 111). The hand-caster is self-contained, and no hoses or permanent installations are necessary. The cylinder, similar to a sport ball air pump, is 8½" long by 2" in diameter and weighs less than 1 pound. The casting flasks are available in 1¼" and 1½" diameters only. Before casting, the pump is actuated to generate air pressure, the flask is removed from the furnace, and the prepared (fluxed) metal is placed in the mold crucible. The pump is then placed over the mold and pressed down until a seal is obtained. This releases the air pressure that forces the metal into the mold. After the flask has cooled for a short time, it is placed in water to disintegrate the investment. The patterns are constructed, sprued, invested, and burned out in a regular furnace in the manner prescribed for lost-wax casting.

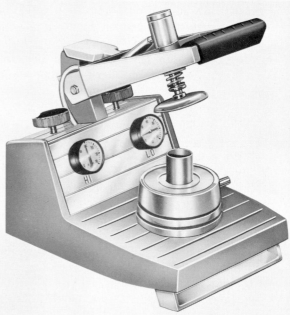

FIG. 108

FIG. 109   Schematic of pressure casting machine

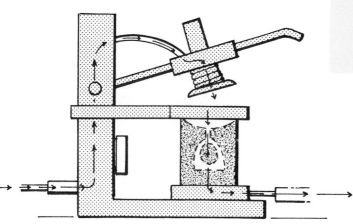

FIG. 110

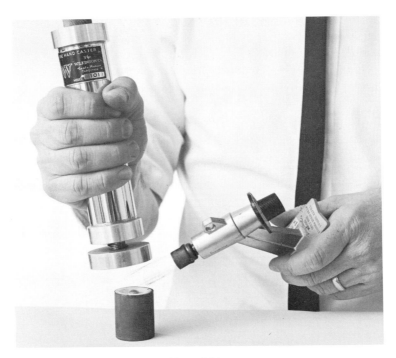

FIG. 111

Balancing the machine before burn-out of the flask

The damp invested casting flask is placed in the casting machine and the counterbalances adjusted so that the arm is balanced before the flask is placed in the furnace for the burn-out (see Figs. 113 and 114). There is no time to balance the machine when the heated mold is removed from the furnace prior to completion of the casting step. A machine balanced without the invested flask in place will not function properly.

The arm is balanced by loosening the retaining nut on the upright shaft until the arm can be rocked up and down. The casting arm is then aligned with the balancing arm. The cradle size necessary to position the mold sprue directly in line with the opening of the casting crucible is checked, and the proper cradle is installed on the machine (see Fig. 71). Large casting rings do not require a cradle. The invested flask is placed in the cradle or on the support arms of the backplate. The heavier end of the entire cross-arm will tip downward. The counterbalances are adjusted and tightened until the arm

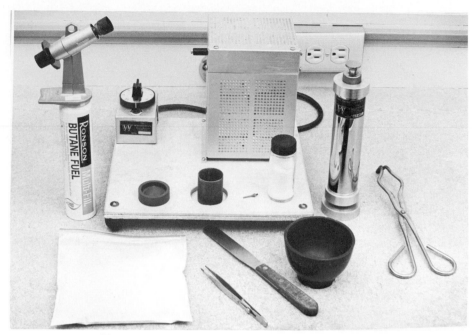

FIG. 112   Complete pressure hand-casting kit
(tweezers, spatula and bowl not included in kit offered by the manufacturer)

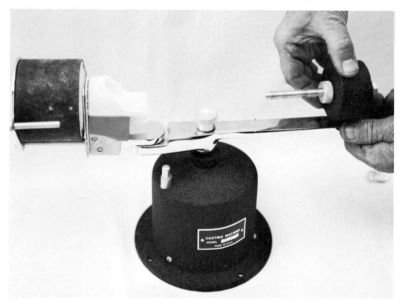

FIG. 113

is evenly balanced before the retaining nut is tightened.

Recording positions of counterbalances does not work, for they are far from absolute. No calibration procedure is such that it will ensure an accurate and static balance. The machine must be balanced for each individual flask owing to the presence of varying amounts of water in the investment mix because of water/powder ratio or lack of sufficient vibration of the flask during investment. This applies to invested flasks of the same size.

Burn-out temperatures

Furnace controls should be set at 900°–1200°F., unless otherwise specified by the investment manufacturer. Furnace temperatures exceeding 1300°F. will shorten the life of the furnace element or muffle, causing a breakdown in the heating coils with costly repair expense. This is in addition to the damage which occurs in and to the mold. A cherry-red color, observed in bright light, indicates that the mold has been heated above 1300°F. and a breakdown in the investment can be expected. Investments contain calcium sulfates which when heated to extremely high temperatures give out sulfur or sulfuric compounds. Occurrence of these gases in the mold brings about a breakdown in the mold cavity and produces a rough surface on the casting. The gases can also combine with the base metal in the cast to form metal sulfides. This reaction is recognizable as a black surface film that is extremely difficult to remove. In addition, sulfur given off by the continual overheating of investments causes a rapid deterioration of the casting flasks, the metal parts of the furnace, and the heating element.

In casting, temperatures of 1200° to 1300°F. are more than ample for heating flasks. Silver melts at 1626°F., and with flask temperatures at 1200°F. an ideal temperature ratio is possible. Gold casting calls for a flask temperature of 1200°F. Some investments can be burned out at temperatures of 850°–900°F., but the heat differential between flask and molten metal is so great that successful castings cannot be guaranteed. Low temperatures prolong furnace life, but require more burn-out time for the flask. Such low-heat molds cool the molten metal before all the metal that is required has entered the pattern chamber. An overheated mold will delay freezing or solidifying of the molten metal until after the machine has stopped and sulfur gases will form the black discoloration. An incomplete casting is the result of either extreme.

Burn-out times are proportionate to the different sizes of the casting flasks (see Fig. 115). The small casting flasks can be burned out in less than 1 hour, while large flasks require as much as 2¼ hours for complete burn-out. Invested flasks may be placed in cold or preheated furnaces. They should touch neither the walls of the furnace nor other flasks if more than one is burnt out at a time.

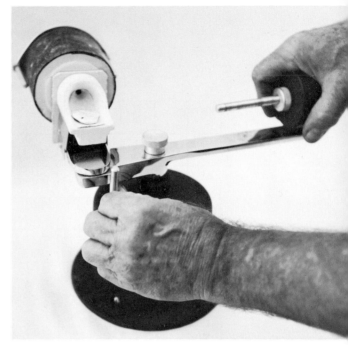

FIG. 114

Placing the flask in the furnace

The casting flask with the crucible opening placed downwards, in addition to permitting easy evacuation of the molten wax, heats the sprue opening so that it becomes the hottest part of the mold (see Fig. 116). The heat helps to prevent the freezing of the molten metal in the sprue before the cavity is filled. Flasks are usually placed in a cold furnace so that the temperatures of the furnace and flask rise simultaneously. Investments heated in this manner will not crack because of heat-shock or uneven expansion; however, the flask requires considerable time (8 hours minimum) to heat because of the build-up of steam pressure in the invested flask. Steam pressure develops from the natural water content of the dry investment plus the water added when the investment is mixed. The flask temperature lags behind the furnace temperature because the water in the investment mass does not turn to steam for escape until it reaches 212°F. (boiling point).

A damp invested flask placed in a preheated furnace will quite often explode because of the build-up of the steam pressure; however, sev-

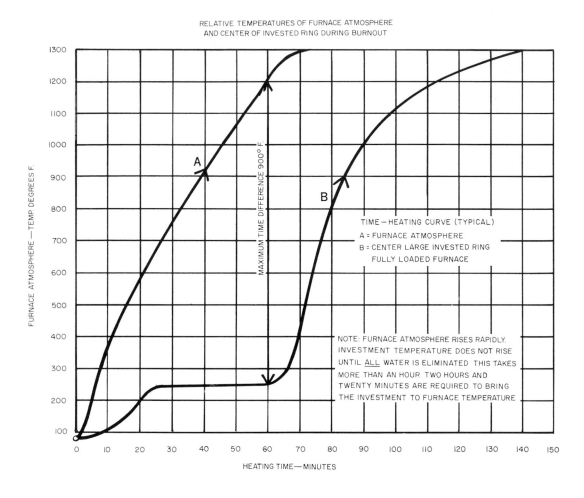

RELATIVE TEMPERATURES OF FURNACE ATMOSPHERE
AND CENTER OF INVESTED RING DURING BURNOUT

FIG. 115

eral investments are offered commercially that work perfectly well when placed in a preheated oven with a temperature of 800°–900°F. To eliminate the possibility of such an explosion and to make all investments effective when the oven is preheated, the invested flask can be completely immersed (after set-up and the sprue base or crucible former is removed) in a container of water. When the air bubbles cease to rise to the surface from the submerged flask, it is removed from the water. The flask should not be submerged for more than 5 minutes' duration.

Often casting time is at a premium and one cannot wait for the furnace to cool to start another burn-out. If you immerse the flask as previously indicated, the furnace can be kept at the desired burn-out temperature and castings made as quickly as wax can be eliminated from the pattern chamber and the mold becomes heat-soaked. Burn-out times vary with mold sizes and wax proportions, but it is possible to eliminate the wax from the pattern chamber completely in less than 45 minutes, so that all that remains is the time required to heat-soak the mold.

FIG. 116

FIG. 117

Burn-out of gem-embedded wax models

Wax models, such as caged pendants with gem-stones that have been placed inside the wax form and invested, must be put into a cold furnace and the heat brought up slowly.

If more than one casting is planned while the furnace is hot and several invested flasks are already prepared for burn-out, each must be wrapped in a damp towel. Semidry molds should not be placed into a heated oven or they will explode because of steam pressure.

Heat-soaking the mold

The mold is not removed from the furnace immediately when the furnace pyrometer indicates the desired temperature. This is the temperature of the furnace and not the inner mass of the invested flask. Burn-out completion is determined by observing the color of the sprue hole in a position shielded from artificial light or daylight. Observation of the sprue hole in a bright light makes it appear darker; because of this the flask temperature is often assumed to be much lower than it actually is. The result is that the mold is heated above the optimum flask temperature necessary for casting. A cherry-red color in the flask indicates that it is about 1373°F., which is too hot. If the flask is heated

to 1000°F., a dull red color is visible at the sprue hole, and the investment is bone-white on the ends. This indicates that the burn-out is complete and the mold is free of carbon. Carbon-free molds produce castings which are much easier to pickle. Black or gray-yellow-colored investment indicates that the wax is not yet completely burned out (see Fig. 117).

The temperature is retained after the wax has been eliminated to heat-soak the mold for at least 30 minutes. This will ensure both the removal of all the water from the mold and the correct temperature of the mold when it is ready to receive the molten metal.

No exact burn-out time can be given for eliminating all traces of replicas from the mold. They usually require approximately the same burn-out time as their counterparts in wax. If casting results are unsatisfactory, it is well to cast samples in scrap metal for confirming more accurate burn-out times. The best burn-out results will occur when the pattern or replica is placed as close as possible on the main sprue of the crucible end of the casting flask. Study of the density of replica items will indicate that some objects take longer than others; for example, a rosebud will take longer than a dog-wood blossom.

Burn-out of large molds

The large wax mold is placed in a kiln, crucible end down, to evacuate the melted wax and to eliminate all moisture as the mold is heated to 1000°F.

CHAPTER 8

Casting

CASTING IS THE THRUST OF MOLTEN METAL into an extremely hot mold by centrifugal force, pressure, or vacuum so that it immediately freezes or solidifies into a form that reflects in metal every detail of the wax model.

Preparing the casting machine

Before the casting flask is removed from the furnace several steps must be taken. These can be accomplished during the heat-soak step of the investment. The balanced arm on the casting machine must be wound the proper number of turns for the particular size of casting flask used (see Fig. 113). (The cradle, already in place, and the arm, counterbalanced before the flask was placed in the furnace for burn-out, are previously completed portions of the casting steps.) The balancing arm is rotated clockwise two complete turns for the small and medium-sized flasks, and four complete turns for the large flask. The arm is held until the releasing pin is raised. This is to prevent the arm from starting its whiplike unwinding action before it is needed. The casting arm section with the crucible is turned at right angles to the balancing arm.

Preparing the casting crucible

The casting crucible is coated with borax and heated so that a complete liner of flux is formed. Short strips of asbestos are dampened with water, which helps form them with finger pressure to fit the crucible (see Fig. 118). The asbestos liner is replaced each time the crucible is used for a new casting. A crucible should always have a new liner; it should not be used either with the old liner or with no liner at all. Residual metal incrustations will contaminate the metal, especially if the crucible is used for several different metals.

Each metal should be melted in its own crucible. Electric bench pots for melting and fluxing of metals preparatory to casting permit molten metals to be poured into the casting crucible while the oxides remain in the pot. These electric pots are expensive; regular crucibles will serve the purpose if properly prepared. The casting crucible, either new or used previously, after being lined with new asbestos, can be placed in the furnace along with the invested flask during the burn-out to heat the metal.

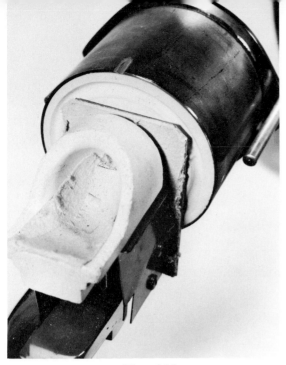

FIG. 118

Reworking used casting crucibles

Crucibles which have a heavy coating of old flux and metal incrustations can be reworked instead of discarded. This can be done by scraping off as much of the old flux as possible and boiling the crucible in a weak solution of sulfuric acid and water. Boiling in water alone will not loosen the flux. After boiling, the crucible is rinsed in clear water to remove the solution and set aside to dry slowly. Crucibles cannot be dried with a torch or by placing them in the burn-out furnace, as they will crack.

The faceplate of the casting machine must always have an asbestos sheet. The crucible should be checked to see that it fits tightly against the faceplate on the casting machine, and that the faceplate fits tightly against the flask (see Fig. 119). The asbestos gasket or pad on the casting machine backing-plate should be moistened before removing the casting flask from the furnace. This provides a cushion for the ring and a better seal.

Fluxing

To eliminate oxides and increase fluidity, correct fluxing steps are important. The casting metal (even if scrap) should be heated in a depression in a charcoal block before being placed in the casting crucible (see Fig. 120).

The investment crucible is used to heat the metal in the final stages of preparation for pressure casting; therefore, the metal must first be premelted and fluxed in a charcoal block. After it is fluxed and free of oxides and contaminants, it is transferred to the investment crucible at the same time the flask is removed from the furnace and placed in the casting machine. Scrap material containing any solder should not be used for casting, as it will not homogenize with the base metals. Solder concentrates in one mass in the metal, creating hard and soft spots.

Copper is an important constituent of alloyed golds which are used for casting. Its exact amount in the alloy is altered or reduced when oxidized or slagged off with plain borax. This upsets the balance of the alloy and its properties. Borax does not mix with the molten metal, but builds up on the sides of the crucible and carries oxidized portions of copper with it. A good reducing flux contains equal parts of ground boric acid powder and fused borax powder, which is available in supermarkets as 99.5% pure borax. The boric acid powder retains the flux on the surface of the metal and is added when the metal is in the molten stage. It can be used on either new or used metal. Flux

FIG. 119

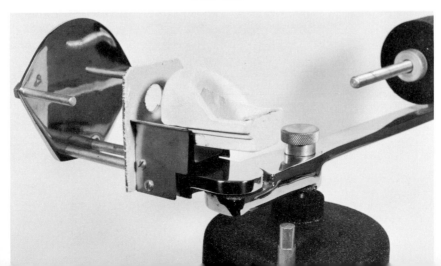

is not necessary when preparing casting metals if the crucible is continually covered with the correct flame. This prevents atmospheric air from contacting the metal and causing oxidation. A commercially prepared pickling solution offered by the dental trade is an excellent oxide preventive, which can be used when preparing metal for casting and when reclaiming and alloying old sprue buttons with new metal.

Selection and use of torches

Torches and blowpipes are designed for specific combinations of oxygen-gas, compressed air-gas, and oxygen-acetylene, and are not interchangeable. An oxygen and gas mixture is best for melting gold and silver (see Figs. 121 and 122). If a torch is difficult to light there is usually too much gas entering the blowpipe. The gas valve should be opened or "cracked" just enough to allow sufficient gas to enter to light the flame. The oxygen is then added slowly, then the gas valve is opened and adjusted to a reducing flame. A harsh hissing flame indicates it is an oxidizing flame. The temperature of the flame should be several hundred degrees hotter than the temperature at which gold is cast. Acetylene mixed with air is even hotter, so that care must be exercised to avoid overheating the metals.

FIG. 120

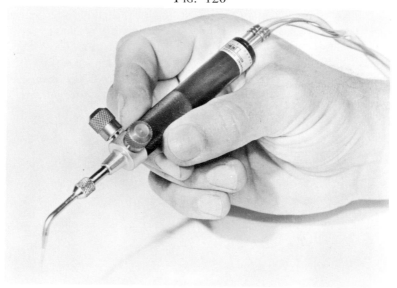

FIG. 121

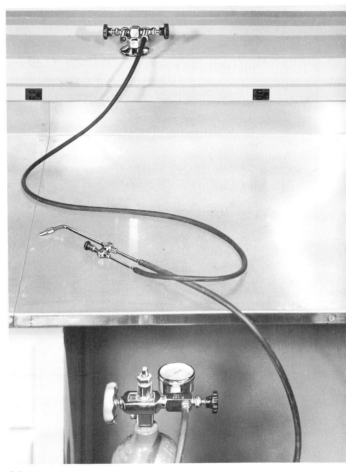

FIG. 122

Flame adjustment

Proper flame adjustment and use can prevent harmful oxidations in the casting metals during the initial fusing, fluxing, and melting of the metal in the casting crucible immediately before casting.

The best reducing flame uses a minimum amount of air (or oxygen) and will not melt metal as swiftly as an oxidizing flame, though it gives better results. All of the air in the mix of the reducing flame is consumed, leaving nothing to combine with the hot metal to form new oxides; the oxides previously formed are reduced.

The oxidizing and reducing areas of the flame can be easily identified (see Figs. 123 and 124). A visible scum, which indicates an oxidizing flame, forms immediately when the dark-blue innermost cone of the flame is directed on the melting button. This flame acts as a reducing flame when it is withdrawn until only the cone of the light-blue center comes into contact with the button. The metal becomes bright, shiny, and mirror-like as the oxide film disappears. When the flame is withdrawn even further, a purplish-blue brushlike flame is in contact with the metal, and the oxide scum reappears. The dark-blue tip, or oxidizing flame, should not touch the metal. The flame is always pointed straight down at the metal. The first dark-blue cone of the flame, issuing from the nozzle of the blowpipe, is air and gas before combustion and is not hot. The second cone, green in color, the oxidizing zone, completely surrounds the first cone and is in partial combustion. The third cone, dim blue, just beyond the green zone, is the reducing zone. This third cone, the hottest part, is held within 1″ of the molten metal in the crucible. The fourth, outermost cone is the low-heat oxidizing zone; the combustion here occurs on contact with the oxygen in the atmosphere.

A reducing flame should always be used for gold and silver. These two metals are affected by oxidation (excess of oxygen) when prepared for casting, but they will not carbonize. Platinum requires an oxidizing flame to prevent carbonization.

OXIDIZING ZONE
YELLOW BLUE
LIGHT BLUE
REDUCING ZONE
DIM BLUE
OXIDIZING ZONE
DARK BLUE

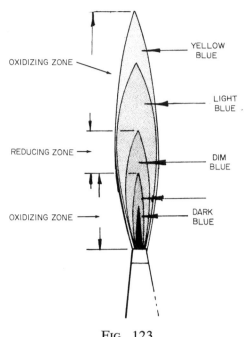

FIG. 123

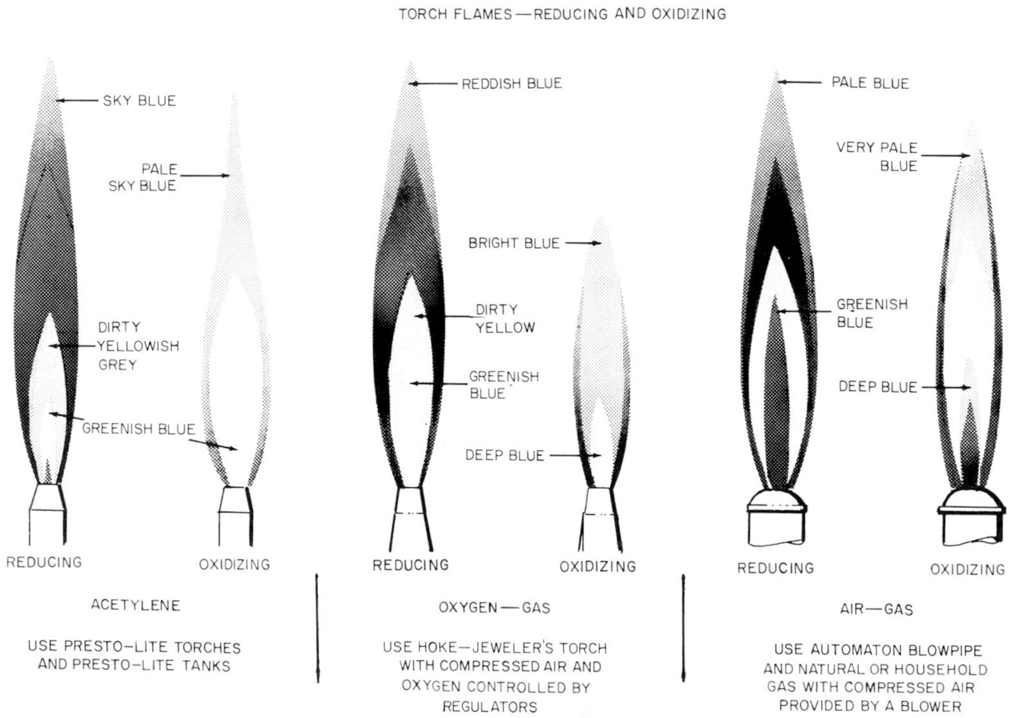

TORCH FLAMES—REDUCING AND OXIDIZING
SKY BLUE
PALE SKY BLUE
DIRTY YELLOWISH GREY
GREENISH BLUE
REDUCING
OXIDIZING
ACETYLENE
USE PRESTO-LITE TORCHES AND PRESTO-LITE TANKS
REDDISH BLUE
BRIGHT BLUE
DIRTY YELLOW
GREENISH BLUE
DEEP BLUE
REDUCING
OXIDIZING
OXYGEN—GAS
USE HOKE—JEWELER'S TORCH WITH COMPRESSED AIR AND OXYGEN CONTROLLED BY REGULATORS
PALE BLUE
VERY PALE BLUE
GREENISH BLUE
DEEP BLUE
REDUCING
OXIDIZING
AIR—GAS
USE AUTOMATON BLOWPIPE AND NATURAL OR HOUSEHOLD GAS WITH COMPRESSED AIR PROVIDED BY A BLOWER

ALWAYS TRY TO OBTAIN A REDUCING FLAME, BUT NEVER A NOISY OR HISSING FLAME.

A reducing flame is easily and quickly obtained by turning on the gas first, then adding oxygen or air, until the yellow tinge just barely disappears except with acetylene—leave a faint tinge of yellow in the flame.

FIG. 124

Metal temperatures

The melting range of a casting metal is the temperature variance between partly melted and completely melted metal. This serves as a guide for casting heat and selection of solder when the casting is being finished.

A thin ingot of fluxed metal will melt faster in the crucible than heavy pieces, thus avoiding the manufacture of the harmful oxides that form in long heating periods. Large quantities of metal must be melted and fluxed in the casting crucible before the casting flask is transferred from the furnace to the casting machine.

Care should always be taken not to overheat metal. Maximum heat should be approximately 100°–150°F. above its temperature when the metal is completely liquid (liquidus temperature). The heated metals when viewed in a shaded light will be visibly red at 900°F., an even dull red at 1200°F., bright cherry-red at 1400°F., pink at 1600°F., and light orange at 1640°F. The correct casting temperature of molten alloy is indicated by a light-orange color. The metal when it reaches this color will spin and follow the torch flame as it is moved slightly.

Transferring the mold

Casting is completed as soon as possible after the mold leaves the furnace. After completion of the burn-out, molds must remain in the hot furnace at a controlled temperature until ready for transfer to the casting machine. These molds, if allowed to cool before the metal is cast into them, will gather moisture, which will appear as pits on the surface of the casting. When transferring the hot flask from the furnace to the casting machine, make sure that the identifying notch is in an upright position (see Fig. 118). When the sprue opening is facing downward, the flask is tapped lightly to help eject any ash residue that remains in the pattern chamber.

The crucible must be covered with the flame to maintain the melting temperature of the metal as the flask is transferred from the furnace to the casting machine with the heavy tongs (see Fig. 125). It is advisable to wear asbestos gloves to protect the hands from the heat and the hot inner walls of the furnace during this procedure.

Casting should never be attempted if a scum or oxide is visible on the surface of the molten metal. Additional flux is added until the surface is bright and shiny, followed by more in a very small amount just before the pin holding the balancing arm is released. The metal should never be overheated, especially to the point where it boils.

Coarse grain structure in cast gold is caused by a slow-cooling mold. This means that the mold temperature is too close to the metal temperature. A finer-grained casting will result if the mold is burned out at 1292°F. and the furnace temperature reduced to 1000°F. for a half-hour before the metal is cast.

FIG. 125

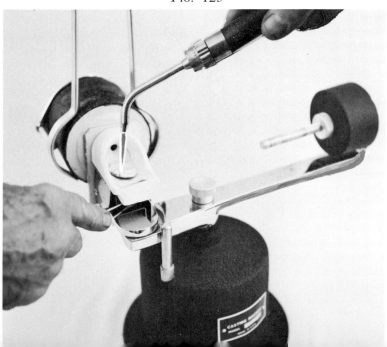

FIG. 126

Casting the metal

The balancing arm of the casting machine is grasped with the right hand and moved slightly to allow the pin to drop while the hand retains its hold on the arm. The balancing arm is joggled slightly to make sure that the button of molten metal rolls freely and no solids or impurities are present. The torch flame is still covering the metal during this step. *The machine must not be released until the metal has stopped rolling, because it rolls on a different plane from the rotation of the casting machine and the metal will splash out of the crucible.* A good rule to follow is to release the arm and lift the torch at the same time. This gets the hands out of the circle of movement and away from the splash of metal (see Fig. 126).

Cooling the mold and removal of casting

The machine is permitted to spin of its own accord until it stops. This allows the metal to cool and solidify. When the machine has stopped rotating and the sprue button loses its red color and turns black, the flask is removed from the machine with the large tongs and immediately plunged into a container of cool water (see Fig. 127). A shaking, sideways motion of the tongs aids in releasing the investment from the flask. The sudden temperature change during the quenching causes a violent reaction in the investment, which makes it become soft and granular, so that it disintegrates and the casting can be removed easily. It is not neces-

sary to cool the flask for a longer period before dunking in the water. A longer cooling period is a heat-hardening process for dental appliances and is not used in jewelry casting.

Molds with gemstones

Molds containing gemstones originally invested with the wax form are returned to the furnace as soon as the casting machine has stopped spinning. The furnace is turned off and the door closed to permit the casting to cool along with the furnace. The flask is not dipped in cold water or cooled at room temperature because the shock of cool air on the hot gemstone will either shatter or craze it.

FIG. 127

Vacuum casting

When the mold has been checked in the furnace and is ready for casting, the casting metal is prepared in the crucible or on the arm of the centrifugal-vacuum casting machine. The hot flask is transferred to the machine, and a trigger action releases the machine so that the molten metal is forced into the mold centrifugally. At the same time, the vacuum on the other end of the flask pulls the air and gases from the mold so that the molten metal does not have to push them ahead in order to flow to all areas of the mold. The vacuum reading should be between 12″ and 20″ for a successful casting. The combined centrifugal and vacuum forces speed the metal to all parts of the mold before solidifying begins (see Figs. 103 and 104).

Pressure casting

Pressure casting machines operate in a similar manner. A lid is placed over the investment crucible containing the molten metal to eliminate air and gases by vacuum from the mold. In this case there will be no metal spillage. Low pressure is applied to initiate the flow of the molten metal and avoid slamming the metal into the mold. It is then followed by high pressure, which forces the metal into all inner recesses of the mold. A minimum pressure of 10 p.s.i. must be maintained for at least 4 seconds. The mold fills and begins to solidify in 1 second, but the hot metal is soft and needs support as it cools further (see Figs. 108 and 109).

Large castings

The large wax mold, after wax elimination, is placed in a pit and surrounded with sand to support the investment during the pour (see Fig. 128). The metal for the large wax mold is heated in a large crucible in a gas-fired melting furnace to 2000°F. When the metal is completely molten, the crucible is removed from the furnace, and the surface of the metal is skimmed to remove any slag or dross. It is then fluxed and poured into the mold (see Fig. 129). When the large casting mold has cooled after the pour, the investment plaster is broken off the casting and remaining particles are washed

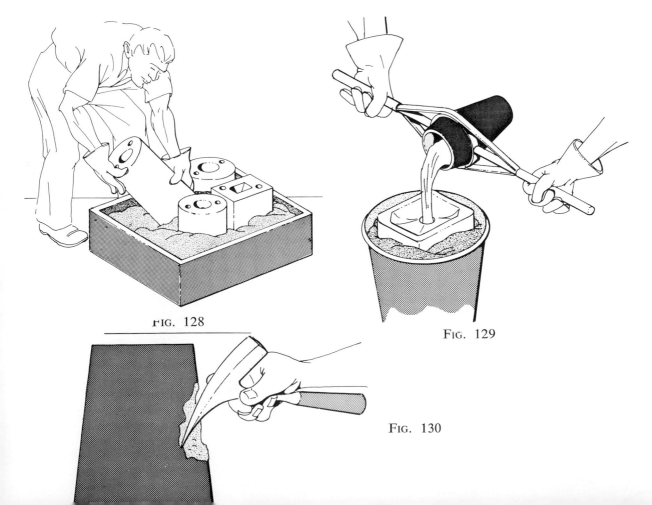

FIG. 128

FIG. 129

FIG. 130

away with water (see Fig. 130). The metal is further cleaned by being immersed in a pickling bath, followed by rinsing in clear water. The sprue and vents are then sawed off the casting and ground smooth with a carborundum wheel on a standard bench grinder. The surfaces are finished by any one of the customary methods: filing and grinding, hammering, welding, buffing, polishing, and affecting the surface color by patina or heat application.

Cleaning the casting

As the casting emerges from the mold, much of the old fired investment is left in the pail, but some investment still adheres to the casting, especially in areas of intricate detail. The casting is scrubbed with a small stiff brush under running water to loosen the remaining particles until every trace of the investment is removed (see Figs. 131 and 132). Small dental scalers, chisels, and picks are used to get at any tenacious bits of the investment that still cling to the casting in intricate or detailed areas. The tools are used gently without gouging or scratching the surfaces. Stubborn bits of investment can be removed by pickling, sand-blasting or ultrasonic vibration.

Pickling the casting

Pickling (dipping in an acid solution) removes investment and oxidation at the same time, and is best accomplished by plunging the article into the hot acid solution, taking care to avoid any splashing of the liquid. Dropping hot castings

into a cold pickling solution may cause the solution to spew out of its container and onto one's hands as well as cause warpage in thin areas of the casting. If the casting must be handled in the solution, tweezers or tongs of quartz, glass, plastic, plastic-coated metal, etc., should be used.

Sparex no. 2 is available for most pickling uses, although sulfuric acid is preferred because of its highly effective action in dissolving oxides. (The sulfuric fumes are less objectionable than those emitted by hydrochloric or nitric acid, which readily affect, by corrosion, all metal tools and equipment in the workshop.) The action of sulfuric acid is increased by the addition of a very small amount of potassium dichromate. This additive immediately attacks gold oxides, but is never added to a pickling solution for silver.

Pickling solution for silver is made from equal parts of sulfuric acid and water (the same ratio is used for a gold pickling solution, but with additive included). *Always pour the acid into the water.* Reversing the procedure will cause the acid to boil violently and cause serious burns if it splatters. Castings should never be heated directly in a flame unless extreme caution is used.

For effective and rapid pickling, the casting is placed in a porcelain or glass pan and the pickling solution poured over the object (see Fig. 133). The pan, placed on a hot plate, is brought to a boil. When the pickling is completed the solution is poured off into another porcelain or glass pan and the casting flushed

FIG. 131

FIG. 132

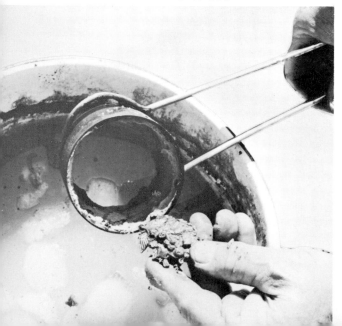

with running water. In this way the casting does not receive a flash copper-plating from a contaminated solution, and the pickle is left clean. The casting is then placed in a solution of sodium bicarbonate (baking soda) and water to neutralize the acids, and flushed again with running water. Tongs (other than copper) should be used to remove the casting from the pickling solution and to hold it under running water to flush all of the solution away. This saves time when casting several items simultaneously and eliminates the time-consuming pour-off of the acid solution. Acids, when not used, are stored in glass-stoppered bottles appropriately marked. The pickling dishes and pans are made of a porcelain-like material called sillimanite, which is highly resistant to acids and thermal shock. Sillimanite, found in its natural state, is a gem-cutting material for cabochons, but its primary value is in serving as the main constituent of porcelain sections of spark plugs.

The solution should be used only as long as it remains colorless. Solutions with a greenish-blue tinge are contaminated with copper salts from previously pickled castings or from continual dipping of the copper tongs into the pickle.

Surface pits

Surface pits in castings frequently attract minute deposits of copper from contaminated pickling solutions, which remain difficult to remove except by sanding or considerable buffing. Such

FIG. 133

deposits can be removed with a bench sand-blasting chamber filled with fine abrasive materials which are forced out through small jets in the blasting machine. Tenacious bits of investment remaining on the casting and oxides can be removed in the same manner so that a bright casting emerges.

Removal of sprue wires and buttons

The excess metal used to ensure a complete casting fills in the sprue passageways and a portion of the crucible cone (now called a button) and is still attached to the casting. These wires and the button are removed from the casting during the finishing steps.

Remelting silver sprue buttons and wires

Sprue buttons and wires remelted for subsequent castings must be cleaned of all impurities such as oxides and old investment. The metal is melted in a charcoal block and the torch left on the metal after fluxing. The air is turned off and the gas flame is left on the metal until it solidifies. If the blowpipe is completely removed after fluxing, the metal absorbs gas from the atmosphere which oxidizes it.

Melting blocks of fire brick, asbestos, and similar refractory materials are not satisfactory, as they lack the reducing action of the charcoal block. Small beads of metal that become entangled in the flux adhere to the refractory materials and are practically impossible to remove. These will contaminate any metal subsequently melted thereon. The charcoal block is scraped clean, and a small depression is made to hold the molten metal and to protect it as much as possible from torch oxidation. The wires and button are placed in the hollow, melted, and kept molten for 15 seconds. A pinch of the same reducing flux used when melting the metal before casting is added. The boric acid powder in the flux retains the powder on the surface until the metal is clean and shiny. The metal is then covered with a teaspoonful of flux as the flame is removed. When solid and cooled to a black color, the hot metal is either eased gently into the pickling solution or placed in a porcelain pan and the solution poured over it. The mirror-like finish on the melted button and wires indicates perfect fusion and the absence of oxides. A cloudy surface indicates oxide contamination from the torch or

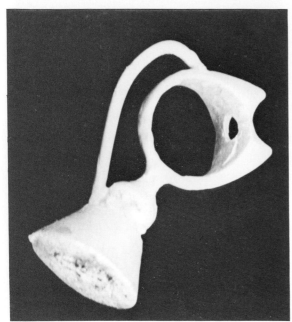

FIG. 134   Pickled ring casting with button
sprue attached

investment. This same method of melting and fluxing is used when combining the melted buttons and wires with new metal for use in another casting.

The ratio of used and new metal combined for casting material is always equal. Melted and fluxed buttons and sprue wires should never be used for subsequent castings, unless a like amount of new metal is combined with the used materials.

Cleaning and remelting gold sprues and buttons

Gold sprues and buttons sawed from castings that are to be used in a subsequent casting are soaked over night in a solution of cold hydrofluoric acid before they are reworked. This solution will attack glass, so it must be kept in tightly covered containers of polyethylene material. The acid dissolves the silica and removes all of the investment material.

When reused for casting, sprue buttons with investment particles remaining release sulfur or sulfuric oxides. The sulfur or oxides are accumulative even in small amounts, so that eventually they will produce a sluggish and brittle casting.

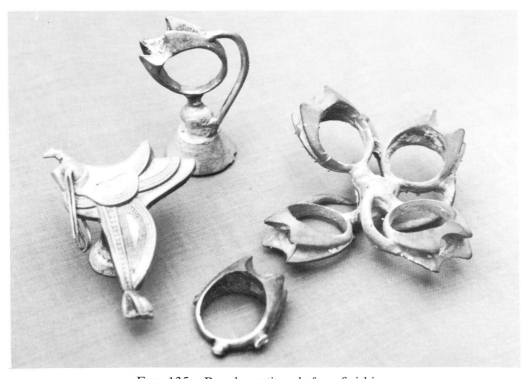

FIG. 135   Rough castings before finishing

CHAPTER 9

Hollow Core Casting

HOLLOW CORE DIFFERS FROM OTHER TECH-niques already outlined in that the complete metal casting is hollow rather than solid. The core is formed of plaster poured around a wire frame, placed in the hollow inner area, and removed when the casting is ready for finishing.

Several types of molds can be made for hollow core castings. Among them are waste molds, used for one casting only because the mold has to be destroyed to retrieve the casting, and piece molds, sometimes reusable, which are used for castings in one piece or for those too large to be cast in one piece. Hollow core casting is a challenge even for the serious craftsman, and should be attempted only after a thorough knowledge of casting principles has been gained through experimenting with other techniques.

Construction of a waste mold, model, and armature

A sketch is made of the planned casting, and a skeletal wire frame called an armature is constructed for the support of the inner core (see Fig. 136). The metal wire frame, when used for small castings, should be made with wire that can be soldered, brazed, or fastened with scrim (a glass fiber ribbon soaked with plaster). All intersections and junctures of wire on the frame must be securely attached. If the model is to be built around a core, the armature is inserted into a small block of wood, or stuck into an opening in a thick block of wood called a molding board. The wire ends of the armature are bent at right angles to the main section. When the investment plaster is poured to form the outer mold, these wires will protrude through the model to hold the core in position during casting (see Fig. 137). On the other hand, if the armature is to be inserted into the inner core area as the core investment is poured, no wires can protrude from the frame.

Core pins

Core pins, often called chaplets, are required to hold the core in position. They are inserted into the hollow wax model, which is encased in investment before the core is filled (see Fig. 137).

The small core pins should be of the same metal as will be used for the casting, so that they can be sawed off the casting after the mold is removed and then finished to become invisible on the finished casting. The use of core pins made of a different metal requires their com-

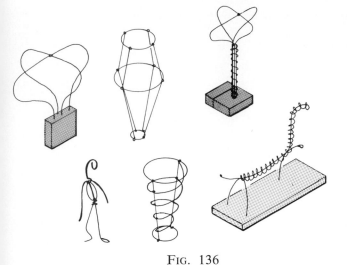

FIG. 136

Reinforcement of molds

Hollow cores too small to permit the insertion of an armature can be reinforced with a thin strip of scrim, twisted to a rod after soaking in investment. The scrim is added when the hollow core is filled with the investment.

Mixing the core investment

Investment for hollow core castings is mixed in a plaster bowl with a spatula in the same way investment is mixed for other types of castings. Large amounts are mixed in pails or plastic wastebaskets, tubs, etc. Investment is mixed in amounts sufficient for the core only. The basic water/powder ratio is 15 cc. of water to 50 grams of investment powder. Investment plaster for the core should be of a consistency that will make it stay in place as it sets up on the armature. Plaster set-up time can be speeded by adding a small amount (a pinch) of alum to each 450 grams of investment powder. Plaster set-up time can be slowed down by adding 1 tablespoon of ammonia or stale beer to each 450 grams of powder. The basic water/powder ratio may vary with different investments.

Build-up of core

For large molds, the core armature is wrapped in newsprint, after which the newsprint is damp-

plete removal from the casting. The holes left after removal of the pins must be filled with scrap bits of the casting metal, filed to fit, soldered into place, and then surface-finished to match the casting.

For larger castings, the core pins should be 1″ to 1½″ long for a casting approximately 9″ high. The holes left by the pins in the mold are called core prints. Place the pins carefully, avoiding detailed and textured areas that would be difficult to finish after the casting is made. Only a few pins (4 to 6) are necessary on small castings made with hollow cores that are cast on centrifugal, vacuum-centrifugal, or pressure casting machines.

FIG. 137

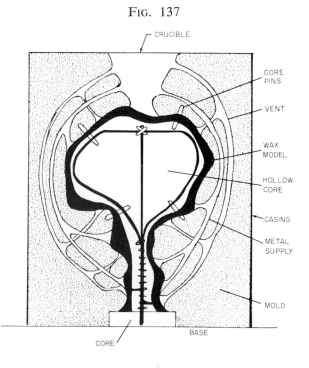

ened. This wrapped armature is covered with a thick viscous mix made of investment plaster combined with regular brickdust. After this investment has set up, the form is coated with liquid wax and the wax model is constructed on the surface. When dry, the combination of the investment and brickdust gives support to the core and is easier to remove from the completed casting than solid plaster.

The investment is applied with a small paddle or spatula and smoothed over lightly until it resembles the general shape of the planned casting, although smaller in size. The core should be constructed so that the wax model will be at least $\frac{1}{16}''$ thick at any place on the casting. This necessitates the craftsman visualizing the completed casting in order to construct the core correctly. The core is set aside to harden but should not be allowed to dry out.

Adding the wax model

When the core has set up, the wax model is built on it. Wax can be poured over the core to give a basic thin wax coating before building it up in needed areas with the heated spatula and other wax molding tools (see Chapter 3). Protrusions, such as arms or legs on models, will require a wire support in the extensions when the plaster is added to form the mold. To preserve the correct form when constructing wax models, all extensions on models of the human form or animals, birds, etc., should be bent at the normal joints.

Plaster molds for hollow wax models

Making a plaster mold of an object is another method by which models can be produced. The object is covered with plaster of Paris or dental stone in mold frames such as those used for the construction of rubber molds (see Chapter 12). The molds can be all-in-one or in two parts, depending upon the complexity of the object. For easy removal from the mold, the object is coated with liquid soap applied with a shaving brush.

When the plaster mold has been completed and the model removed, the mold surfaces are painted with shellac or sodium silicate (water glass) to make a smooth surface which will permit easy lifting of the wax section with tweezers. Wax can be poured into the half-sections, and the excess wax in the center area removed to produce a hollow inner area of the model (see Fig. 138). The two wax half-sections, when removed from the mold, are attached to each other with the heated spatula.

Two-part mold sections of plaster can be held together and partially filled with molten wax, which is immediately sloshed around inside to coat all of the mold surfaces with a layer $\frac{1}{16}''$ thick. The excess wax is poured out, leaving a one-piece hollow mold which does not require the removal of wax from the inner area. The wax-coated hollow mold is then filled with the armature and investment mix. When the investment has set up, the outer mold is removed and the wax model is ready for the addition of sprues, vents, and core pins.

Fig. 138

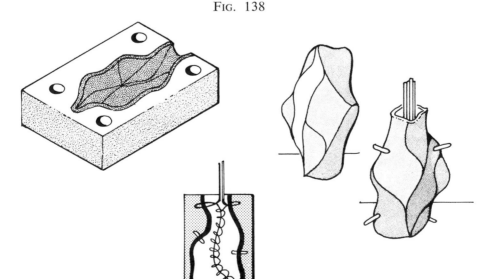

Rubber molds

In the same manner, melted wax can be poured into a rubber mold which has been dusted with talc for the easy removal of the model. As soon as the wax has sloshed around enough to coat the inner area of the mold, the excess wax is poured out and the mold set aside to harden. After the wax has hardened in the mold, the core plaster is poured into the hollow center. When this core has hardened, the plaster-filled wax model is gently removed by peeling the mold away from the model.

Attaching sprues, pins, and vents

After the wax model has been constructed by any one of the methods described, sprues and vents are attached to it, and also core pins. The core pins hold the core in proper position as the wax model is being eliminated in the furnace. *The core must always be stationary and securely fastened.*

Sprues and vents are added to the wax model before it is encased in the outer mold investment mix, just as they are in other casting methods (see Fig. 139). The sprue wires should be as large in diameter as the thickness of the casting walls. The vent wires should be one-third smaller than the sprue wires. The main sprue is attached to the end of the wax model opposite the core opening.

Adding the armature

The armature wire that was inserted in the wood block or molding board is inserted in another hole on the molding board which is not as deep as the first hole. This is necessary to keep the base of the model ¼″ above the molding board (½″ above the board if a pressure casting machine is to be used). In this way the investment depth required for an invested flask is maintained (see Fig. 137). Because the model size will usually preclude the use of a crucible former, the sprue and vent wires will have to be brought up and fastened together temporarily above the model. When the poured investment has set up around the sprued and vented model, the crucible is carved with the bench knife and the wax wires will be in their correct positions (see Fig. 86).

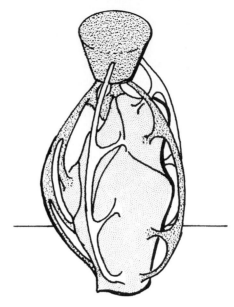

FIG. 139

Spruing large models

Larger lost-wax molds that produce castings by gravitation require sprues as large as ⅜″ in diameter and vents ¼″ in diameter. Wax wires for such models are made by making plaster casts. Dowel wood of the appropriate size for the models is used for the wax wire molds. Melted wax is poured into the cavity of these molds. Wax rods can also be made by heating a large chunk of wax and rolling it out on a smooth surface lightly coated with a very thin oil (too much oil will let the wax slide rather than roll). Wax rods must be as round as possible when used for sprues in order to eliminate turbulence in the sprues when the gases are exiting from the mold ahead of the molten metal. These wax rods can be used for making plaster molds for additional rods when larger castings are planned.

Hollow core models from plaster blocks

Hollow core models can be cast in dental stone, investment, or pumice blocks. The sprues and vents are carved and cast in half-sections of pumice stone, in dental plaster, or investment contained in boxed frames. The mold sections are separated and coated with a thin, even layer of melted wax. The armature is placed in the assembled mold sections, and the inner area is filled with plaster. When the core has set up, the mold sections are parted and the wax is removed from the core (see Fig. 138). The surfaces are dusted with talc and placed together (alignment nubs and depressions should be constructed in the mold halves), and the object cast. The core is removed in the same manner as that used for other hollow core casting techniques.

Waste-piece molds

Waste molds are made in as many sections as desired. This type of mold construction requires considerable planning, and is usually used for very large castings, such as busts and other statuary.

The model

The mold is constructed around a rigid model of plaster, wood, plastic, etc., but not generally of wax. The model is placed on a molding board, and the planned sections of the mold are lightly marked on the model.

Fencing a mold area

A fence of clay is made of thin flat strips, which are stood on edge on the marked line around a mold section, as they are constructed, one at a time. The fence is held upright and supported by small bits of clay pressed on the model and against the base outside the fence (see Fig. 140). The fences are 1″ to 1½″ wide and ⅛″ thick for models that are approximately 9″ in height. The sizes are reduced in proportion to the model used. Smaller models can be fenced with wax instead of clay. A small amount of very thin oil is mixed with the clay or wax as it is formed into strips so that it can be easily removed from the model. A spatula can be run over the surface of the strips to make them as flat as possible—the flatter the better, because the strips form the faces of the mold sections that mate with the adjacent portions.

Metal fences can be used, but they must be cut from a flat sheet of thin metal to the general outline of the model. They are then pressed into the wax model. Usually these fences are trimmed to fit the model and imbedded in it so that they will have sufficient strength to stand without the support of the clay chinks.

The portion of the model with the most de-

tail should be fenced off and constructed first. Models of heads should be fenced so that the mold section comes either in front or in back of the ears. In order to prevent any possible leakage of the plaster, the fence is checked to make sure that there are no gaps between it and the model.

Preparation of model for later mold sections

Core pins must be placed so that when the mold sections are removed there will not be any restriction (see Fig. 140). The portion of the model outside the fence is covered with dampened tissue paper, paper towels, or newsprint to prevent any splattering of plaster onto the surfaces (see Fig. 141).

FIG. 140

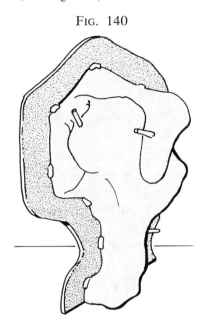

FIG. 141

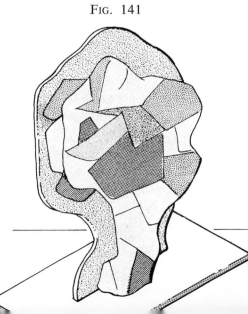

Coating the fenced section

The investment plaster is mixed to a thin creamy consistency (22 cc. of water to 50 grams of powder) and flicked onto the model surface with the fingers. The detailed areas are filled in first, and the plaster is then blown or spread on with a paint brush until the coating is approximately ¼″ thick. The plaster should not be smoothed at this time. After the initial coating has set, small mold sections are coated with a thicker plaster mix until the coating is either at least ½″ thick in all areas or level with the fence. This outer coating is smoothed with a spatula.

Reinforcement scrim and rods and second coating

Large mold sections need reinforcement wires or scrim (plaster-soaked glass fiber cloth) for support. Scrim is usually used for minimal extra support, and the reinforcement wire or iron for heavier support of larger castings. The scrim is applied to the mold section before the second, thicker coating of plaster is added (see Fig. 142). The glass fiber cloth is available in several weights, which can usually be identified by appearance. The fine tissue fiber cloth looks much like ordinary tissue paper and is the lightest type. Bonded glass fiber strands used for resin embedment projects have a matted appearance and are slightly heavier. The heaviest scrim is woven glass fiber cloth such as that used for boat hulls, etc. Broken molds that can be repaired are reinforced with woven ribbon (thin strapping of the glass fiber material) or strands (similar to loose-woven rope) called roving. The scrim, regardless of the type used, is soaked in thin creamy plaster and applied to the mold section which has its initial coating completed and is set up. A small roller is used to press the scrim into place. After it has set up enough to stay in place, the second coating is added to the mold section.

A frame of wires or reinforcing iron (size depends on the casting) is constructed to cage the mold section. The loose ends or junctures are tied together with strips of plaster-soaked scrim. There should not be any loose, floating wire ends. When the frame is completed, it is placed on the coated area, and the second, heavier coating of plaster is applied to the enclosed area up to the level of the fence (see Fig. 143).

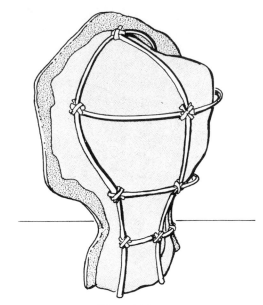

FIG. 142

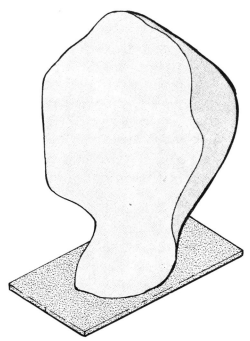

FIG. 143

Preparation for second mold section

When the completed section has set up, the wet paper is stripped from the model, and the fence is carefully removed so that the mold is not chipped or damaged in any way. The section remains on the model and is not removed until surrounding portions have been completed. Mold sections should be kept damp until all parts are finished.

The exposed portion of the model is covered with a damp cloth, and V-shaped notches are cut in the edge of the completed mold section. Small depressions, similar to countersunk holes, are made in the faces of the mold section (see Fig. 144). The mating mold section is constructed over the model; the plaster fills in the depressions. When the sections are parted small nubs will remain on the second mold section. These nubs and depressions mate to align the sections. The dampened cloth placed over the exposed model prevents the deposit of chips and shavings from the notches and depressions.

Detail of mold sections

The second mold section is constructed in the same manner as the previous section with scrim or reinforcing rods if necessary. The mold section faces are coated with clay and water mixed to a paint consistency or brushed with a thin coating of Vaseline. Clay or wax wedges are made to fit the V-notches (see Fig. 144). The clay or wax is removed later when the mold sections are completed and wooden wedges are inserted to pry the mold apart gently so that the model can be removed.

Addition of a crucible to the mold section

A small clay crucible is attached to the exposed model at the top for the entry of the molten metal (see Fig. 144). No sprues or vents are used in piece molds, because the mold could not be removed for subsequent use if these were placed on the model. The thickness of the casting (between the core and the mold) is large enough to carry the metal to all areas. Venting is accomplished through the joints of the mold sections, which, even if fitted as closely as possible, will still permit some escape of air and gases.

Molds without a crucible

If a metal such as pewter with a low melting point is used for the casting, the crucible is not added to the model before completing the second mold section. The mold sections without a core are held together with rope, steel strapping, or string until the entire inner surface is coated with molten metal that has been poured into the hollow mold from the melting crucible. The excess molten metal is quickly poured back into

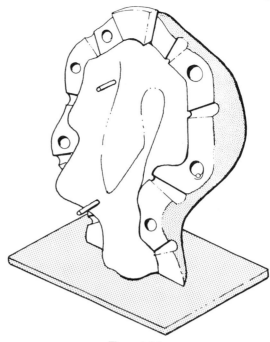

FIG. 144

the crucible. This method is called slush casting and is similar to slip casting in ceramic work.

The mold, after completion of the final section (which has set up), is carefully pried apart to remove the model. The core pins must remain in the mold sections (see Fig. 137). Any area damaged during this step can be repaired with investment plaster, which is spatulated until almost ready to set up. It is applied with small spatulas, paddles, or other tools and molded to match the model. After setting up, the mold surfaces are coated with liquid soap, thin oil, or sodium silicate mixed with water to a thin paint consistency. They are then allowed to dry.

Permanent plaster models from molds

A permanent plaster model can be cast from the mold, but the mold should be soaked in water so that it will not absorb any moisture from the casting plaster.

Making the wax model

The mold sections are fitted together and held in position with heavy twine, rope, webbing, or steel strapping, depending upon the size of the mold (see Fig. 145). Wooden wedges are forced under the binding material to maintain a tight fit. Melted wax is then poured into the mold and sloshed around to coat the inner surfaces. When the wax begins to harden around the center, the remaining melted wax is poured out, and the inner wax coating is permitted to harden further.

A fence of clay is constructed around the base of the assembled mold sections, and small depressions are made in the bottom surfaces of these mold sections to act as alignment posts for the core section. The mold sections are

FIG. 145

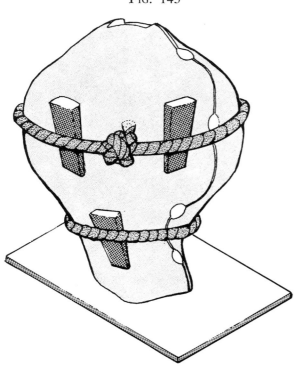

coated with liquid soap, the armature or core frame is placed in the hollow area of the wax-lined mold, and the core is filled with freshly mixed plaster.

When the core has set up and hardened, the mold sections are separated and the wax gently removed from the core. The entire assemblage is then bound together again and set aside until it is time to cast the metal. Molds that are to be heated for casting high-temperature metals must be held together with wire that will withstand the heat of the furnace without melting. Metal wedges are used to maintain tension on the binding wire.

Reclaimable piece molds

Piece molds having extreme detail as a part of the model are constructed in smaller sections. Built piece by piece, they are constructed with sloping walls or faces, so that they will not fall inward when assembled without the support of the model (see Fig. 146). They should also be numbered for easy identification when assembled. The final section (keystone) will lock the entire mold together. The mold will not come apart until this section is removed. This final section should be fitted with a piece of wire bent into a loop at the end so that it can be lifted out easily (see Fig. 147). The small mold sections are made with depressions or nubs for alignment, and the joints between the sections are beveled on the outer surface (see Fig. 147).

FIG. 146

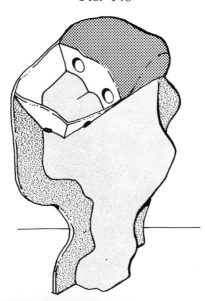

FIG. 147

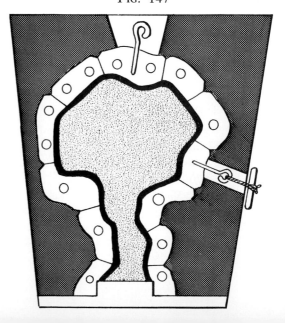

Mold surface treatment

When the core is in place, the mating faces of the mold sections are coated with liquid soap and fitted onto the core. The assembled sections are then coated with a clay-water mix before a complete outer layer of colored (regular vegetable coloring can be used) plaster is applied (see Fig. 147). Molds constructed of many small sections need an outer casing of plaster to hold them together during casting. Large molds will require a wire or scrim reinforcement in the outer shell.

When the casting is completed, the outer layer of colored plaster is chipped away (the clay-water coating prevents it from adhering to the mold sections). The keystone mold section is removed to permit the separation of the remainder of the mold.

Retention of small mold sections during casting

Small mold sections that may fall inward, even after careful construction, can be held in place by a wire loop like the one constructed for the keystone piece threaded through a hole drilled in the mold section. The loop is covered with clay before the outer casing of plaster is added to the assembled sections. When the outer plaster layer has set up, the clay is removed from the opening and a length of string or wire is hooked through the loop. The inner mold section is then pulled outward and held in position with a string or wire wrapped around a short length of dowel wood or drill rod (see Fig. 147).

Sectional or piece molds that are to be used for higher-melting metals do not have to be disassembled to remove the wax model, as it is eliminated in the furnace.

Fig. 148

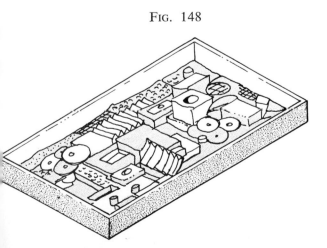

The preceding techniques for making molds have been detailed to produce a complete casting in one operation; however, molds can be constructed to produce complete sections of large castings.

Constructing piece molds is a highly specialized technique. If successful results are to be assured, the procedure should be thoroughly understood before any attempt is made to cast metals.

Casting panels

Panels can be cast in investment plaster waste molds (see Fig. 148). The model is placed on a smooth hard surface and both the model and the surface are coated with a mold release of a thin water-clay mix (4 parts water to 1 part clay). A fence that will be the outline of the panel is constructed around the model, and its inner surfaces are also coated with the mold release. The fence should be 1″ higher than the highest part of the model. The plaster is mixed and poured over the model and allowed to set up. Scrim can be added for reinforcement if necessary. When the mold has hardened, the model is removed and damaged spots in the mold are repaired with a thick viscous investment mix.

Mold surface treatment

After the mold surfaces have been repaired and smoothed, the surface is scrubbed with soap and water, which is left to dry on the surface. The surface is then painted with sodium silicate to give a high gloss to the casting.

Casting the metal

The metal is heated in the crucible, and oxides are removed from the surface of the metal with a metal skimmer. When the molten metal has a bright mirror-like surface, it is quickly poured into the mold.

Removal of mold

After cooling, the model is either gently lifted out of the mold, or the mold, with the casting intact, is turned over and lifted off the casting. This is possible if the mold surfaces were properly prepared prior to casting. Otherwise, the mold must be chipped off the casting, with care taken not to damage the cast metal surfaces. Smaller models are pickled to remove adhering plaster. The casting is finished in the same manner as that described for other castings.

Selection of metal

Any metal can be used for articles cast with hollow cores. Low-melting-point alloys can also be cast in a slush technique (see appendix for metal alloy contents). Metals are prepared in the same manner as that given for other casting techniques; however, to prevent oxidation, bronze, the customary casting metal for large objects, is cleaned with aqua regia (any combination of hydrochloric and nitric acid) or nitric acid alone, then rinsed in running water and buried in sawdust until it is ready to be melted.

Metal preparation

Metals for larger castings, which are poured into the mold from large ladles held by shank rings, are cleaned of oxides by skimming the surface of the metal as it melts in the crucible or ladle with a skimmer made from an iron rod. This rod can be used as an indicator to determine when the metal is hot enough to pour. If the metal is just at its melting point, it will stick to the rod. A higher temperature will permit it to run off, leaving the rod clean. The metals must always be heated at least 100° hotter than their molten stage because of the drop in temperature as the metal is poured into the mold.

Crucibles for large castings

Metal crucibles for large casting are numbered according to their capacity in increments of 1–4000. For each successive number, 3 pounds of metal is added; for example, a no. 5 crucible will hold 15 pounds of casting metal. (A 9″ torso would require 15 to 20 pounds of bronze for a solid casting.)

Furnaces for large molds

A furnace for the elimination of wax from large molds can be built by constructing a square enclosure of fire brick on a fire brick base (see Fig. 149). A grate placed on the furnace floor holds the coke used to heat the

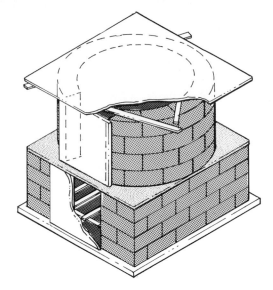

FIG. 149

mold. The brick enclosure is covered with an iron plate on which the mold is placed.

Supports under the mold permit the flow of molten wax from the mold. This area is enclosed by a round wall of brick that is smaller in area than the lower portion. Strap iron is placed across the top rim of the bricks to support the roof or iron sheet. The front openings are covered with sheets of iron to contain the heat.

Casting in the large mold

When the large mold is ready for casting (all traces of the model have been eliminated by the 1000°F. heat), it is transferred with large crucible tongs to a sand-filled box for the pour of molten metal. During this time the metal is being prepared in a crucible in a gas-fired melting furnace at a temperature of 2000°F. The slag or dross is skimmed from the metal surface after the crucible is removed from the furnace, and the metal is immediately poured into the mold. This procedure is usually too complicated for one person to handle. It often takes two persons to transfer the mold from the furnace and one or two persons to pour the metal into the mold.

Casting in small molds

Small hollow core molds are cast in the usual manner by placing the heated mold in the cradle of the casting machine and following through with the regular casting steps (see Chapter 8).

NOVELTY. Silver octopus.
Replica.
By Sharr Choate.

RING. Silver with faceted
synthetic emerald.
Sand-cast.
By Sharr Choate.

RING. 18 kt. gold with faceted
smoky quartz.
Lost wax.
By Sharr Choate.

GEMSTONE CARVINGS AND INTARSIA.
Agate and jade leaves from Germany.
Turquoise *Kwan Yin* from Persia.
Gem intarsia from Italy.

PIN. Silver sea horse
and starfish with coral.
Replica.
By Lou Binkley.

PIN. Gold-plated silver with opal.
Lost wax.
By Ruth Noble.
(*Photo by Ruth Noble*)

PIN. 18 kt. gold funerary mask from Mexico.
Lost wax.

Removal of casting from the mold

After the casting is completed, the mold is either destroyed to retrieve the casting or gently separated for subsequent castings. The core is removed by using dental chisels, scalers, explorers, awls, large probes, or any similar sharp instrument to loosen the core plaster so that the wire armature can be removed. If the opening is small the armature can easily be removed by cutting it apart with pliers.

Slush castings (hollow core)

Slush castings are made by pouring molten metal into molds and rotating the mold in a rocking and rolling manner to coat the inner surfaces completely with a layer of metal. The excess metal is poured out of the mold and back into the crucible before it solidifies.

A reservoir should be constructed on a slush casting model at the end opposite the gate or crucible so that the entire casting will be hollow (see Fig. 150). Otherwise the excess metal does not leave the mold when poured out before solidification, which produces a thick solid area inside the casting that often makes it top-heavy.

Slush molds must be heated before a hollow casting is made. This is accomplished by pouring a solid casting of the metal into a room-temperature mold. The casting is removed immediately after solidification, the metal is quickly poured into the heated mold, and the excess metal poured back into the ladle. An unheated mold cools the metal, causing it to solidify too quickly for it to be poured back into the ladle. After the first hollow core casting has been completed, additional castings can be made in rapid succession. As fast as the metal cools and solidifies, the mold can be separated to remove the casting and reassembled for the next pour.

Finishing of castings

All castings require some finishing after removal from the mold. Large castings will require power-driven grinding, sanding, and polishing equipment. Hollow core models are finished in the same manner as other castings. The core pins are removed from the surface, and any flashes (fins or feathers from improperly fitted mold sections), sprues, gates, vents,

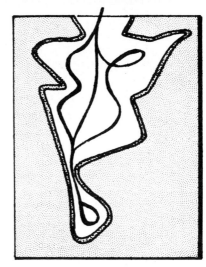

FIG. 150

or other extraneous material are removed, including any particles of investment. Sectional pieces are soldered or brazed together, and the surfaces finished before any coloring or surface decoration is added (see Chapter 16).

COLD CASTING

Cold castings differ from other metal castings in that they do not require molten metal but are produced by making a casting material with a combination of fine powdered metal (100 to 300 mesh) and resins. The combined mix produces a casting in a regular mold. After curing and hardening, the casting, because of the high metal content, can be surface treated, finished, and colored in the same manner as that described for regular metals. The only restriction is that they can be neither soldered nor subjected to any heat such as is required for enameling and some plating processes.

Molds and models

Molds are constructed using any one of the techniques previously described for casting processes. Molds can also be constructed of silicone rubber, either hot pour or cold pour compounds. A vinyl base mold material called Vinagel, which is cured in the kitchen oven for molding purposes, can also be used. Small molds should be cast solid. Models can be as varied as the mold materials.

Gel coats

A thin gel coat of resin is applied to molds before the resin-metal mix is poured (see Fig. 150). This produces a high luster on the surface of the casting. However, if the casting is to be colored with a dipping or a painting solution to obtain an antique or patina finish, the gel coat should be either omitted or sanded before any attempt is made to color the casting.

The gel coat (about $\frac{1}{100}$" thick), if used, is usually mixed of resin and catalyst (hardener) in different proportions from a normal mix. An accelerator is added to the resin before the catalyst is added. The accelerator is cobalt, a fine-ground metal added in the proportion of 1 drop of accelerator to 1 ounce of resin. This accelerator is added to the thin gel coat, which produces internal heat in the mix, curing the resin quickly. The catalyst is added to the resin after the cobalt. If the catalyst is added to the cobalt it might explode. Many resins are sold with the accelerator already added, and if the manufacturer's label on the resin container indicates the presence of cobalt as an accelerator, no more should be added. The catalyst is MEK peroxide (methyl-ethylketone peroxide). The gel coat is mixed in the proportion of 6 drops of catalyst to 1 ounce of resin. The catalyst (usually a 2% amount), when used at normal humidity and at an average temperature of 70°F., requires 1 ounce (by volume) of catalyst to 1 quart of resin (1 ounce is equal to 6 teaspoons in measure). Higher humidity, due to the season or geographical location, will require additional catalyst (up to 100%) to cure the mix. Lower humidity or higher temperatures will require less catalyst. Resins should always be mixed in the containers recommended by the manufacturers.

The thin gel coat can be used as a surface finish on mold frames. After curing, the mold frame surfaces are sanded with steel wool, wet-or-dry paper (320 grit and 6/0 paper). The surface is then buffed with Tripoli (used for metal buffing) and a mold release is applied to the frame surfaces.

A gel coat should be added to any regular or panel mold that can be reached and treated just as when a gel coating is applied to mold frames. This thin coating will permit the casting resin mix to adhere to the surface without any air bubbles.

Mixing the mold material

The resin material and the metal are combined in proportions of 5 parts of metal by weight to 1 part of casting resin to make a pouring mix. For each ounce of resin add 8 drops of catalyst. This is a basic formula, which can be varied for a thicker, thixotropic paste or a thinner mix for casting panels. Before large amounts of resin and metal are mixed, test batches should be mixed and small casts made first to determine optimum mixture amounts.

Metals used for cold casting include bronze (100 to 300 mesh), lead (200 mesh), gold and brass (300 mesh), silver (200 mesh), nickel silver (100 mesh), and aluminum (200 mesh). The mesh (fineness) refers to the number of openings in a linear inch. The materials must not be combined before the mold is ready to cast. They have a pot life or working time of 35 minutes in a room temperature of 65°F. after mixing. However, this is not extremely important in pouring a small mold, but may be crucial in pouring a large panel.

Resins, metals, and catalysts should be mixed in batches of 1 quart or less, unless a large panel is being poured. It is important that the metal be added to the resin before the catalyst is added. In this way the first two constituents can be combined thoroughly so that any additional mixing is done for the sole purpose of combining the catalyst with the two materials. Mixed resin and the metal that is not needed for the casting is never poured back into the resin supply because it would harden the supply, making it unusable. Resins have a shelf life of approximately 4 months; therefore amounts should be purchased that can be used within this period of time.

Panel molds

Panel molds are constructed of a plaster negative mold confined in a boxed frame; however, the inner surfaces should be lined with Formica or a similar laminated material to permit easy removal of the frame when the casting has completely cured. The mold surfaces are coated with liquid wax or a commercial mold release for the removal of the casting. To make press panel molds from Vinagel material, knead it into a mass and then press it against the object to produce an impression. The mold duplicate is gently separated from the object and the resin is poured.

The casting resin and metal powder are combined to a thin painting layer of mix by using

30 drops of catalyst and 6½ ounces of powdered metal to 3 ounces of resin. Enough of the resin-metal should be mixed at one time to coat the entire surface in one operation. The mix is painted onto the mold surfaces, and a thicker or more viscous mix is added when the painted coat is slightly tacky when touched. Large panels should be reinforced with glass fiber rods, thin wooden slats, or plastic strips to prevent warpage.

Molds for large cast panels and other uncomplicated patterns can be constructed in a manner similar to those perfected for aircraft molding projects (see Fig. 151). The mold contours are built up from a base of plywood with stringers called "formers" placed to support the contours. These formers are covered with heavy burlap or fine mesh screen. Plaster of Paris is poured over the burlap and worked down into the fibres to produce a smooth contoured surface. After the plaster has been applied and completely covers the burlap or screen, it is set aside to cure. During the curing time, some of the rough surface can be smoothed with sandpaper or a scraper. Final sanding is done after the mold has completely cured.

The mold contours and surfaces can be sealed for casting by coating them with a mold release and a wax film, but preferably they should receive a thin protective gel coat or a laminated layer of glass fiber cloth. This is accomplished by applying a gel coat, and, when it is partially gelled, adding the cloth, which should be tacked around the outer edges to hold it tight. A second gel coat is then added, air bubbles worked out, and the complete mold section allowed to cure. The mold surface is finished in the same manner as casting surfaces. When casting the resin into a gel-coated and laminated mold, coat it first with a mold release and then a paste wax to permit removal of the casting after curing.

Curing time

The casting is left in the mold for 12 to 24 hours, according to the size of the mold, its thickness, and whether or not it is hollow core or solid cast. After removal from the mold, the casting should cure for at least another 6 hours before being worked. The casting can be finished just as though it were cast of molten metal, except that it cannot be soldered or subjected to any heat. It can be surface-colored the same as any other castings.

Insufficient metal was used if the casting has a weak metal look with too much resin showing. If the surface is pitted with air bubbles, the metal portion is too great. Dry, powdery, or tacky surfaces indicate improper mixing of materials.

Assembly of cast sections

Sectional parts of cold castings are attached to each other with a fresh mixture of resin, which is sanded and filed after curing to eliminate traces of a seam or joint.

Final finishing

The casting is sanded with files, sandpaper (1/0, 3/0, 6/0), and then with wet-or-dry paper (320 to 400 grit). It is then buffed with Tripoli with an 8″ to 10″ muslin buffing wheel running at 1725 rpm. After buffing and coloring, a coating of paste wax is applied and hand-polished with a soft cloth.

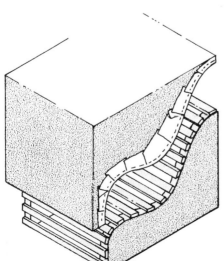

Fig. 151

CHAPTER 10

Sand Casting

SAND CASTING IS ACCOMPLISHED BY THE construction of a mold composed of fine jeweler's sand rammed or tamped around a rigid uncomplicated model and placed in a two-part metal frame without a top or bottom. The mold sections are gently parted and the model or pattern drawn away, leaving a replica impression in the sand. The sections are then reassembled and molten metal poured into the mold through an opening made in one end. When the hot metal cools, the mold is separated and the casting emerges identical in detail with the original pattern.

Preparation of the equipment

The model or pattern used to make the impression in the sand for the casting (similar to a rubber mold) can be made from any rigid material that will maintain its shape as the sand is packed around it. Objects previously cast in precious metals or low-fusing alloys polished to a mirror-like finish can be used as models (see Fig. 152). Models constructed of plastic must also have the same high polish. Wood models are generally constructed of mahogany or cherry. Other close-grained woods can also be used if available.

Wood models should be given several coats of shellac or varnish and rubbed with steel wool between each coating to protect the wood from moisture and to give a smooth finish. This is necessary so that the model can be drawn from the mold easily without damaging the impression surfaces in the mold sections. Note that sand casting can be used only for objects with simple detail. Models with undercuts and draws cannot be removed without damage to the mold.

The flask and mandrel

The flask or mold frames used in sand casting consists of two half-sections, either round or rectangular, with neither top nor bottom (see Fig. 153).

Two small pins attached to and parallel with the outer walls of the "cope" (top section) extend above the surface on each side. Two small "lugs" or ears protrude from the sides of the "drag" (bottom section). These alignment devices are placed so that the two parts of the mold will engage in one position only.

Mandrels

Two types of mandrels, round and half-round, are used to construct ring molds (see Fig. 154). Round mandrels of metal or wood are turned on lathes to match the inside diameter of the

ring model and are then sawed lengthwise to
make half-round sections. Mandrels can also
be made from thin-walled metal tubing, left as
is for full round forms, or split lengthwise for
half-round forms. These mandrels support the
ring model when the sand is rammed into the
mold frames.

Sprues

The half-round mandrel is perfectly flat on the
bottom. To form the sprue or tunnel that carries the molten metal from the crucible to the
pattern chamber, a hole is drilled in the center
of this mandrel at right angles to the flat base,
so that when a small tapered sprue former is
inserted, the former will stand vertically in the
hole (see Fig. 154). (Sprue formers should not
be made of any material that will rust or cor-
rode. Particles from erosion will cling to the
walls of the sprue and be carried into the mold
by the flow of the molten metal.) Additional
half-mandrels may be constructed with two
sprue pins so that two rings can be cast simultaneously in one mold. The sprue pin must protrude above the upper edge of the cope far
enough so that it can be turned and twisted
gently up out of the sand-packed frame.

Flat models

Flat models, such as coins, belt buckles, or bas-
relief carved items, do not need a half-mandrel,
but do require a sprue. A metal base ¼″ thick
with a hole drilled in the center for the tapered
sprue pin is constructed for this purpose (see
Fig. 154). Flat castings, although requiring no
backing, present a more finished appearance
and a smoother back if a top mold section is
used. To ensure an adequate flow of metal to
all areas, the sprue pin should be constructed
with multiple gates (see Fig. 154). Position
the cope section over the drag and hold the
sprue pin in one hand while adding a small
amount of riddled (sifted) sand to hold the
sprue pin upright so that the frame section can
be completely filled with the sand and the sand
rammed firmly. When the cope is filled,
rammed, and struck off, the sprue pin can be
removed by gently twisting it in an upward motion. A cover of wood or metal is placed over
the cope so that the cope can be removed and
turned over without spilling any of the sand.

A short length of steel wire of 6 gauge is
pushed from the mold surfaces toward the
sprue opening to produce additional gates in the
sand for the entry of molten metal (see Fig.

FIG. 152

FIG. 153

155). The sand, if rammed tightly, will not crumble, and smooth gates can easily be made. Venting holes are made from the top or opposite side of the cope with the same wire.

Rings

Ring molds, in which the round and half-round mandrels are used to support the model during ramming, require a core to fill in the void left when the mandrel is removed (see Figs. 155 and 156). Tubing with an inner diameter identical to the diameter of the round mandrel is packed tightly with sand, and the hard-packed core is ejected gently from the tubing with a length of wood doweling (see Fig. 155). The core must be the same length as the round mandrel, or equal to the inside diameter of the mold frame. The only remaining space in the mold, which is to receive the molten metal, is that left by the impression of the original model.

Casting sand

Casting sand, also called "French" or green sand, is a very fine grit loam or quartz sand (silicon dioxide) with reducing agents added. It resembles finely powdered pumice, which is often used for the same purpose. Water-tempered sand is preferred to oil sands, because water is easily added to temper it, and if too much water is added it can be dried out in the kitchen oven. Test the sand by squeezing it in the hand (see Fig. 157). When the hand is opened the sand should retain its shape without separating (see Fig. 158), so that when it is broken apart gently the pieces will retain sharp corners and not crumble. If too dry, the sand

FIG. 156

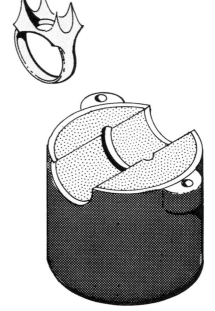

FIG. 154

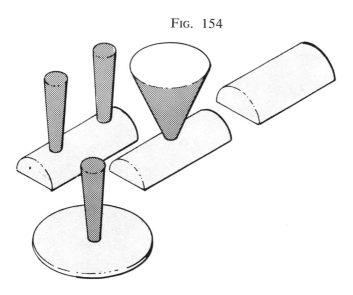

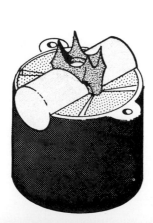

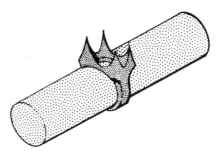

FIG. 155

will produce a weak mold, and corners or extending areas of the pattern chamber will be broken by the flow of molten metal into the cavity. On the other hand, sand which is excessively moist, giving a soggy feeling when squeezed, creates steam pressure in the mold. This pressure has to escape from the mold, and in doing so creates "blowholes" in the casting and roughness on the surfaces. Venting takes care of a normal amount of pressure, but the excessive moisture of overdamp sand creates blowholes.

Ramming the mold frame

The cope section of the casting mold is placed on a smooth, flat surface of wood, metal, or glass. The sprue pin and base, either flat or half-round, depending upon the object to be cast, is also placed on the flat base, which is called a molding board. The sand is riddled (sifted through wire screening or a small sieve) into the cope until the model is covered (see Fig. 159).

The sand is rammed or tamped with light blows of the rammers (short tapered lengths of wood doweling in various diameters) to pack the sand carefully into every area (see Fig. 160). Numerous light taps are better than a few heavy ones. The flask is filled with riddled sand until completely covered and additional sand is placed on top of the flask to a depth of approximately 2″. Unsifted sand can be used after the model is covered with a thin layer of riddled sand, but the practice of using the riddled sand alone prevents its contamination with foreign particles, which would result in imperfect molds. The sand is rammed until tight. Scrape the excess material off the top of the cope rim by working around the protruding sprue pin with a strike-off iron (a flat piece of steel or metal rule).

Removing the half-mandrel and adding the round mandrel

When the cope has been rammed sufficiently, it is picked up and the sprue pins are gently twisted up and out of the sand. The frame is then inverted and placed back on the molding board. The half-mandrel is eased up and out of this packed mold frame. The ring model is then placed on the round mandrel and both are dusted with a parting powder. Unscented talc

FIG. 157

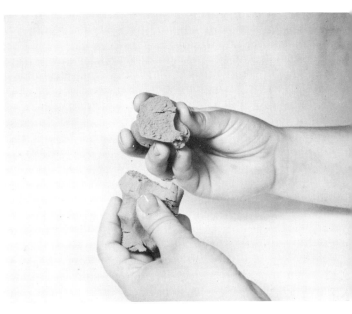

FIG. 158

FIG. 159

FIG. 160

FIG. 162

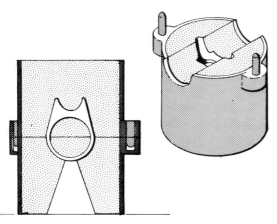

FIG. 161

(used for rubber mold releasing agents), lycopodium powder, or graphite (sold for lubricating locks and door catches) is dusted onto the mold and pattern surfaces. This permits easy parting of the mold sections and removal of the model without damaging the pattern impression. The round mandrel, with the ring positioned mounting side up to align with the sprue opening, is then placed in the packed mold frame and is pressed down into the rammed sand so that the ring model will make its impression.

Ramming the drag

The drag is positioned on the cope, the upright pins on the outside aligned with the holes in the ears on the cope (see Fig. 161). The exposed mandrel and ring are then covered with a thin layer of riddled sand and rammed. Additional sand is added and rammed, as described in packing the drag section, and the excess is struck off the rim of the flask with a strike-off tool.

Removing of the model

Separate the two sections of the mold gently by lifting the drag up and away from the cope sec-

tion. The mold may be tapped lightly on the outside before the mold sections are separated to loosen the model slightly for easy removal. The model can then be lifted carefully from the mold by the fingertips or with tweezers, after which any loose particles of sand must be blown away. A small rubber bulb with a tapered point, which is generally used to dust flowers or minute objects, or a rubber-bulb dental syringe (see Fig. 162) are ideal for dusting out these small areas and can also be used for dusting the surfaces with the parting agent.

Air vents

Air vents are carved in the surface of the drag section of the mold to permit the escape of air and gases and prevent back pressure, so that the mold pattern chamber will fill completely with molten metal. The venting can also be accomplished by darning needles or short lengths of steel wire placed on the surface of the rammed drag section. These needles or wires must touch the model and radiate to the outer perimeter of the mold frame.

After the core has been rammed and the round mandrel has been removed, the needles (or wires) are removed, leaving small grooves for venting. Loose particles of sand must always be blown away gently from the mold surfaces and the model impression surfaces.

Preparing the core

The core, usually made with the same sand as that used in the mold, replaces the round mandrel in the mold, preventing the flow of metal to any area other than the model impression. The core must fit the mold exactly. Equal portions of beach sand added to core sand will strengthen the core; however, the used core sand must not be mixed with used molding sand for subsequent molds or cores.

The sand is rammed evenly into a section of tubing and packed harder than in the mold sections. The tubing is the same length as the round mandrel, with the inside diameter equal to the diameter of the round mandrel. The tubing must be free of any burrs on the inner edges, so that the rammed core can be pushed from the tube with a short length of wood doweling. The core, after removal from the tubing, is dusted with the parting powder and placed in position on the drag section of the mold.

Reassembling the mold

When the core is in place, the mating surfaces are checked again for any loose particles of sand which, if found, must be blown away. Either broken sections must be repaired or the complete mold sections repacked. The cope section is placed with the alignment pins set in the holes of the drag extensions.

The reassembled mold is set in a tray of sand for the "pour." In this way any sand that may break loose and separate from the mold frames when the casting is removed remains in the tray. This eliminates waste, time-consuming clean-up of working area, and contamination of the used sand with foreign particles, which occurs when it has to be swept off the working area into a tray for reclaiming.

Metal requirements and preparation

Sufficient metal to complete the pour and fill the mold is always melted in one operation. The amount of metal needed to ensure a complete casting is determined by the same method as that used for centrifugal casting (see Chapter 5). A glass cylinder is used and the water level observed; however, because sprue weight has not been considered, additional metal is required for the sprue and button (see Figs. 73 and 74). To ensure adequate metal for the casting, sprue, and button, add more metal until the water level is 3 times the amount needed for the casting alone. For example, if the model alone raises the water level 10 gradations above the original level on the graduate or container, additional metal must be used to bring the water level up 3 times that number to 30 gradations above the original level on the grad-

uate. If a model previously cast in precious metal is used, the model is weighed to determine the amount of metal required to duplicate the casting and twice as much extra metal for the sprue and button is added. The specific gravity chart (see Appendix) can also be used to ascertain metal requirements.

Crucibles

Special crucibles are available for sand casting, which keep the metal, except during stirring or checking, covered during the melting steps. Crucibles are made of sand, clay, and graphite, silica quartz, zirconium, alumina, and magnesia. Gold and silver casting metals are melted and prepared in sand, silica-quartz, or clay graphite vessels. Gold can be, and platinum refining usually is, done in zirconium crucibles. White gold and nickel are prepared in magnesia or alumina vessels. Nickel, a high-percentage alloy metal in white gold, attracts carbon from graphite crucibles. The metal must be stirred with any one of the following only: a piece of charcoal held by tongs, a graphite rod, or a stick of green wood. The crucible should not be overheated. The metal is heated quickly and poured as soon as the surface is rolling and free of oxides.

Metal that is not completely molten should not be stirred. Additional metal added to partially molten metal must be heated before being added to the molten mass, as cold metal dropped into molten metal may damage the crucible. The torch, with the reducing portion of the flame in correct position, is held on the metal during all the melting steps. When the metal is molten, reducing flux is added. A circular motion with the tongs that hold the crucible rolls the metal, forcing any oxides forming on the surface to slag off on the edge of the crucible. The metal should have a mirror-like finish when poured. With the torch flame held on the metal, the crucible is moved to the mold sprue opening in a rolling motion. The metal is poured slowly and continuously into the mold before the flame is removed. Sudden up-ending of the crucible when pouring the metal or turning it upside down is as foolhardy as an interrupted pour.

Silver, when heated to the molten stage, attracts oxygen from the torch mixture and dispels it as the metal starts to freeze. This produces a spitting or spluttering effect even during the pouring, for the metal is already beginning to solidify.

Goggles should be worn for working close to the mold. If the metal splutters and gurgles after it is poured, air and gases are trying to escape from the mold chamber out through the sprue opening, rather than through the vents, which probably have been either improperly placed or omitted entirely. Another possible reason for the splutter is over-moist sand.

The extra metal (provided for the button) that remains in the sprue after the pour will, because of its weight, force the molten metal into all areas of the model impression in the mold, so that a small dimple or depression will appear in the center of the button as it cools.

An incompletely filled mold usually indicates either inadequate sprue openings too small to carry the metal to all areas before it solidified, or that the metal was not hot enough and solidified or cooled before flowing to all areas.

The crucible must be emptied with each pour. Metal should never be left in the crucible to cool for later use. If more metal is melted than is needed, the excess is poured off into a depression in a charcoal block for cooling; it is then pickled and realloyed with new metal for a subsequent casting.

Removal of the casting from the mold

When the button has lost its red color and turns black, the mold frames can be separated with tongs curved to fit the shape of the mold frame. The casting can then be lifted from the sand with tongs and eased into room-temperature water to cool. If the metal is quenched while still hot from casting, it will be in an annealed state for finishing. The casting should be allowed to cool if there is a possibility of warpage in the thinner areas, which often occurs during immediate quenching. It is then scrubbed under running water to remove any remaining sand. Sand trapped in draws or undercuts, or stubborn particles adhering to any surface will be removed if the casting is dipped in a solution of 4 parts water to 1 part hydrofluoric acid.

The dipping solution is mixed, used, and stored in a rubber-lined container or plastic bottle, for it readily attacks glass, metal, and enamel surfaces. The casting is rinsed in clear water after dipping. Castings with any oxidized surfaces are dipped in the same pickling solutions used for centrifugal casting.

After cleaning, the casting is ready for the finishing steps. The button and vents are sawed off as close to the casting as possible. A short length of sprue left attached to a ring shank will provide additional and identical metal if the ring needs to be sized larger.

Reclaiming the casting sand

When the mold is separated and the casting is removed with the tongs, a properly rammed mold will remain virtually undamaged, unless reckless removal of the casting breaks portions of the mold. *This mold must not be used for another identical casting.* The used casting sand is pushed out of the cylindrical flask sections with a large section of dowel wood. The sand is then riddled through a large mesh screen to remove the lumps and foreign particles and riddled a second time through a very fine mesh screen to return it to a uniformly fine grain sand. *It must be mixed with new sand for ramming a new mold.* Core sand, if mixed with any other binder to maintain its shape after ramming, cannot be mixed with the new or used casting sand. It must be discarded completely.

Preparation of molds for large castings

Single and split models other than jewelry and large pieces of jewelry can be cast in larger mold frames. If a split model is used, it must have its own pins and mating holes in the two sections for perfect alignment. The model is placed on the molding board and the drag is placed over it. Riddled sand is dusted over the model and packed into every minute area. Additional riddled sand is added to fill the drag and is firmly rammed. The excess sand is struck off or scraped level with the upper surface of the drag, and a molding board is placed on top of the frame. This holds the sand in the frame as it is inverted and becomes the molding board and support for the drag, so that the cope, with alignment pins, can be placed into position.

The mold surface is dusted with parting powder. If a split model is used, the remaining section is also dusted before it is aligned with its mating part, already embedded in the sand-filled mold frame.

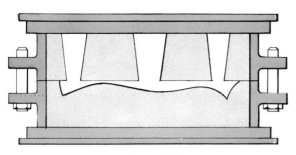

FIG. 163

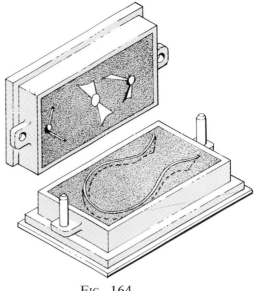

FIG. 164

Sprue pins are positioned upright at the outer edges of the model, so that the impression chamber will receive an equal flow of molten metal into all parts of the impression (see Fig. 163). The exposed area of the model is covered with riddled sand and rammed firmly. Additional riddled sand is added to fill the flask above the rim of the frame. The sand is rammed firmly, and the excess molding material is struck off the top of the flask. The sprue pins are removed, and the lip edges of the sprue are rounded off so that the molten metal will not carry loose sand from these edges into the mold. The molding board is placed over the cope, and this section of the mold is lifted gently up off the drag.

The larger molds are dampened around the outer edges with water and then either lifted out with tweezers or lifted by a rod inserted in a predrilled hole in the model and screwed into the pattern. The mold is tapped lightly, and the lifting rod is used to ease the model up out of the drag section.

Gates are cut from the sprue holes to the pattern impression (see Fig. 164). The gates are deepened as they reach the sprue holes. The mold surface and impression area are blown free of sand particles with bellows. The surfaces are dusted with the parting powder and the cope is replaced on the drag.

The metal requirement, determined previously in the same manner as that used for smaller castings, is placed in a large crucible, fluxed, and the dross slagged off the molten metal surface just before the metal is poured into the center sprue hole. This is the "pour" hole, and the remaining two sprue holes are called "risers." These act as vents and indicate that the mold is completely filled with metal.

When the button or metal in the pour hole has changed from bright red to black, the mold can be separated with the heavy tongs and the casting cooled by being gently submerged in water. Finishing details follow according to the requirements of the particular casting.

In addition to standard foundry techniques for sand casting large objects, a new method was discovered in 1956 by Louis Beardslee of California. Primarily for large architectural forms of sculpture, it can also be used to create small-scale decorative pieces for the home, office, and studio.

Constructed of Styrofoam, the pattern is sculpted into shape with hand and power tools. The process is like stone cutting. Heated tools are also used to form the material and to create a design. This must be done outdoors or in a well-ventilated room with a fan in operation, because the gas produced by burning the Styrofoam is extremely toxic if inhaled.

The Styrofoam pattern is tightly packed in the usual foundry sand, which is contained in a metal frame or flask. In this casting method the pattern is not left to be removed, but is replaced by the molten metal. Sprues or gates made in the sand permit the entry of the molten metal, which is usually bronze or aluminum. Venting is necessary just as it is for small castings.

The metal is poured from a melting crucible into troughs, which carry the mass to the sprues and into the sand-covered model. The troughs or runways for the molten metal are necessary because of the highly toxic gas formed by the disappearing Styrofoam pattern. The metal thus replaces the Styrofoam and flows down into all interstices, crevices, and detailed areas as well as into the main portions of the pattern.

The size of the pattern determines whether or not the casting is to be made in a foundry or in a home outdoor work area. Founding equipment is expensive, and large castings can be executed only in a foundry. The craftsman should follow the casting through to completion. Any unforeseen difficulties that arise can thus be controlled by on-the-spot design changes. Sometimes sprues left attached give added interest and also help to display the object to better advantage.

After casting the object of course requires the usual finishing and patinization to bring out its character.

Though this type of casting can be considered a sand casting technique, it is akin to the lost-wax method because the pattern is destroyed and in case of an unsatisfactory pour must be completely reconstructed.

Pumice block or Indian-type casting

Single-piece castings with one or two surface details can be cast in patterns carved in pumice or tufa stone (see Fig. 165). Molds may be made by regular casting investment poured over a wax, wood, or plastic model placed in a boxed frame. Plaster of Paris should not be used as a mold material; it is too finely grained to breathe and vent air and gases as the molten metal is poured into the pattern area. Collapsible or breakaway mold frames can be used to hold the investment or plaster from the time it is poured until it is set. This is the method employed by the Navajos to cast silver pendants, belt buckles, bracelets, and concha belt links.

The surface of the stone is ground or sanded smooth and the design is carved in the surface, usually in a V- or U-shaped depression (see Fig. 166). Small vents are cut away from the design, but not necessarily to the outer edges of the stone block. A gate or sprue is cut in one end of the stone mold. A cover plate, made to match the mold block, must be sanded smooth to make complete contact with the mold block. The two sections are held together with wire, or placed between thin sections of wood and tightened together with large "C" clamps (see Fig. 167). Vents and gates may be omitted if the casting is made without the cover. The molten metal is poured from the crucible over the carved impression. When the metal has cooled, it is lifted gently from the mold with a pointed rod and is eased into the pickling solution with copper tongs, and then rinsed in running water.

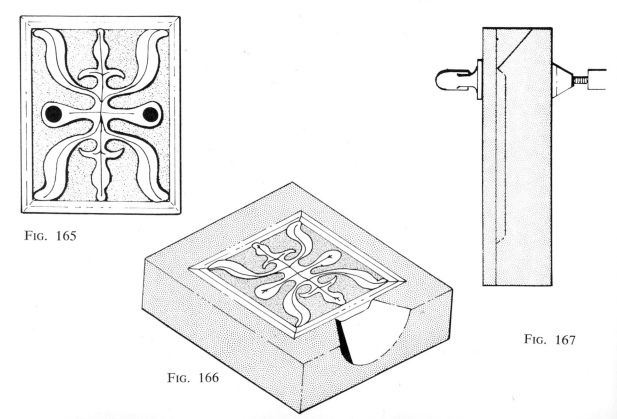

FIG. 165

FIG. 166

FIG. 167

CHAPTER 11

Cuttlefish Bone Casting

CUTTLEFISH BONE CASTING IS IDENTICAL TO sand casting in many respects. A simple rigid model without intricate detail is pressed between prepared half-sections of cuttlefish bone to produce an impression replica or mold chamber in the shell. Sprues, vents, and gates, carved or formed in the shell mold, perform the same operations as in sand casting. If the correct process is followed carefully, molten metal (prepared in the same manner as for sand molds), when poured into the mold, will produce single piece castings with excellent results. Expensive equipment is not required. Although the cuttlefish bone can be used for only one casting (casting sand can be reclaimed for multiple use), the procedure is much easier and quicker than that for sand casting.

Preparation of the model and the mold

A model can be constructed of any rigid material, such as wood, plastic, metal, or any other material capable of retaining its shape. Smooth or highly polished surfaces on the model are required to aid in removing it after the impression is made on the shell. Cuttlefish bone casting, unlike sand casting, is not limited to the reproduction of duplicates of previously constructed models. The mold sections, after sec-

tioning and sanding steps have been completed, may be carved free-hand with a sharp pointed knife to produce an impression chamber. This requires visualization of the shape and form to be produced as an impression rather than as an actual object.

The dried shell of the cuttlefish resembles the oyster shell. The cuttlefish is a member of the mollusk family, which includes snails, clams, squid, and oysters. Large shells required for the casting process are sold by casting supply houses for the use of the jewelry craftsman. The large shells, 12″ to 14″ long, are split equally by being sawed lengthwise (they must be sawed completely, as the bone does not break evenly), so that two flat oblong half-sections are produced (see Fig. 168). Larger castings may require two complete shells for a single mold, though the mold is prepared in the same manner as when a single shell provides the entire mold. The inner portion of the bone is softer than the outside and is sanded smooth on a piece of sandpaper placed on a flat, hard surface. A circular motion is used in sanding to avoid rounding of the edges of the mold. The second half-shell is sanded in the same manner. The two half-shells should not be rubbed against each other to smooth the mating surfaces, because this does not produce as close

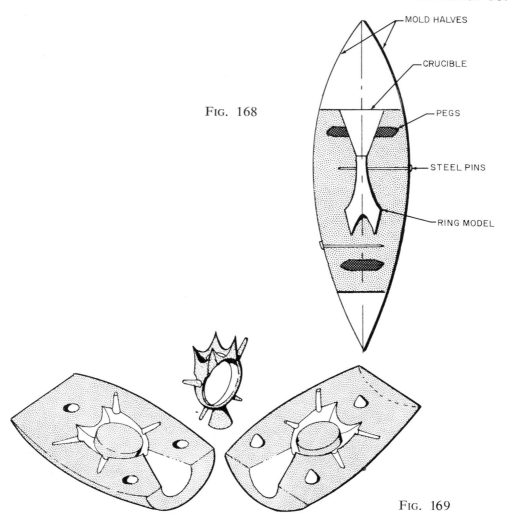

FIG. 168

MOLD HALVES

CRUCIBLE

PEGS

STEEL PINS

RING MODEL

FIG. 169

a fit as when each shell is sanded on a flat surface. The two sanded halves are then placed together. The shell sections and the model must be measured to locate the approximate center of the thickest part of the mold, where the model is to be positioned. This is necessary because the maximum wall thickness must be maintained to contain the molten metal in the shell.

When the model impression area has been ascertained, several small wooden pegs are placed in one of the sanded surfaces of the mold (see Fig. 168). These make indentations in the mating half of the mold and act as alignment pins, which are necessary when the mold is separated and reassembled. The alternate method is to insert steel wires through both mold sections when making the impression chamber, but these are not as accurate as the small wooden pins.

The original model or pattern is placed in the predetermined area on one of the sanded surfaces and pressed halfway into the shell. The remaining half-shell, aligned on the tapered wooden pins, is pressed slowly and firmly against the first section until the sanded surfaces make complete contact with each other. Knee pressure may be needed to close the mold sufficiently. With the model or pattern in place and the wooden pins maintaining proper alignment of the two mold sections, the ends of the cuttlebone are sawed off flat and the remaining edges are faced off with a rasp or vixen file so that the mold can stand upright on either end (see Fig. 168).

Removal of model or pattern

When the mold impression is completed, the two sections are carefully separated, and the model is lifted out with the fingertips or with a pair of tweezers. The impression chamber should be checked at this point to make sure that the mold is complete and identical to the model.

A funnel-shaped channel is cut in each mold section with a sharp carving knife or scalpel. The mold sections are cut one at a time. This channel or sprue, also called a gate, is for the flow of molten metal into the pattern chamber and is cut into the surface of the mold sections on the shank end if a ring is the model. Directing the flow of molten metal to the ring shank end preserves any detail in the mounting portion of the ring, but a sprue cut to the mounting portion destroys much of the possible detail of the casting and necessitates extra bench-time for finishing the mounting.

Vents

Small thin grooves, which act as vents for the escape of air and gases when the molten metal enters the mold, are cut radially from the impression chamber, halfway or less to the outer edge of the mold (see Fig. 169). (All loose shell particles must be blown away.) If the grooves are cut to the exterior of the mold, they will permit the escape of molten metal, so that an incomplete casting will result.

Treatment of the mold surface

The impression chamber is dusted with powdered graphite or lycopodium through a rubber-bulb dental syringe; the model is replaced gently in the impression, and the two mold sections are pressed together again. This forces the dusting powder into the surfaces of the impression and produces a smooth surface on the casting.

To achieve the same results, the assembled mold, without the model, can be held over a candle or alcohol-lamp flame to "soot" the inner surface. A third method is to use castor oil which, when brushed lightly over rough model surfaces, produces a smooth cast surface and aids in the removal of the model after the impression has been made.

A fourth, and perhaps the preferred, way is to paint the impression chamber with a heat-resistant solution consisting of equal parts of hard-soldering flux (borax and boric acid) and sodium silicate (water glass). After the surface

has dried, it can be coated with a layer of strong liquid household wax and a second coating of 1 part water to 1 part sodium silicate. This second coating is only used if a very high polish is desired on the surface of the casting. A maximum of 1 teaspoon of solution is used in each half-mold. The mold sections are placed together and allowed to dry for several days in normal room temperatures or in a low-heat oven to eliminate all moisture before the metal is cast into the mold.

Reassembling the mold

The parts when dry are placed together on the aligning pins and held together with iron binding wire wrapped in both directions around the mold. The assembled and wired mold is placed upright in a container of sand, which catches any unexpected escape of molten metal from the mold seams (see Fig. 170).

Preparing the metal

The metal is prepared in the proper crucible depending upon the type of metal to be used. The metal is heated quickly, the oxides are removed with a reducing flux, and the pour is made in the same manner as that described for sand casting.

Charcoal crucibles

The outer convex surface of one mold section is sanded down flat at its sprue or gate end, and a small square of charcoal with a crucible-

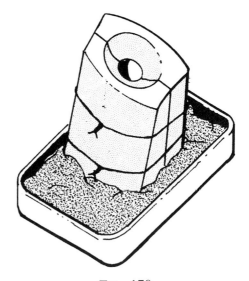

FIG. 170

like depression is sanded to fit flush against this surface. A small channel or groove can then be cut from the depression in the charcoal block through the cuttlefish bone mold section to the main gate or sprue that has been previously carved in the mold section. The charcoal block is wired to the cuttlefish bone mold, and the entire assemblage is placed upright in a container of sand. The metal is heated in the small charcoal crucible, fluxed if necessary, and the whole assemblage tilted with the tongs so that the molten metal runs directly into the mold sprue (see Figs. 171 and 172).

Removal of casting from the mold

The binding wire is clipped, the mold sections separated, and the casting placed in the pickling solution to remove any oxides, after which it is rinsed in clear water. If the metal is quenched while still hot from casting, it will be in an annealed state for finishing. The casting must be allowed to cool if there is any possibility of warpage in thinner areas, which is apt to occur when the metal is quenched immediately. Several additional castings of pewter can be obtained from the same mold if the cuttlefish mold is handled carefully when separated to remove the casting.

After the sprues and vents are sawed off, the casting is ready for finishing (see Chapter 13).

Three- and four-part molds

Original models with more intricate detail can often be reproduced by the cuttlefish bone casting process. The model is studied to determine which area of detail or undercuts and draws need split mold sections to allow the model to be removed. The shells are split, sanded, and then sawed crosswise to permit removal of a small section of the mold separate from the main mold half-section. This requires some trial and error efforts, and many more aligning pins are required to hold the mold sections securely in position for casting.

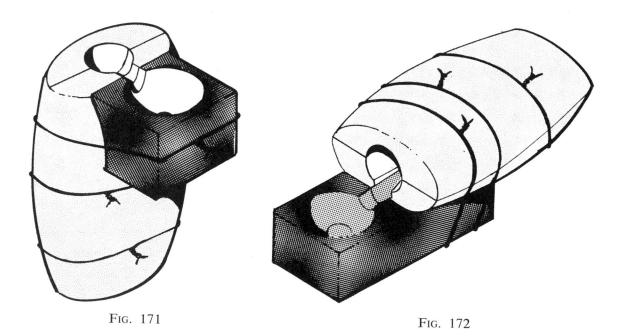

FIG. 171   FIG. 172

CHAPTER 12

Rubber Molds

A MOLD MADE OF SILICONE OR VULCANIZED rubber is a form containing an impression of an original model. It is filled with melted wax to duplicate identical models of the originals, which are always constructed of any material except wax. The inherent characteristics of the silicone or vulcanized rubber constituents dictate the life of the mold. Some molds may produce from one to approximately one hundred duplicate models in wax before a breakdown occurs because of handling and/or the continual impact of hot melted wax on the mold surfaces. Original wax models must be cast in precious metal or a low-fusing alloy before they can be used as a mold pattern. Small objects required in quantities that are too small to be constructed of wax by hand are also originally cast in precious metal or low-fusing alloy and a rubber mold made from the castings. Assorted shapes, such as half-domes, small leaves, acorns, rosebuds, teardrops, etc., can be formed in one rubber mold to produce identical wax models of the original casting. The technical limitations of centrifugal casting, which forces the craftsman to construct a new model for each casting, is overcome in part by the use of rubber molds.

Molds made with silicone or vulcanized rubber permit the use of a low-fusing alloy (consisting of percentages of lead, tin, cadmium, and bismuth for a casting metal) and precious metals, or any material capable of maintaining rigidity during the pour and set-up of the rubber substance in the mold frame (see Fig. 152). Silicone and polysulfide molds withstand heat up to 600°F. and will produce in perfect detail five to ten wax patterns before the mold begins to deteriorate from contact with the molten wax. Vulcanized rubber molds, which withstand heat up to 275°F., are capable of producing a minimum of ten times as many patterns as a silicone mold, retaining the exact detail of the original model. Hot pour compounds, unlike silicone and vulcanizing rubber materials, are completely reclaimable and can be reused many times. A comparison between the three principal mold materials shows that silicone rubber is expensive even in small amounts, but does not require expensive equipment. Vulcanizing rubber is inexpensive, but requires an expensive press. Hot pour compounds require neither expensive materials nor equipment, though they produce excellent detailed duplicate wax patterns. However, the greatest degree of accuracy in duplication is credited to the silicone or polysulfide rubber materials.

Silicone and polysulfide rubber molds

Silicone rubber impression compounds applied to casting processes are limited only by the imagination of the craftsman, and the technique is easily mastered. The material will produce every minute detail of the model even to the slightest imperfections.

Silicones and cold mold compounds have a short shelf life and because of this are sold in dated boxes. The base material tube and the reactor container have identical "batch numbers." Base material compounds should be polymerized only with reactors having the same batch numbers. This prevents unsatisfactory molds being compounded from mismatched materials. The shelf life averages 4 to 6 months, and each container is stamped with a 3-, 4-, or 6-month expiration date, but the materials should always be checked before being discarded. A small amount of out-dated material should be mixed to see if it is usable; if it is, pot life and curing times will be normal. Batch numbers are never interchangeable.

These impression materials have a synthetic rubber base of silicones or polysulfides, the silicone base material being the most popular. Both are liquids and polymeric compounds in that they must be mixed with a chemical reactor called a catalyst to polymerize them. Thus, identical elements in equal proportions but with different molecular weights and physical properties are combined to form the mold compound. Silicones are called R.T.V.s (room temperature vulcanizing), and the polysulfides are called cold mold compounds (the abbreviation C.M.C. refers to a trade name of one of these compounds). The polysulfide rubber is packaged in tubes, as is its reactor. Silicone rubber is also supplied in tubes, but the reactor is usually a bottled liquid. Silicone materials are the best of the two types because of color, odor, and clean handling. However, flexible positive and negative duplications are possible with either the R.T.V. or cold mold compounds when used with the proper technique. Of course, the mold will be an accurate duplication of the original model in either compound.

Three types of commonly used molds can be selected to fit particular needs (see Fig. 173). The diagrammatic illustrations should be studied to ascertain which type best fits the need. The versatility of the material enables the craftsman to utilize materials and equipment in many ways.

FIG. 173

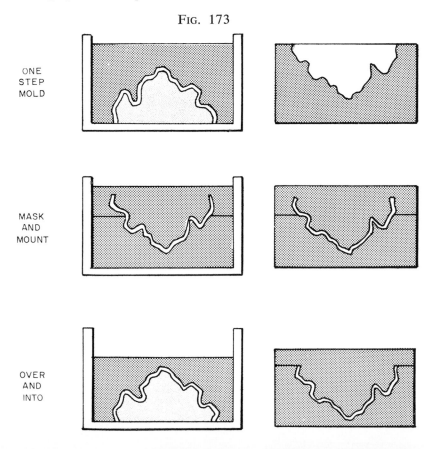

ONE STEP MOLD

MASK AND MOUNT

OVER AND INTO

Preparation of models and molds

Models may be constructed of any material such as metal, wood, plastic, polyurethane, plaster of Paris, or objects of natural origin such as seedpods, nutmeats, shells, etc. The pattern must be clean and free of oils and grease, and the undercuts and crevices free of dirt and foreign matter of any kind. Models other than those with an affinity to acetone may be dipped in acetone for a degreasing and set on a paper towel to drain.

One-step mold

Collapsible, breakaway mold frames (see Fig. 174) are used to contain a thin silicone mix until it sets up. The box is constructed of plywood or lucite notched at the corners and held together with a large rubber band cut from an old inner tube. A slotted base may be used to hold the frame walls, or the topless and bottomless frame can be placed on a smooth, flat surface and sealed around the base with sticky wax or floral clay to prevent leakage of thin silicone rubber compound.

A dam or boxed area can be quickly constructed of wallpaper cleaner, a claylike material that is kneaded into shape for use (see Fig. 175). This material, much cleaner to use than clay or wax, can also be used as a seal between the boxed frame and a flat Formica-covered surface or a glass slab. Breakaway dental flasks can also be used for mold frames (see

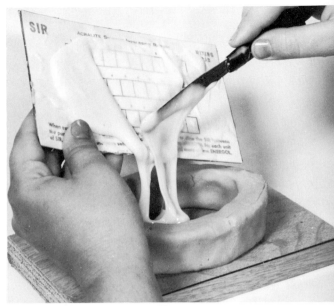

FIG. 175

Figs. 176, 177, and 178). The model and all surfaces inside the boxed frame coming into contact with the rubber compound should be coated with a parting agent. This is easily made of 5% household detergent mixed with tap water. A brush can be used, but preferably the solution should be applied by spraying (window spray bottle can be used). The frame and model must be dry before the compound is poured.

Parting agents

Other parting agents equally effective include castor oil thinned with coconut oil, oil dag (colloidal graphite) mixed with kerosene, water-soluble waxes, non-rub wax furniture polishes, and vaseline thinned with lighter fluid. The liquid in the Vaseline solution evaporates and leaves a thin film of lubricant on the mold surfaces. Any excessive amount of the parting agent remaining on the mold surfaces should be blown away gently before additional rubber compound is poured over the coated mold section. Models or patterns with extreme undercuts, crevices, and draws should always be coated to ensure their removal without damage to the mold.

Spatulation pallet

The compound is mixed and spatulated on a disposable paper that is imprinted with mark-

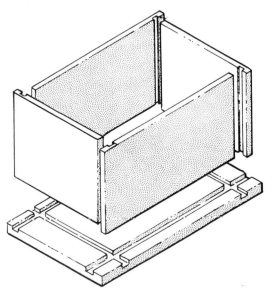

FIG. 174

FIG. 176

FIG. 177

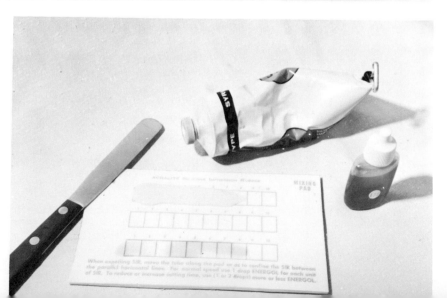

FIG. 178

FIG. 179

ings for correct combinations and which is, therefore, preferred over unprinted paper pallets or glass slabs (see Fig. 179). A measure of compound is squeezed from the tube onto the pallet over the imprinted strip as indicated. On the same pallet the reactor is measured by drops onto a separately marked strip as indicated. Large molds require that the mix be measured by weight into a container. The standard mix ratio is 4 parts of reactor to 100 parts of compound by weight. This ratio should be used if no other recommendations are given by the manufacturer, or if previous mixes tried were unsatisfactory. It should always be kept in mind that there are many factors that may contribute to an unsatisfactory mix.

A thinner can be added to the mix to lower the consistency of the compound, but only the one recommended by the manufacturer of the specific compound should be used. Use the thinner as needed instead of adding additional catalyst. This reserves the reactor for subsequent compound polymerization. By using thinner, the craftsman is afforded additional time to pour the mold, since pot life or working time is extended, whereas viscosity, strength, and hardness of the mold decrease unless the added thinner is limited to 10% by weight of the complete mix.

The reactor should be smoothed onto both sides of the spatula on the pallet before working it into the silicone paste. This allows easier cleaning of the spatula, for the reactor will not adhere to the tool as easily as does the unpolymerized base material. The compounds are mixed with the spatula (see Fig. 180) until a homogeneous mix is indicated by a uniform color with no streaks of the reactor visible in the base material. Spatulation should always be accomplished in no more than 1 minute, or just until the streaks disappear. Under-spatulation prevents complete polymerization and over-spatulation shortens the set or curing time. The pot life, determined by the amount of reactor used, is all the time available for pouring the mix after the compound has been polymerized. Varying the amount of reactor used will lengthen or shorten the curing time (with some materials this is not necessary, as increased temperatures and humidity will have the same effect). Reactors are often called accelerators, but they should be more specifically referred to

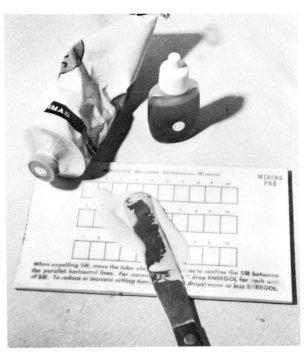

FIG. 180

at all times as reactors, because they alter the structure of the material during polymerization. This pot life varies from 1 minute to several hours, depending on the materials used and the manufacturer's recommendations.

Large molds require containers for mixing the materials and a spatula or paddle that will reach the sides and bottom of the container so that a completely homogeneous mix is obtained. Drill presses and hand drills can be adapted for excellent mixing results, but care must be taken to prevent overmixing. Compounds vigorously overmixed by hand or mixed mechanically at excessive speeds will create air bubbles. This causes voids or craters on the surface convolutions of the mold. To ensure an air-free mold material, catalyzed compounds should be de-aired with vacuum equipment (used for investing models) before the mix is poured into the boxed frame (see Figs. 89 and 90). The mold can be coated with a thinned layer of the polymerized compound just as a wax model is coated with thinned investment before the casting flask is filled. This also aids in eliminating air bubbles from the model surfaces.

When the mix is properly prepared it is poured into the mold frame, which has been placed on an angle so that the compound will flow around the model, thus pushing out any air from under it. The mold is half-filled with the mix and then allowed to set for several seconds so that the pour will level out. The remainder of the mix is then poured into the frame until the model is covered with the compound at least ½" thick at its highest point.

Curing time

The mold frame, after it is filled, is set aside to cure or vulcanize. Curing times vary from 10 minutes to 24 hours at 70°F., although some molecular change may continue to take place for as much as 4 to 7 days. Manufacturer's specification sheets usually list set-up or curing times along with the pot life time. The average pot life indicated is 3 to 5 hours, tack-free time is 8 to 10 hours, and 24 to 48 hours for complete cure from the time that the mix was polymerized under average temperature and humidity conditions. A rule of thumb for set-up, cure, or vulcanizing time is to allow 24 hours for each ¼" thickness of the mold material, with adjustments and compensations for the various thicknesses of the mold areas. The curing or vulcanizing time is largely influenced by both the degree of confinement and the shape of the model. Minute portions of volatile by-products are formed during polymerization of the compound and are released during the curing time through the top or unconfined area of the mold. The distance these volatiles must travel through the unconfined masses of the mold is the thickness gauge of the material and is used to determine the curing time for a satisfactory mold. Curing time is extended as surface exposure is reduced. A boxed frame almost completely confined with only a small vent will, more often than not, refuse to cure.

Curing or vulcanizing can be stepped up by the utilization of heat, but because of variances in time and temperature relationships, the mold, after pouring, should stand at room temperature for 2 to 4 hours before the heat is applied. Early heat application results in voids or "artifacts" and "sponging" in the mold because trapped air has not been allowed to escape. If the mold has been de-aired by a vacuum process immediately after polymerization, it can be heat-cured after pouring without standing at room temperature for any specific length of time. Heat must be applied slowly; rapid heating will

cause porosity and, in some instances, a reversion of the RTV to a semifluid mass that is no longer rubbery or stabile in consistency. The mold is heat-cured at temperatures 25° to 30° greater than the highest temperature of the casting material to be used in the rubber mold. The heat-curing time will vary from 15 minutes to several hours.

The mold is removed from the boxed frame and twisted slowly and gently to release the model.

Repair of broken or damaged molds

Molds broken during the removal of the original model or molds damaged by use can be restored, and any imperfections found in a mold section can also be taken care of at this point. The damaged section is cut away with the sharp wax carving knife. The model and mold surfaces are cleaned with acetone. The model is returned to the mold and then replaced in the boxed frame. Freshly mixed compound is generously poured into the removed section of the mold, then set aside to cure. When the vulcanization is complete the mold will be as good or better than the original mold in strength, stability, and workability.

Mask and mount molds

A boxed frame is constructed around the model, or the model is placed in a half-section of a bronze dental flask. The frame is sealed to prevent the leakage of any liquid material. Melted paraffin is then poured not over but around the model until the upper half alone is exposed (see Fig. 173), and set aside to harden. The R.T.V. compound is spatulated and poured over the exposed portion of the model, and then set aside to cure. Only enough mix is prepared to cover the exposed part of the model completely.

When the mold has cured, the boxing frame or flask section is removed. The mold section is then separated gently from the mold, and all of the paraffin is completely eliminated. This can be done by placing the model in near-boiling water. Special care must be taken if the model is made of plastic.

Notches are cut in the completed half-mold for exact alignment, and the mold is replaced in the boxed frame or flask, cavity side up, after which the model is replaced in the mold section. The surfaces of the exposed model and mold section are coated with a liquid called a parting agent, a die-lube or a mold release. Some parting agents are not effective on certain types of rubber, and the model becomes completely encapsulated in a one-piece mold. In such cases, remove the model by slitting the mold (see removal of models from vulcanized rubber molds, Fig. 202).

Freshly polymerized molding compound is required for the second pour. *Any previously mixed compound must not be used at any time.* The exposed part of the model is now covered with the fresh compound until it is ½" thick at the highest part of the model, and set aside to cure or vulcanize.

When this second section of the mold is vulcanized, the two frame or flask portions are separated and the model is removed. The indentations or notch marks made when the first section of the mold was completed form interlocking nubs on the second mold section to permit perfect alignment.

In the first section of the mold a sprue hole is cut from the outer edge of the mold to the pattern cavity in the side opposite the notches, and a small air vent is cut between the notches. Small notches are cut on the outside of the two mold sections and, if constructed in an oval or circular frame, the sprue side of the mold is cut off flat (see Figs. 181 and 182). Rubber bands are placed in the small notches to hold the mold sections together when the hot wax is poured or injected into the mold.

Mold clamps can be constructed of small squares of ¼" plywood attached one to the other with a rubber or webbed cotton strip, which acts as a hinge (see Figs. 183 and 184). The mold is placed between the two wood sections and hand-held during the injection of the wax. In order to avoid distorting the pattern chamber, care must be taken not to compress the two halves of the mold.

Over-and-into molds

The model and boxing frame are prepared in the same manner as that used for one-step molds (see Fig. 173). Freshly polymerized compound is poured over the model until it is

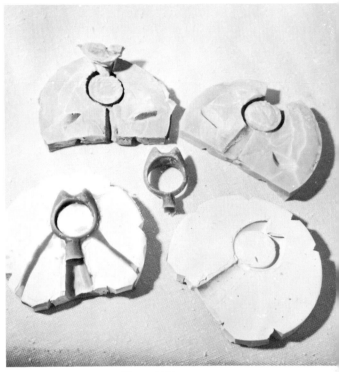

FIG. 181

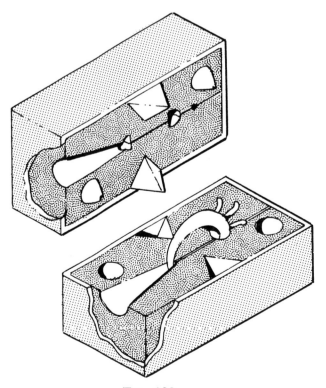

FIG. 182

completely covered at least ½″ at the highest point. The mold is set aside to cure. After vulcanizing is complete, the mold and the model, kept intact, are removed from the flame or flask. Notches are cut in one end of the mold for exact alignment, and the mold, with the model still intact, is placed back in the boxing frame with the exposed side facing upward. The surfaces of the exposed model and the mold section are coated with a parting agent. The exposed portion of the model is covered with a freshly mixed compound and set aside to cure. When vulcanized, the complete mold is taken from the frame, and the two mold sections separated to remove the model. A sprue opening is cut in the first mold section after the separation, and an air vent is cut opposite the sprue. Again, the two sections will align perfectly because of the notches cut into the first section.

Fabric reinforcement of molds

If desired, a mold can be reinforced for greater strength and stability by placing a piece of fabric in it when half of the compound required for the mold section is poured. Allow the compound to level off before completely covering the model (see Fig. 185). If casting materials with temperatures above 350°F. are poured into the mold, a glass fabric must be used.

Hot pour compounds

Another mold material, mentioned briefly at the beginning of this chapter, is a synthetic rubber material called a hot pour compound. It can be used for one- and two-part molds and also to repair or reinforce silicone rubber molds as previously outlined. The material has the appearance of green or pink wrinkled rubber worms (see Fig. 186). To change it to a liquid

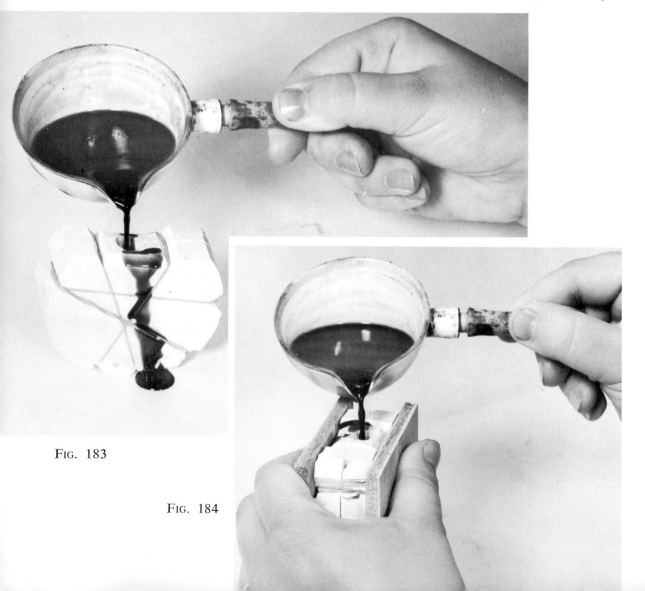

FIG. 183

FIG. 184

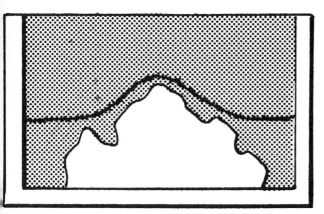

FIG. 185

state, place it in a metal container (such as an aluminum pie plate) in an oven and heat to pouring state at 340°–360°F. The alternate method is partially to fill the bottom section of a double boiler with castor oil or petroleum oil such as Golden Shell No. 40 and fill the upper portion with the rubber material. The oil boils at a higher temperature than water and so equals the oven heat required to change the material to pouring consistency. The material is poured into the mold frame and set aside to cure (see Fig. 187). The maximum pot time is 2 minutes, and the curing time is as little as 1 hour, depending on the thickness of the mold. When the mold has served its purpose, save the material by thoroughly cleaning and then degreasing it by dipping it in acetone and placing it on a paper towel to drain. The material is then returned to the double boiler or oven for immediate reliquefication. This process may be delayed until the material is required for a new pour.

Petrolatum (Vaseline) or liquid soap should be used as a parting agent when two-piece molds are made with hot pour compounds.

FIG. 186

FIG. 187

Vulcanized rubber molds

To make vulcanized rubber molds, suspend a metal model in a two-section metal frame of aluminum, brass, or steel (see Figs. 188 and 189) and fill the surrounding area with bits and ⅛″ sheets of uncured natural rubber. The metal frame or flask is placed in a vulcanizing press consisting of electrically heated plates, similar to jaw vises, which are tightened during the process (see Fig. 190).

A small flask can be constructed (see Fig. 191) or purchased from suppliers of casting equipment.

When the flask is constructed, alignment pins are placed in opposing corners by inserting a ⅛″ drill rod tightly into predrilled holes until ¼″ of rod extends from the frame surface. Holes in the other half-section of the flask mate with these pins for alignment of the two sections. A cradle is formed in one end of each mold section for a rod or tube, which is attached to the original model and suspends it in the mold frame (see Figs. 188 and 189). When the original model with rod attached is removed, the rod leaves a tunnel or sprue for the entry of the molten wax into the pattern chamber. A conical section of metal ⅜″ long is constructed to fit snugly over this tube and against the inner walls of the frames. This cone forms a crucible opening in the completed mold (see Fig. 192).

FIG. 188

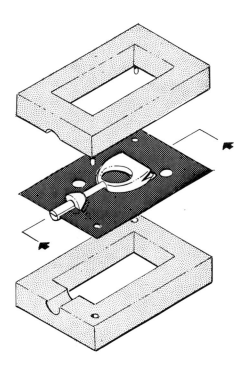

FIG. 189

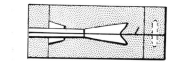

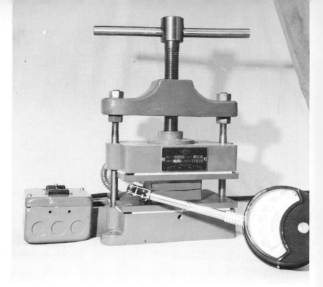

FIG. 190

FIG. 191

FIG. 192

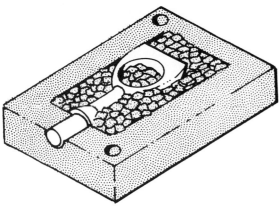

FIG. 193

Packing the frame and vulcanizing the mold

One section of the frame, cradle and pin side up, is placed on a flat surface, and the frame is fully packed with cut sections of uncured rubber (see Fig. 193). The model, attached to a short length of metal rod, is placed in the cradle. The remaining half-frame is dusted with talc and positioned on the first section. Tiny bits of uncured rubber are firmly packed around the model and down into any under-crevices. Larger rubber pieces are then placed up to the top of the second frame. It always takes more material than seems necessary, because the rubber is compressed by the force of the press.

To complete the packing, pieces of uncured rubber are cut to the size of the inner opening of the frames. One piece is placed against the rubber on the outside of the upper flask section. The other is placed against the rubber bits exposed in the lower frame section.

The frame surfaces that will come into contact with the press plates are dusted with talc and placed into position on the press (see Fig. 190). The entire assemblage must be kept together as a unit when placed in the vulcanizer, or it will have to be removed and repacked. The press is switched on, and the jack handle is turned only enough to hold the flasks loosely together. After 10 to 15 minutes in the press, the plates are partially tightened, then after 25 minutes, securely tightened. Vulcanizing is usually completed in 45 to 70 minutes. Checking the press with a portable pyrometer, which gives instantaneous readings, will show that the flask periphery heats to 300°F. in about 20 minutes. A well-vulcanized mold will usually result if the flask is left in position for at least 60 minutes. Molds are completely vulcanized when the thumbnail pressed into the surface leaves a permanent mark.

The kitchen oven can be used to vulcanize the rubber in the mold frames; however, metal plates must be used to contain the uncured rubber in the frames. Thin but rigid metal plates are positioned over the mold frame openings, and the entire assemblage is held together with several large "C" clamps.

After the flask is vulcanized, it is removed from the expanded press plates with tongs and placed in room-temperature water to cool for approximately 15 to 20 minutes. A sharp carving knife is inserted along the inner walls of the frame section faces to loosen them from the rubber mold. The two sections can then be gently separated. Because the support rod is positioned between the two half-sections and encased in the rubber, the mold can never be pushed out from either side of the metal frames.

Removal of the model from the mold

When the flask has been removed, the mold is slit open along the sides with an extremely sharp scalpel or modeler's knife (see Fig. 194). The mold should be cut as nearly as possible into equal parts. An initial cut is made around the support pin. For exact alignment in case the mold is completely separated into two parts, notches are cut at this point in opposite corners of the mold. Because vulcanized rubber is tough and difficult to handle, it should be placed in a small bench vise when the initial cuts are made (see Fig. 194). The mold can be completely separated into two parts, or one end left uncut to act as a hinge for the mold sections. After the first cut is completed, the mold is removed from the vise and the openings dusted with talc to prevent sticking. The mold is returned to the vise so that the rubber can be pulled and stretched slightly to open the mold enough to insert the separating knifeblade. The shape of the model will determine the number of additional cuts required to open the mold and remove the model.

Ring molds are cut along one side of the finger space and up around the mounting. If

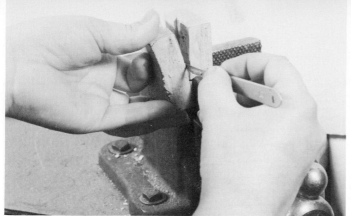

Fɪɢ. 194

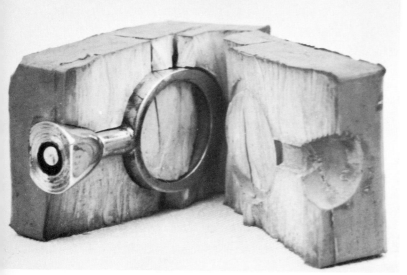

Fɪɢ. 195

Fɪɢ. 196

Fɪɢ. 197

possible, the mounting section should remain in one side of the mold. Extremely intricate detail requires absolutely equal sections of the mold in order that the wax model can be removed easily. As each area of the mold is exposed by cutting, it must be dusted with talc. To open the mold further, cuts at right angles to the main direction of the model and into the outer areas of the mold can be made. These extra cuts act as double hinges in the mold (see Figs. 195, 196, and 197).

Two-part molds with metal separator

To make molds with metal separators, which eliminates much of the slitting after vulcanizing, a piece of 30 gauge copper sheet is placed across the inner surface of the lower flask section and down over the alignment pins before it is packed with rubber. The upper section of metal is placed in position, and the excess copper sheet that extends outside the mold is trimmed away. The top section of the flask is then removed, and the model, with the short length of metal rod attached, is placed on the copper sheet so that the outline of the model can be traced onto the copper sheet. The outline of the model is then cut from the copper sheet, and the rod is slit to allow it to slide over the copper separator. The copper separator is removed so that the lower section can be packed with rubber as previously described (see Fig. 193).

The model, with the copper separator attached in the slot, is set into place in the cradle. The upper portion of the flask, positioned and filled with bits and pieces of uncured natural rubber, is then covered with a full sheet of rubber the same size as the inner opening of the flasks. The two flask sections are then turned over as a unit and the procedure repeated, after which the filled mold is vulcanized. Often, when they are tightened, the press plates push the model off center, but this is of small consequence and does not affect the usefulness of the mold.

When the mold is completed, if a ring mold is being made, only the finger opening needs cutting, plus a few small thread-like connections of rubber, which must be severed before the mold frames are parted.

Center positioning the model in the mold

If difficulties arise in centering the model in the mold, or if an absolutely center pattern chamber is required, the model, with pin attached, may be embedded in a flask that has been coated with oil and then filled with dental plaster. Small dowel pegs are placed in the plaster for alignment pins. As this material sets up quickly, the suspended model can be held by hand or clamped to the flask section until completely set.

When the plaster is set, the surfaces of flask, plaster, and model are dusted with talc, and the upper flask section is placed in position. This upper section is then packed with bits and pieces of uncured natural rubber, and the half-section is vulcanized before anything else is done. When vulcanizing is complete and the flask has cooled, the mold sections are separated. The model is removed from the plaster, which, in turn, is removed from the bottom flask section. The rubber half-mold and the model are replaced in the metal frame, and the procedure reversed. The mold surfaces and the exposed model are dusted with talc. The other half-flask section is then added, packed with the rubber, and vulcanized. When the second vulcanizing step has been completed and the flask is cool, the mold is removed from the metal sections and the model from the mold.

Casting a wax model in a rubber mold or low-fusing alloy

Rubber molds must have a sprue opening or crucible unless they are negative exposed molds with single surface impressions, which permit the hot wax to be poured directly down into the pattern cavity.

The pattern chamber and mating mold surfaces are lubricated with liquid soap or dusted with talc. Small plastic containers that are sold for catsup or mustard are ideal to use for dusting the mold convolutions, because the pointed nozzle emits just enough powder for small areas when the bottle is gently squeezed (see Fig. 198). The mold should be redusted with talc after every five wax models have been made, or after each alloy model.

The mold sections are placed between the

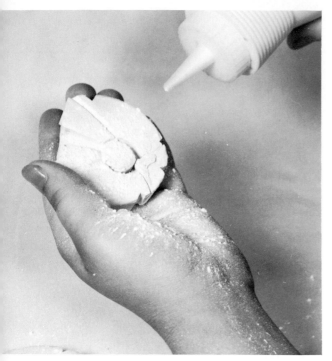

FIG. 198

FIG. 199

FIG. 200

FIG. 201

flat boards (see Figs. 183 and 184), held together with rubber bands or "C" clamps, and the wax injected into the cavity through the crucible or sprue opening. Shallow molds, or those with simple detail, can be filled with hot wax fed by gravity and poured from the small porcelain melting pot (see Figs. 183 and 184).

Wax injectors

Molten wax cools too quickly to permit a gravity flow into all the inner parts of a deep mold or into a mold that has considerable detail. Such molds necessitate a mechanical injection of molten wax. Wax can be injected into the predusted mold by air, centrifugal, or hydraulic pressure. However, the simplest way is to use a small electricity-heated hydraulic injector (see Figs. 199, 200, and 201). This consists of a small container with an upright nozzle extending above the rim. A plunger on the opposite side of the container, when forced downward, drives a thin stream of hot wax into the mold. The mold is placed between two boards, as previously mentioned (see Figs. 183 and 184) and held tightly over the nozzle. When the wax has cooled sufficiently, the mold is parted and the wax model eased gently out (see Fig. 202). The less intricate side of the mold, separating more easily from the model, should be identified so that it can be removed first. The complicated or detailed portions of the wax pattern can then be seen as the model is separated from the mold, thus preventing breakage or distortion of the wax.

The mold should be redusted or lubricated after every five wax castings have been made.

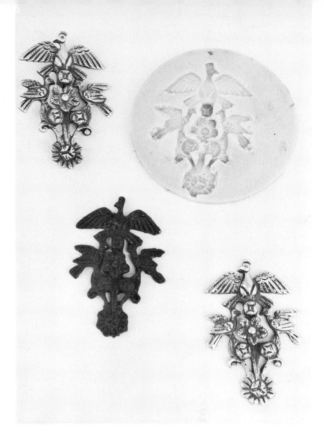

FIG. 203   Single one-piece molds

FIG. 204   Single one-piece molds with original wax model and casting

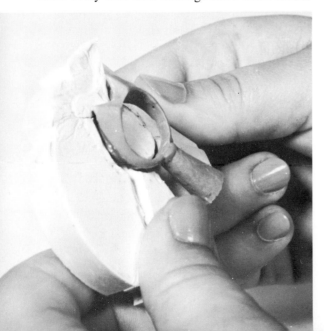

FIG. 202

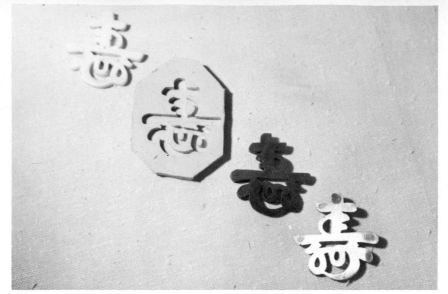

FIG. 205 Single one-piece molds with original wax model and casting

FIG. 206 Single one-piece molds with original wax model and casting

FIG. 207 Two-piece mold with original and castings

CREATIONS IN JEWELRY,

SILVERWARE,

AND SCULPTURE

120

Created by EDNA SAYRE

RING. (child's). Silver.
Lost wax.

NOVELTY. Silver African violet leaf.
Replica.

PIN. 14 kt. gold roses.
Lost wax.

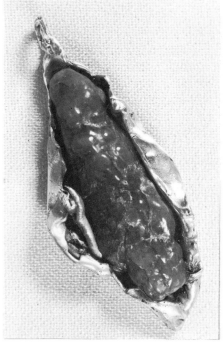

PENDANT. Silver with botryoidal jade.
Lost wax.

NOVELTY. Silver orchids.
Replica.

Created by JAYNE SMITH

PENDANT. Gold-plated silver.
Lost wax.

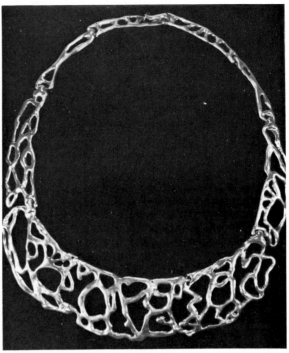

NECKLACE. Silver, nine sections.   *Lost wax.*

NECKLACE. Silver and ebony,
combined cast and handwrought metals.

Lost wax.

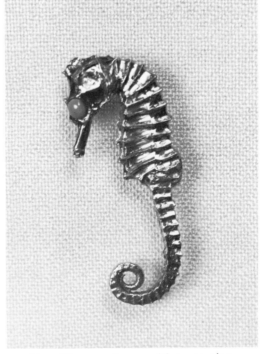

PIN. Silver sea horse with turquoise.
Lost wax.

Created by HELEN PEGRAM

BRACELET. Silver dogwood blossom, combined cast and handwrought metals. *Lost wax.*

BRACELET. Silver pelargonium leaf with pearl. *Replica.*

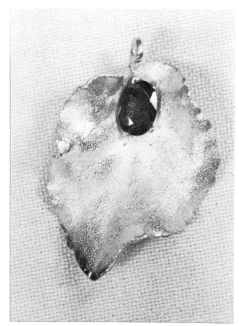

PENDANT. Silver African violet leaf with faceted garnet. *Replica.*

NOVELTY. Silver orchid. *Replica.*

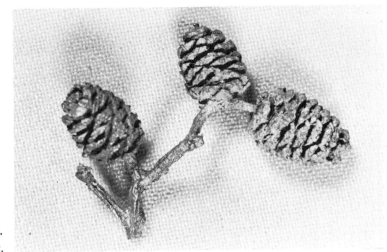

NOVELTY. Silver alder cones.
Replica.

NOVELTY. Silver scorpion.
Replica.

PENDANT. Silver and
petrified coral with
cast dandelion blossom.
Replica.

PIN AND EARRINGS.
Silver begonia leaves.
Replica.

Created by SHARR CHOATE

NECKLACE. Silver, twelve wishbone rings on a velvet cord. *Lost wax.*

RINGS. 14 kt. gold with faceted smoky quartz. *Lost wax.*

PIN. Silver with stone inlay. *Lost wax.*

BRACELET. Silver with turquoise.

RING. 18 kt. white gold with star sapphire.   *Lost wax.*

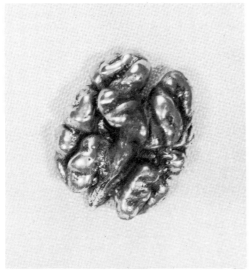

NOVELTY. Silver walnut meat.   *Replica.*

RING. 14 kt. gold wishbone with fire opal.   *Lost wax.*

NOVELTY. Silver octopus, 2″ high.   *Replica.*

Created by ROBERT COLEMAN

PIN. Manganese bronze, "Big-beaked bird." *Lost wax.*

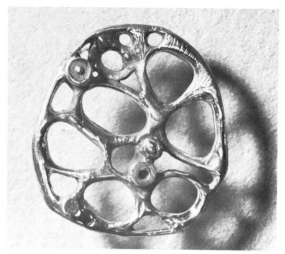

PIN. French gold, "All Circles." *Lost wax.*

PIN. Silver, "Belly Button Bird." 2″ high. *Lost wax.*

PENDANT. Silver, "Honeycomb." 2″ high. *Lost wax.*

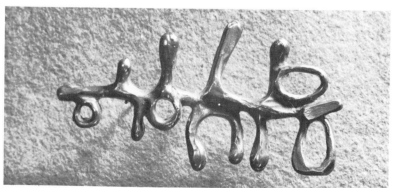

PIN. Silicon bronze, "Growth." 2¼″ long. *Lost wax.*

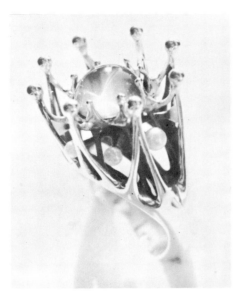

RING. 14 kt. gold with star sapphires.
Lost wax.

FIGURE. Silver.   *Lost wax.*

PIN. 14 kt. gold with rose quartz.
Lost wax.

RING. 14 kt. gold
with gemstone carving. *Lost wax.*

Created by ANNE DONNELLY

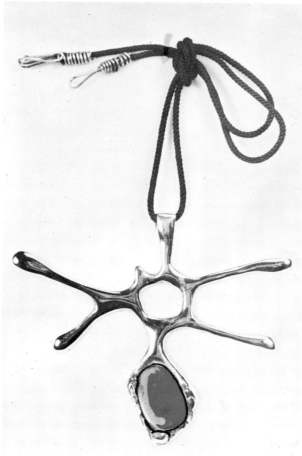

CUFF LINKS. Sterling silver with jade.
Lost wax.

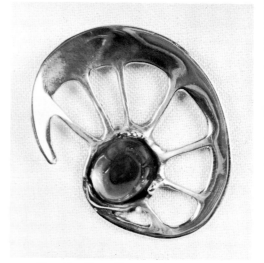

PENDANT. Sterling silver with amethyst.   *Lost wax.*

PIN. Sterling silver with amethyst.
Lost wax.

RING. 14 kt. gold with smoky quartz.
Lost wax. .

PIN. Sterling silver.   *Lost wax.*

PENDANT. Sterling silver and black
coral with black and white pearls.
Lost wax.

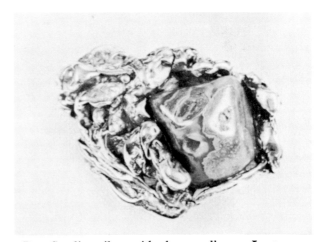

PIN. Sterling silver with chrysocolla.   *Lost wax.*

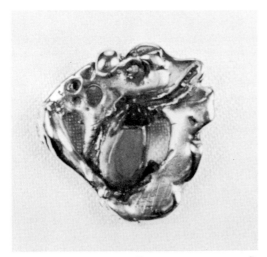

PIN AND EARRINGS. Sterling silver with amethyst.   *Lost wax.*

EARRINGS. Sterling silver with chrysoprase.   *Lost wax.*

PENDANT. Sterling silver. *Lost wax.*

Created by TED HAMMOND

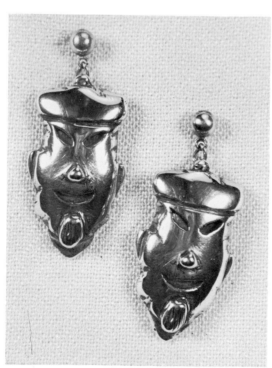

EARRINGS. Silver Chinese masks.
Lost wax.

Created by STANLEY LECHTZIN

GOBLETS. Sterling silver.   *Lost wax, hollow core.*

Created by EARL KRENTZIN

LION CANDLESTICK. Silver and enamel. 2½ " high.   *Lost wax, hollow core.*

Box. Gold-plated sterling silver
and garnets. 2½" high.

Lost wax, hollow core.

SPICE BOX. Sterling silver and tourmalines. 2" high. *Lost wax, hollow core.*

"MADELINE." Henri Matisse. Bronze. 23½" high.
Courtesy San Francisco Museum of Art,
Harriet Lane Levy Bequest.

"THE SERF." Henri Matisse. Bronze. 34" high.
Courtesy San Francisco Museum of Art,
Harriet Lane Levy Bequest.

"ANDALUSIAN GAMES." Richard O'Hanlon. 28½" high. Bronze.
Courtesy San Francisco Museum of Art,
the SFMA Collection,
gift of the Membership Activities Board.

"WAR LORD." Ernest Mahlke.
Cast sterling silver with ebony base.

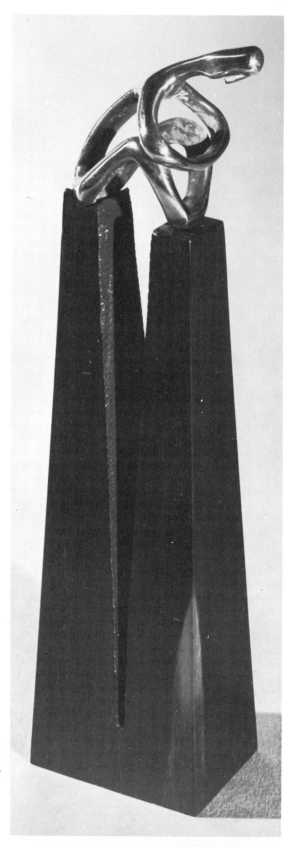

"SUCCESS." Ernest Mahlke.
Bronze casting on ebony base.

Part II
FINISHING

CHAPTER 13

Basic Finishing

ALL CASTINGS REQUIRE THE REMOVAL OF ANY undesired surface roughness and finishing where the sprue wires and vents were attached. Finishing is a vital part of a successful casting. Careful attention is needed in order to assure a completed article that can be pointed to with pride.

Removal of sprues and vents

The casting, after removal from the investment, sand, cuttlefish, or hollow core mold, and the pickling solution is placed in a small bench vise or the V-slot of the bench pin, and the button, sprues, and vents sawed off (see Fig. 208). To hold the casting during the sanding, sawing, and filing, ring clamps are also available (see Fig. 215b), which fit into a small bench vise. It is advisable to leave the button and sprue attached to give a holding place for articles too small or too difficult to hold in the fingers, in a ring clamp, or a hand vise (see Fig. 209). Large castings or sections, also difficult to hold, are worked in the same manner, after which the unwanted metal is removed and only the point of contact refinished. This small con-

tact point is usually finished with small Swedish or Swiss files, small wooden sticks wrapped with emery or garnet paper, or by sanding and grinding with carborundum or rubber-bonded abrasive wheels, which are mounted on mandrels and used with "Handee" grinders, flexible-shaft-driven handpieces, or standard cord-driven dental handpieces (see Figs. 210, 211).

Use of the saw

The sprue, button, auxiliary sprues, and vents are sawed off with the jewelers' saw. Coarse saw blades should be used for bulky sections, although they leave marks, which must be filed away. Fine-toothed saw blades will do the job satisfactorily, leaving little evidence of the saw mark, but usually break in the process. Standard machinists' hacksaws can be used on large castings, if space permits their use without damage to other parts of the casting. Such hacksaw blades are placed so that the teeth point away from the handle and the blade cuts with a pushing motion, whereas the jewelers' saw is always

Fig. 208

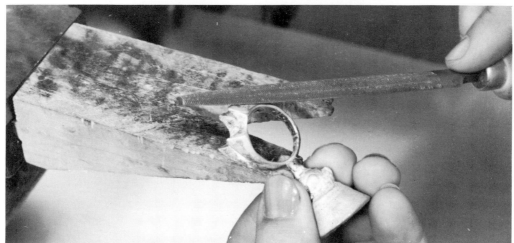

Fig. 209

Fig. 211

Fig. 210

Fig. 212

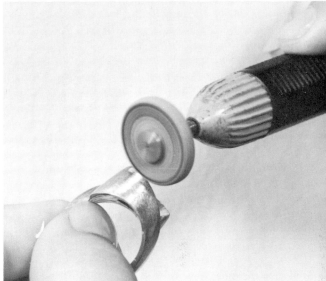

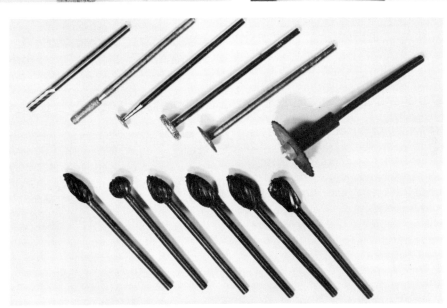

Fig. 213b   Diamond wheels, saws, and metal burrs used with flexible shaft or dental handpieces.

used with the teeth pointing toward the handle.

The blade, after the first end is securely tightened under the clamp, is inserted in the jewelers' saw so that one end just touches the edge of the remaining clamp. The saw frame is pressed against the work bench, and the loose end of the saw blade inserted in the clamp and tightened. A small hole should be drilled in the bench edging for this purpose to prevent the saw from slipping sideways. The saw is released from the pressure holding it against the edge of the work bench, allowing the blade to become taut. Over-taut blades will break as easily as loose-fitting blades. The jewelers' saw is worked in a vertical motion with the force applied on the downward or cutting stroke. If pressure is applied to the return stroke, the blade will either break or wear out quickly. If the work must be stopped for a while, the sawing action should stop so that the frame rests on the metal, as it is much easier to resume sawing with less likelihood of blade breakage if the saw is started from the downward position. In turning a corner, the saw action continues in an up and down motion without moving forward. Gradually, as the blade turns, the sawing continues with pressure applied in a forward motion.

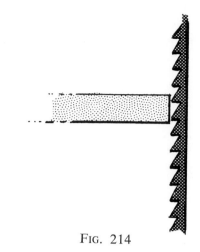

FIG. 214

While the thickness of a casting permits the use of almost any size of saw blade, a good silversmithing rule to remember is: The distance between the points or teeth on the saw blade must be less than the thickness of the metal to be sawed (see Fig. 214). Sawing very thin sections of a casting with a heavy-toothed blade will cause the metal to buckle and chatter, with resultant unwanted bending in the casting extensions as well as blade breakage. Changing to a smaller blade for sawing will eliminate this problem, just as it does in hand-wrought metal techniques. A new saw blade inserted into an old cut will break if too much pressure is used or if the blade is bent sideways at the end of the stroke.

Saw-blade lubricants are usually mentioned in most silversmithing books, with beeswax as the most highly recommended. However, if the sawed edges are to be soldered to others, all greasy or waxy lubricants forced into the fine striations made by the saw blade deter the flow of solder. Because these minute groovings are difficult to clean, the best lubricant is saliva, which leaves no contamination or coating in the microscopic groovings of finely sawed edges.

Broken blades, if still long enough, can be saved and used when there is no immediate supply of new blades. The saw frame is simply adjusted to a smaller opening, and the shortened blade is inserted in the same manner as a full-length blade.

Much of the hand-filing and hand-sanding can be eliminated by developing finesse with the saw blade. A little practice will illustrate the versatility and value of this tool as an auxiliary rasp or file. The blade can be inserted into hard-to-get-at areas that are too small for the Swedish files or rotary cutting instruments.

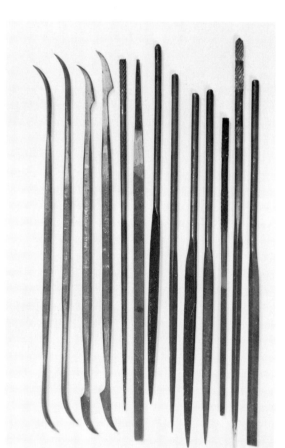

FIG. 215a

Areas of a casting which have emerged solid or webbed because of technique inequalities can be opened by center-punching, drilling a small hole in the webbed area, and inserting the loose end of a saw blade. The loose end after insertion is securely fastened in the saw frame, and the excess metal sawed away.

Filing

The sawed edges and sprue locations are filed with regular flat, mill, half-round, and round files, 6″ to 8″ long, with second or smooth cutting surfaces. Small files, either Swedish or Swiss, are used to obtain a smoother surface and to reach intricate or detailed areas. Die-sinkers' riffler files are also used for this purpose (see Fig. 215b).

Files are moved across the surface of the metal in one direction only. When the stroke is completed, the file should be lifted and returned for another pass across the metal. Pulling the file backward dulls the cutting surface quickly. Files should never be laid one on top of another, allowed to touch, or be touched with the fingers. Moisture, dust, and skin oils collect dirt.

Files rubbed with blackboard chalk will not clog easily with metal particles. The cutting surfaces when clogged are cleaned with a file card or by pushing a short section of copper wire across the file in the same direction as the cuts. This pushes the metal out of these serrations. Files loaded too heavily with metal particles to be cleaned by either of the aforementioned methods, yet worth reclaiming, can be resharpened by removing any grease and placing them for a half-hour in ½ gallon of room-temperature water which has been mixed with 31 ounces of commercial sulfuric acid (or 28 ounces of c.p. sulfuric acid). The acid is poured into the water and stirred with a glass rod, after which one pound of textrol is added. Files, when removed from the acid bath, are rinsed in clear water and coated with a light-weight grade of oil.

Using the Scotch stone

File marks or any other tool marks in hard-to-get-at areas can be removed with a Scotch stone (see Fig. 216). The slatelike stone, available in various sizes, is filed to a taper and is always dipped in water before being rubbed on the metal surface in the direction of the scratch, never across it. This is used for small areas only.

Fig. 215 b

Fig. 216

Filling surface pits

Surface pits in the metal that cannot be filed
and sanded away without altering the desired
shape of the casting can be ground out smoothly
and filled with new material soldered in the depression. The additional metal to fill the pits
should be taken from the sprue button, which
has been sawed off of the casting, because this
metal and the casting metal match.

Annealing

Castings that require considerable work after
emerging from the investment must be annealed
(to soften) and pickled (to remove fire scale)
several times to soften the metal as the finishing steps proceed. The metal is annealed by
being heated on a sheet of asbestos, an asbestos
coil, a charcoal block, or a magnesite block,
all of which are supported by several fire bricks
(see Fig. 217). A soldering and annealing
pan, filled with scraps and bits of asbestos,
charcoal bits, 12 grit carborundum, or pumice
lumps, can also be used for softening the metal.

An excellent soldering and annealing pan is
improvised from a "wuk," a round-bottomed
steel cooking vessel used in Chinese cookery
(see Fig. 120). The convex shape and the rim
handles permit the pan to be rotated as the
metal is heated with the torch. The metal is
heated with a reducing flame deployed with a
brush-stroke motion instead of the torch being
applied directly to one area.

Gold, silver, brass, and bronze are heated to
a dull red. This color should be observed in a
shaded light. Copper is heated to salmon red,
and aluminum to a soft pink. Care must always
be taken so that thin, small, delicate parts and
extensions are not melted by the flame.

Gold (less than 14 kt), silver, and brass
should be allowed to cool slightly before they
are quenched in the pickling solution. The sudden change in temperature between the heat
necessary to anneal the metals and the temperature of the pickling solution will cause the
metals to crack if immersed too soon. Platinum
and high-karat gold can be immersed immediately, but it is preferable to use alcohol rather
than pickling solutions for gold. Copper can be
cooled slightly or immersed right away, and

FIG. 217

FIG. 218

FIG. 219

steel is always cooled as slowly as possible without quenching.

Pickling

Metals, after being heated to the recommended color, should be allowed to cool for several seconds before being quickly immersed in the pickling solution in order to prevent surface cracks which hinder polishing. Slow quenching results in warpage.

The metal must be pickled to remove the black fire scale, which is cuprous oxide. The metals emerge from the solution in bright shades of their own color. Copper is bright pink; gold, a soft yellow; and silver, pure white. The pure white surface on the silver indicates that a thin layer of pure silver covers the surface of the casting, because the pickling solution has dissolved the surface copper that is part of the alloy. The white surface will be lost if the item is filed, or heavily buffed and polished. To recapture the white color, the casting must be reheated and pickled after all surface finishing is completed. This will give the article a frosty surface. The red cuprous oxide (often the result of copper contamination in the pickling solution when iron tweezers or binding wire are dipped in the liquid) or the deeper fire scale is removed with a bright dip (see Chapter 16).

Because pickling splatters when heated articles are thrust into the solution, care must be taken to guard one's clothing and skin from the acid. Larger castings or metal sections should be dropped into the solution by holding them with tongs at arm's length. Smaller items held with tweezers or smaller tongs do not splash as violently. As an added protection, goggles may be worn. Acids on the skin or clothing should be flushed off immediately with running water and then neutralized with sodium bicarbonate (baking soda) either in its dry form or as a solution.

When pickling solutions are prepared, the acid is always poured into the water. Reversing this step will cause the water to boil and splash vigorously.

The pickling solution is used in a copper or porcelain pickling pan (see Figs. 218 and 219). Small articles requiring annealing or pickling are cleaned of surface oxides by being dipped into the acid bath in a basket constructed of copper wire screen bent into shape and held with copper wire. The basket is removed with copper tongs or a wire handle. The articles are then rinsed under running water while still in the basket, so that everything, including the basket, is completely free of any acid.

When pickling solutions no longer perform satisfactorily, they must be discarded. New acids or solution mixtures are never added to old pickling fluids.

Silver and copper are pickled in a solution of 10 parts of sulfuric acid to 100 parts of water. Gold can be pickled in this solution, but a small amount of sodium bichromate should be added to aid in removing stubborn fire scale. Gold of over 14 karats is pickled in a solution of 1 part of nitric acid to 8 parts of water. A solution that can be used to remove fire scale from almost any metal is formulated of 1 gallon of water, 7 ounces of sodium bisulfate, 9 ounces of monosodium phosphate, 16 ounces of 70% phosphoric acid, ¼ ounce of sulfonated castor oil, ½ ounce of glycerine (see Appendix for other formulae).

Sizing rings

Ring shanks, generally constructed one size smaller in wax, are filed with half-round and round files, small carborundum discs mounted on mandrels, or mounted stones in small shapes used with power driven handpieces. Should the ring be oversized, it will be necessary to saw the shank and remove a section of metal to achieve the correct size and then solder the joint together again (see Chapter 15). If the ring is undersized and cannot be enlarged sufficiently by sanding, the shank is sawed and a section of the cast metal fitted and soldered into the opening. Excess metal from the sprue or button should be used for perfect matching. This is absolutely necessary when sizing gold rings.

Rings that have been sized and are still too small must be sawed on each side of the soldered joint, which must be completely removed. A larger section of metal is inserted and soldered into place. The parts should always be filed to fit perfectly before soldering.

Rings can also be enlarged a size or so without the sawing, fitting, filing, and soldering steps

FIG. 220

by the use of a ring mandrel. The center of the ring shank between the two sides of the mounting or top is hammered lightly while placed on the mandrel, which is held in a bench-pin, vise, or hole drilled in the bench edge (see Fig. 220). This stretches the metal slightly. When tapping, the hammer travels out a short distance from the shank center and then returns and travels outward to the other side of the shank center. The ring is tapped onto the tapering mandrel with gentle side blows of a rawhide mallet so that it will fit snugly and its size can be gauged as the stretching progresses. To remove the ring, it is tapped lightly from the other side and reversed on the mandrel so that the inner surface is not tapered.

When the sizing step has been completed, the ring shank edges are filed and sanded so that the shank width is either uniform or tapered in accordance with the design.

Prongs, or any other kind of gem mounting that has been made an integral part of the casting, are filed and sanded to the desired shape and size. Castings that are to have gem mountings attached after all other rough finishing steps are completed are buffed and polished, just as are plain castings.

Bracelet forming

Bracelets and belt buckles are formed by bending them around bracelet stakes, which are mounted on the bench pin, or held in a larger bench vise (see Fig. 221). They can also be

formed on the horn section of the anvil. The bracelet or buckle viewing surface is tapped lightly with a rawhide or wooden mallet so that the gradual curve or circular shape is formed without the casting being strained or cracked. The metal may need annealing during this forming step. When the desired shape is obtained, the article is checked for surface scratches, which should be removed before you proceed to the buffing and polishing steps. If used, gem mountings are added only after the forming step is completed.

Surface sanding by hand

Sanding the surfaces of the casting with garnet paper or emery paper follows the sawing operation. The sandpaper in small pieces is held under the thumb or wrapped around ⅛″ to ¼″ wood doweling or orangewood sticks. Wooden tongue depressors or ice-cream sticks split lengthwise into narrower strips (if desired) and then wrapped with sanding paper make excellent flat instruments. For larger castings, sanding boards of wood or plastic with clamps and a lockscrew for holding the paper in taut position are handy tools for this phase of the finishing procedure (see Fig. 222).

String sanding

Strong string or nylon cord coated with Vaseline and various carborundum grits is used for sanding small curved surfaces of open areas in the casting. The string is securely held at one end by being clamped in the bench vise; the loose end is threaded through the opening in the casting and held with one hand, as the other hand, using pressure, guides the casting along the string (see Fig. 223).

FIG. 221

FIG. 222

FIG. 223

CHAPTER 14

Fine Finishing

AFTER THE BASIC FINISHING STEPS HAVE BEEN completed, finer finishing is easily accomplished by the use of power equipment. Dental lathes or ordinary electric motors with shafts adaptable to mandrels or chucks can be utilized and outfitted with various buffs to speed the final finishing of the casting.

Power sanding

Further hand-sanding and filing is eliminated by using a flexible shaft handpiece powered by a small ⅛ h.p. electric motor capable of 14,000 rpm. Cord-driven dental handpieces on standard dental engines that are capable of speeds to 100,000 rpm can also be used (see Fig. 224). Two types of handpieces, slip-joint or standard with Jacobs chuck, are used on the flexible shaft. The slip-joint handpiece accepts only $\frac{3}{32}''$ mandrels or shafts. The chuck handpiece is capable of accepting all small drill sizes. A smaller chuck mounted on a $\frac{3}{32}''$ shaft and inserted in the Jacobs chuck enables one to hold the smallest drills (to size 80) without slippage during use (see Fig. 225). The regular dental handpieces accept only $\frac{3}{32}''$ shafts or mandrels,

but this is not necessarily a limitation because the small mandrel-mounted chuck can also be used here.

Standard and heavy-duty mandrels are used with numerous varieties (see Figs. 211 and 212a) of emery discs, carborundum cut-off discs, sandpaper discs in three grit sizes, rubber-bonded abrasive discs in coarse, medium, and fine, small diamond drills, carbide rotary files, mounted rubber-bonded abrasive stones, carborundum stones, and diamond or carbide saw blades. Another type of mandrel has a rubber cylinder at the end onto which are slipped cardboard sleeves coated with various grits of carborundum. Standard mandrels are also used with small wire scratch brushes, 1″-diameter carborundum grinding wheels, and 1¼″ diameter muslin wheels used for buffing and polishing hand-held castings. The carborundum, emery, and rubber-bonded abrasive wheels, while available in large and small diameters, should be purchased in the ¾″ size as they eventually become small wheels anyway. To form knife-edged, wedge-shaped, or curved wheels, hold the small rotating wheels against a coarse carborundum stone until the desired wheel shape is obtained.

The small heatless carborundum wheels can be used for quick sanding of inner ring surfaces. They are selected as near in size as possible to the inner ring diameter and then reduced (as mentioned in the previous paragraph) so that they just fit inside the ring. A circular motion with the moving wheel will sand the areas correctly.

Diamond wheels and diamond drills operate with optimum results if water is used with them. A small nozzle attachment fits on the handpiece nose and is connected to a water supply positioned above the work area for gravity flow (see Fig. 226). The water can be contained in a small plastic wastebasket or tub with a drain tube added, or in a discarded glass bottle such as is used for intravenous glucose feedings (see Fig. 227).

Bench grinding

To make a small light-duty bench grinder and buffer-polisher, mount a saw mandrel on a 4″ × 4″ × 8″ block of wood, which is bolted to the workbench. A Jacobs chuck is mounted on one end of the mandrel, and a standard V-type pulley is mounted on the opposite end. The pulley size and the belt length will be determined by the engine used. Electric motors from discarded washing machines work fine, as these are usually 1750 h.p. motors. A larger pulley is installed on the motor shaft to bring the chuck speed up to 3500 rpm. Small 3″-diameter cotton and muslin buffs, wire scratch wheels, and felt wheels are mounted on a ¼″ mandrel or on tapered spindles, which are mounted on the saw mandrel shaft instead of the Jacobs chuck.

Surface texturing

All castings, except those with special surface textures, are buffed and polished according to personal taste. The articles may be surface-textured after buffing and polishing by means of tools, sand blasting, wire-wheel buffing, burnishing, or by dipping in solutions to effect a matte or frosted finish. The matte surface is the texture that appears when the metal is removed from the first pickle bath. This surface can either be retained or, if lost, replaced later on

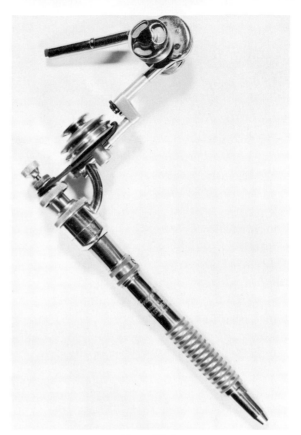

Fig. 224

Fig. 225

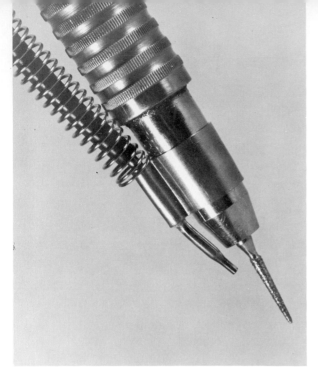

FIG. 226

FIG. 227

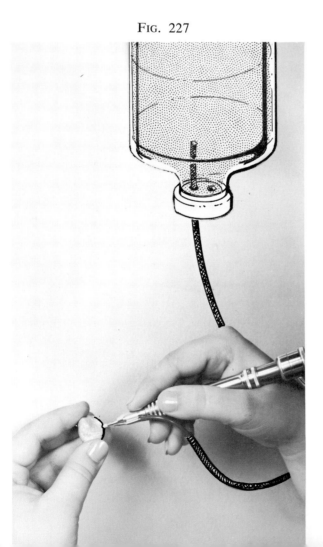

during the final finishing steps. Standard buffing and polishing, used in most instances, is done either by machine or by hand-rubbing.

Buffing and polishing equipment

Machinery for buffing and polishing can consist of a polishing lathe that has chucks or tapered spindles for wheel attachment (see Fig. 228), by arbor and motor combinations, or by smaller power-driven handpieces (see Figs. 210 and 224). Regardless of the method used to achieve the finished appearance on the castings, a specified surface speed must be obtained to permit the buffing and polishing wheels to perform with the best results. Various charts list lathe engine speeds and electric motor speeds that are correlated with wheel sizes and motor and arbor pulley combinations (see Appendix).

To obtain best results, an electric motor or lathe engine must produce a speed that rotates a wheel at a surface speed of at least 5000 sfpm (surface feet per minute). Speeds rated in rpm are used for rotating surfaces that do not change their diameter, such as shafts, spindles, pulleys, etc. Buffing and polishing wheels, which wear to a smaller size, are rated in speeds calculated on surface feet per minute. A new 8″ buffing wheel will rotate at a surface speed of 5025 feet per minute if the motor is rotating at 2400 rpm. But as the wheel wears down to a 7½″-diameter size, the same motor speed of 2400 rpm produces only 4387 feet per minute. Therefore, it is necessary to use a two-speed polishing lathe rated at 1750 and 3500 rpm or a motor and arbor polishing head with two-step pulleys in order to speed up the rpm, which increases the sfpm. The motor and arbor set-up, both equipped with 2″-diameter pulleys, will produce 1750 rpm. Identically sized pulleys used together will still produce the basic motor rpm even if 5″ pulleys are used.

The motor pulley must always be larger in diameter than the arbor pulley to increase the rpm. The speed of the arbor increases approximately 280 rpm for every ¼″ increase in diameter size of the motor pulley, providing a 2″ pulley remains on the arbor shaft. A 5″-diameter motor pulley turns a 2″-diameter arbor pulley 5040 rpm. This will turn an 8″-diameter buffing wheel 10,000 surface feet per minute. A three-step pulley with the smallest groove of

2¾" diameter and the largest groove of 4" diameter will produce speeds ranging from 5000 to 8000 sfpm.

Smaller, slower pulleys are used for polishing wheels, and the larger, faster pulleys are used for buffing wheels (see Appendix for method of determining surface speed and pulley size).

A variety of wheels, cones, brushes, and buffs can be used for the various buffing and polishing steps, all of which are available in standard and special shapes in sizes to fit the smallest handpiece mandrels.

Muslin wheels (see Fig. 228) stitched in rows or circles to make them more sturdy are for buffing. The same wheel without stitching but attached at the center only is used for polishing. Other wheels offered commercially are leather for buffing, cotton flannel and cotton yarn for polishing, and hard felt for buffing and polishing. Knife-edged felt wheels are excellent for getting into grooves, crevices, and around bezels. Bright-boy wheels (rubber-bonded grinding wheels) are similar to the smaller rubber-bonded or abrasive impregnated wheels used with the small dental handpieces. Ring buffs are made of the same materials and also of hard felt for polishing.

Bristle wheels charged with buffing compounds are used for hard-to-get-at areas or for texture finishing. Scratch wire wheels of brass or steel are used for texture finishes. The brass wheel should not be used on silver, as it leaves a faint yellowish tinge on the surface of the casting.

Felt cones and cotton goblet buffs for both buffing and polishing have special shapes for specific jobs.

To make substitute wheels, tear used fabric materials (colored prints, etc.) into 8" squares. The center of each square is marked and a small slit made on this mark so that the square will just fit over the threaded buffing or polishing mandrel. (Tapered mandrels should not be used for these wheels.) After the fabric squares are packed on the spindle until they are ¾" to 1" thick when compressed, the flange and nut are added and tightened. The motor is then switched on and a sharp knife blade held at right angles to the fabric edges. As the fabric rotates, the knife edge "trues" it into a circular shape.

Muslin and cotton buffs can be charged with

FIG. 228

a coating of vegetable glue, rolled on edge through a tray of carborundum grit and hung on a rod to dry (see Fig. 229). The small buffs used with the mandrels in handpieces can be charged in the same manner. These grit-charged wheels used for sanding are excellent for scratch or satin finishes, especially when finer grits are used to charge the wheels.

A separate buff should be used for each buffing and polishing compound. Buffing wheels that have inadvertently been charged (coated) with a different material should be either discarded or washed in an ordinary washing machine and hung up to dry. Drying may take as long as a week for tightly stitched wheels.

Dust collectors, shallow metal pans with hoods and cutouts to fit over engine shafts, serve as a catch-all for buffing dust and the metal casting, if it should be suddenly snatched from the operator's hands (see Figs. 230, 231, and 232 for gold). The hoods, often equipped with a small incandescent bulb for greater visibility when buffing, can be attached to vacuum-cleaning units. This eliminates much of the buffing and polishing dust, which flies around the shop, to be inhaled by the operator.

Buffing the metal

Before buffing a casting, the article should be pickled, scrubbed with warm detergent suds,

FIG. 229

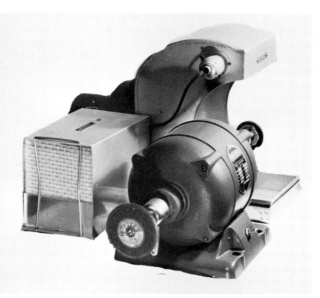

FIG. 230

and rinsed in running water. The buff is charged with Tripoli that has been dipped in kerosene. This permits the compound to adhere more readily to the buff. The article *must* be held firmly in both hands against the wheel just below center, (the imaginary horizontal line from the shaft or hub out to the edge of the buff) (see Fig. 233). It is then moved downward, sideways, rolled, rotated, or positioned so that the buffing wheel reaches all possible areas of the casting. If the wheel portion either above or too far below center is used, the wheel will grab the metal from the hands. The tendency to work lower on the wheel with its resultant grabbing must be avoided, as many almost completed pieces are damaged when grabbed and slammed against the bench top or the dust collector.

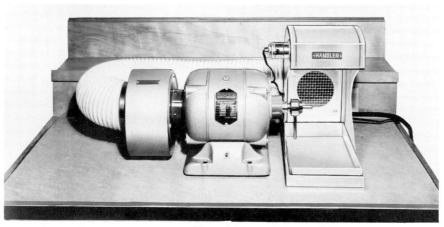

FIG. 231

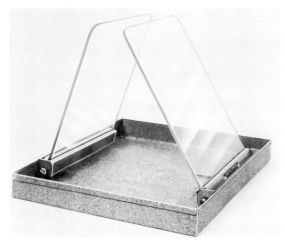

FIG. 232

FIG. 233

Areas that cannot be reached by wheel buffs are finished by a buffing with the bristle brush charged with regular or white diamond Tripoli.

When the buffing is completed, the metal is scrubbed in warm detergent suds, and a small amount of ammonia is used with a soft bristle brush to dislodge any evidence of Tripoli in crevices, draws, or detailed areas of the metal form. The articles must always be thoroughly dried before the polishing step is started.

Polishing the metal

Polishing wheels are charged by any one of numerous rouge bars that have been dipped in kerosene. Rouges are formulated to produce a dark luster on white gold, platinum, and silver, and for regular finishes on all metals. Loose, unstitched buffs of cotton yarn or muslin are best for all-around polishing on all metals, but chamois buffs work best.

Rouge appearing in smears on the casting indicates that the surface speed is too slow or that too much rouge has been used. The use of pressure on an overloaded wheel will heat the metal and rouge so that the latter will be doubly hard to remove. The polishing can be continued with light pressure applied to the wheel, or another article can be polished to use up the excess rouge. The piling up of rouge usually occurs near the end of the polishing stage.

Linde A polishing powder, usually used for polishing gemstones, can be used as a polishing agent for metal, but the article should be hand-polished.

Polishing compounds are removed by scrubbing in the same manner as that described for buffing.

Polishing findings

After the casting has been buffed and polished, any findings that are not a part of the casting are soldered into place, and any gemstone mounts are constructed and soldered into position. The previously mentioned buffing and polishing procedure is done before soldering to eliminate problems that often arise later. Backings or undersides of castings cannot be buffed easily when mountings are in place. Hard buffing may wear down some of the findings in addition to clogging the working parts with compound. Base areas around bezels or gem mountings are often grooved with the edges of the wheels when excessive pressure is applied at the polishing lathe.

Chain links, rings, and other round objects, which are often difficult to hold, can be slid over the outer surface or held in the jaws of a ring clamp (see Fig. 234) during the final buffing and polishing steps. Articles can also be held on tapered sections of dowel wood or on shortened sections of old hardwood chair legs. Flat or semiflat articles, such as leaves, etc., can be supported during buffing and polishing if you place them on a thin board and hold them in place with the thumbs (see Fig. 235).

Final buffing and polishing should be done,

FIG. 234

FIG. 235

if possible, on small wheels driven by hand-pieces on flexible shafts or on dental engines, so that some control can be maintained over the article to avoid damage, which often occurs when using large wheels (see Fig. 236).

All traces of polishing rouge must be removed from the finished casting, or the metal will discolor and tarnish. After scrubbing, the casting is placed in a box of maple, mahogany (not Philippine), or boxwood sawdust to avoid streaking or spotting the metal as it dries. (Other woods are never used, because they contain soluble matter which can tarnish metals.)

The metal is removed from the sawdust by hands encased in cotton cosmetic gloves to avoid fingerprinting the surface.

FIG. 236

CHAPTER 15

Soldering

SOLDERING IS A METHOD OF ATTACHING METALS one to another with an alloyed metal (solder) of a lower melting point than the metals that are to be joined but similar to them in color and content. A soldered joint when completed will be as strong or stronger than the metals that it connects.

Cleaning the metal

Before soldering, all parts must be absolutely clean, free from any dirt, dust, grease, and buffing and polishing compounds. The solder itself must also be cleaned before use. If oxidation is evident, the article is either pickled or cleaned with steel wool; however, it must be remembered that steel wool scratches the surface as it cleans. Clean and brightly polished surfaces on gold will permit better soldering results.

Gold solders

Gold solders must match the karat of the metal in the casting. A 14-karat solder does not mean that the material is 14-karat gold, but that it is alloyed to work perfectly with articles cast in 14-karat gold. Solder should melt at temperatures that are $150°–250°F$. below the melting point of the metals to be joined. The flow point of solder is $45°–85°F$. higher than its melting point, according to the type of solder used. The melting points of gold solders are: 10kt—$1340°F$., 14kt easy—$1310°F$., 14kt hard—$1463°F$., 18kt easy—$1300°F$., 18kt medium—$1386°F$., 18kt hard—$1517°F$.

Silver solders

Silver solders in sheet or wire form are alloyed to become fluid at specified temperatures and are a combination of silver, copper, and zinc in proportions of 50 to 80 parts of silver, 34 to 16 parts of copper, and 4 to 16 parts of zinc, depending upon the melting temperature desired. The four melting temperatures of silver solder are: hard—$1450°F$., hard no. 1—$1425°F$., medium—$1390°F$., and easy-flow—$1325°F$.

Soft solders

Soft solder is usually alloyed of equal parts of tin and lead by weight. The melting point is approximately $442°F$.; it should never be used on quality jewelry. Soft-soldered parts are never pickled, but after brief cooling, the article is immersed in clear water only. Soft solder should be removed before any joint is hard-soldered. The soft solder will burn into the metal when heated to the higher temperature necessary for hard-soldering.

The various grades of solder should be marked with a metal scribe, indicating their respective melting points. The solder should be placed in individual metal or plastic containers properly labeled as to melting points. The solder sheet is cut into narrow strips $\frac{1}{32}''$ to $\frac{1}{8}''$ wide and approximately $1\frac{1}{2}''$ deep across one end. The sheet is cupped in the hand so that the small squares (called pledgets or paillons) are caught as the snips or shears are used to cut the solder (see Fig. 237).

Fluxes

Fluxes are applied to the metal parts to keep the metal clean and to prevent oxides forming. The flowing properties of the solder are in the solder and not in the flux. The flux should become fluid at a temperature just below that of the melted solder. Boric acid and borax, combined in equal parts either in powdered form or paste, is an excellent flux, which becomes

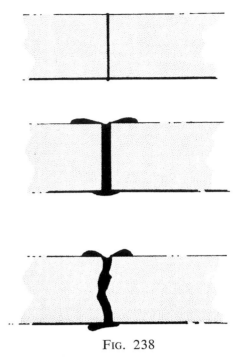

FIG. 238

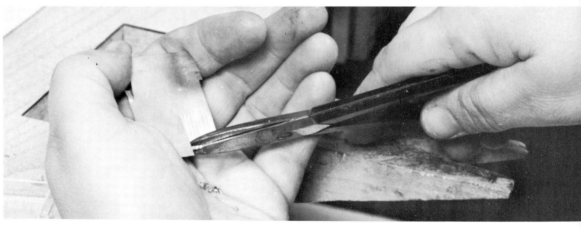

FIG. 237

FIG. 239

fluid at 1400°F. If the flux is used in paste form, alcohol is preferred to water for the liquid constituent.

The ratio of the two constituents can be varied to produce fluxes that melt at different temperatures. Increasing the boric acid proportion to 75% lowers the fusion point considerably for low-heat soldering "joins." Lowering the boric acid proportion to 25% obtains a high-fusing flux. Solders alloyed in gold content to match a high-karat gold casting have higher fusion points, requiring a flux with a relatively high fluidity point. Silver solders with a high melting point of 1450°F. require a flux with a lower fluidity point.

Commercial fluxes, which produce excellent results, are also available. Fluxes for divergent metals, such as platinum and pewter, should always be purchased commercially because of other additives that are needed to produce satisfactory results.

Anti-fluxes

Surfaces that are not to be soldered are painted with an anti-flux (anti-oxidizer), so that the solder will not flow to these areas. Commercial preparations can be purchased for this purpose, or the areas can be coated with a rouge paste or yellow ochre. An alternate anti-flux is a saturated solution of boric acid and alcohol. The mixture is painted onto all metal surfaces except where soldering is to be done. The surface is ignited so that the alcohol is consumed. The dry coating that remains will prevent oxidation. When one article is subjected to a multiple-soldering operation, it is coated with anti-flux after each soldering to prevent oxidation when lower melting solders are added to other areas.

Fitting the joints

The areas to be soldered are fitted closely by filing and sanding so that no light is visible through the seam or joint. Solder will not fill an irregular separation in the joint, regardless of how small the separation may seem (see Fig. 238). The soldered joint, if fitted properly, will be strongest where the least amount of solder flows through an area of contact between two metals. The solder will flow freely into the smallest carefully fitted joint, alloy with the metal, and "freeze" smooth and clean without pits or pinholes.

Heating the metal

Observance of the colors of heated metals will indicate the metal temperatures. The first visible red color appears at approximately 990°F., an even dull red at 1200°F., a cherry-red at 1400°F., and a pink glow at 1600°F.—the danger point.

In soldering, the sections should be joined in sequence, the solder with the highest melting point being used first, with a gradual descent to the lower melting points for final steps such as findings, etc. If a casting requires no soldering steps except for findings, the easy-flow solder is used.

Solder flows to the hottest part. The area around the joint must be heated also, or the solder will flow but not alloy properly. The joint is heated after being coated with flux, and the solder is picked up with a damp sable paintbrush and transferred to the solder area, so that the heat of the metal heats the solder. It can also be transferred by pushing the finely filed point of a 1/8" section of drill rod into the solder and carrying it where desired (see Fig. 239). As flux bubbles when heated, it may lift the solder and transfer it to an undesired area; therefore, a new piece of solder should be picked up and applied to the fluxed joint.

If the solder becomes overheated before the metals to be joined are heated, it will roll up into a ball and will not flow until the metals reach the temperature at which the solder melts. Balling also occurs if the surfaces are not clean and free of oils and grease.

Refilling gaps

If a gap or separation appears in the soldered joint, it should not be filled with additional solder. Instead, a piece of metal remaining from the casting must be cut to the shape of the gap, fluxed, and soldered into place. The excess solder is removed later. Soldered joints, except soft-soldered ones, are as strong as the metal they hold together.

Soldering different metals together

If combining casting sections of two or more different metals, use a silver solder for joining the metals. The melting point of gold solder is greater than the melting point of the cast silver section and, if used, will melt the silver portion.

FIG. 240

FIG. 241

FIG. 242

Pickling

After the soldering is completed, the metal is dipped in a pot of pickling solution to remove the flux and fire scale (oxidation), then rinsed under running water. Pickling solutions (1 part sulfuric acid to 10 parts water) are the same as those used for annealing (see Fig. 240).

To dislodge stubborn flux, gold articles can be dipped in a stronger cold solution of 1 part nitric acid to 8 parts water. If it is necessary to resolder any portion, the article should first be neutralized by being boiled for 5 minutes or so in sodium bicarbonate dissolved in water, followed by a rinsing in running water.

Removal of excess solder

Excess solder is removed by gently scraping the surface of the solder with a hollow scraper (see Fig. 241). The area is then finished with files, sandpaper, and the usual buffing and polishing steps. A solder scraper can be made from a cast-off or clogged taper file. The three sides of the file are ground smooth on a bench grinder, with a sharp cutting edge left on each side.

Soft solder on an article is removed by heating the area and then scraping away the excess material. Any remaining film of solder can be removed by dipping the article for a short time in strong hydrochloric acid.

Addition of gem mountings

To solder gemstone mountings to the casting, first fit the mounting area and clean the mating parts, and then proceed with the soldering. To add wire prongs, drill small holes to accommodate them so that they can be soldered into place.

Findings

Earring, cufflink, and tietack parts can be fluxed and coated with solder for attachment before being positioned on the casting. Earrings that have a cup base instead of a flat pad must be fluxed and the cup filled level with solder to achieve a good join. Tweezers, third hand soldering instruments, and locking tweezers, staples, cotter pins, or welding clamps can be used to hold the articles upright (see Figs. 242 and 243).

Pin backs or brooch clasps are soldered into position without the pin portion of the clasp, as it will melt during soldering. The pin portion is best added after all final buffing and polishing has been completed, because it usually needs to be shortened to fit and filed to a sharp point which is then buffed and polished.

Soldering ring shanks

Ring shanks are soldered on a carbon ring-soldering mandrel. This tool can also be used in soldering the bezel mounting or any other additional parts on the ring (see Fig. 34).

Soldering aids

Gum tragacanth in powdered form mixed with isopropyl alcohol makes an excellent paste to hold small metal parts in position on concave, convex, sloping, and angular surfaces while the flux and solder are applied and heated. This is the same paste as that used to hold enamels on the surface for firing.

Soldering investment

Sections difficult to hold for soldering, even when held with the aforementioned soldering aids, can be joined together while embedded in investment plaster (see Figs. 244 and 245). The sections are cleaned by being scrubbed in soap and water, then rinsed in running water, pickled, and rinsed again. This removes any buffing and polishing compounds and any casting oxidation.

The metal parts are fluxed (fluxing could be done just before soldering) before being joined with sticky wax (see Chapter 5). The sections are then embedded in soldering investment or standard casting investment and set aside to dry so that only the joints are exposed (see Chapter 6).

Soldering investment is preferable to casting investment, because it is compounded of ingredients with cristobalite at a minimum proportion. The water/powder ratio should be

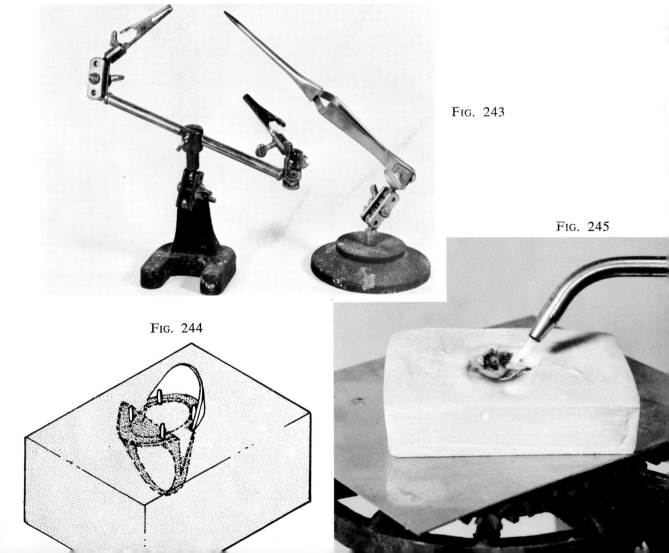

FIG. 243

FIG. 245

FIG. 244

according to the manufacturer's recommendation. It should be a thick viscous mass that will hold together on the glass slab without confinement in a ring or boxed frame. The wax-joined cast sections are held in this mass during the soldering.

The investment can also be dried and heated with the Bunsen burner or torch; however, it must be placed on an asbestos sheet on top of a wire grid on the soldering tripod. The investment must not be heated excessively, or contamination of the casting and solder will occur. This is produced by the overheating and the disintegration of the investment.

The clean joints are fluxed at the join area only. Anti-flux, to confine the flow of solder to critical areas, is applied in the form of rouge (or whiting) and alcohol paste. Ordinary graphite lead pencils can be used to mark off an area for solder containment, but they are ineffective if temperatures soar too high.

The torch is adjusted to a reducing flame and applied gradually to the exposed joints of the casting. When the flux begins to flow, the torch heat is increased to soldering temperature, and the solder is added without the flame being removed from the join area. The reducing area of the flame should be adjusted to its smallest possible cone, so that only the join area is heated. The solder must flow smoothly and quickly into the join area. If it does not flow thus, the flame is removed and the metal allowed to cool, so that it can be recleaned of oxides or other contaminants. Continual heating of the flux when it is evident that the solder is not going to flow freely will fuse the solder with the metal and make it difficult to get a flow of solder in the join. The distances between the sections should be minimal, or soldered joins will be weak and porous.

A good soldering flux is made by a mixture of boric acid and borax powders and petrolatum (white Vaseline), forming a paste flux that will stay on the metal. The grease prevents the air from contacting the metal. After the soldering is completed, the metal and its investment case are dipped in water, which disintegrates the investment so that the soldered article can be removed. Remaining particles of investment are scrubbed from the metal, and the article is ready for the pickling and finishing steps.

Indirect investment soldering

Another type of investment soldering, called the indirect method, is accomplished by investing cast or other metal sections in the investment and adding the solder and flux where needed (see Fig. 246). The investment is dried in the furnace and heat-soaked for 30 minutes. It is then removed and placed on the wire mesh grid on the soldering tripod and heated with a Bunsen burner. When the investment turns a dull red, the torch is applied from below until the solder flows (see Fig. 247). The blowpipe flame does not touch the soldered area. When the solder has flowed, the flame is passed over the soldered sections to raise the flux to the surface and prevent pits forming.

FIG. 246

FIG. 247

CHAPTER 16

Treatment and Surface Decoration

A METAL CASTING MUST BE ABSOLUTELY clean before surface coloring. The article should be scrubbed in a solution of warm detergent suds and rinsed in clear water, followed by pickling or bright-dipping. If an acid dip is preferred, a cleaning solution that can be used in place of the detergent suds is made of 1 part sulfuric acid to 50 parts water. After the article is cleaned, care must be taken not to touch it with the bare hands.

Satin finishes

There are four different ways to obtain a satin finish on metal. The first and simplest way is to dip the article in a "satin" finish solution consisting of 1 part hydrofluoric acid and 3 parts water, followed by a rinsing in running water.

The second method is to wire-brush the surface with a steel or brass wheel brush charged with a paste of pumice mixed with thin oil (see Fig. 248). It should be kept in mind that the ends of the bristles do the work. When too much pressure is applied, the bristles tend to curl over, which produces a poor surface. If this occurs, the brush should be immediately discarded. Brass wheels should never be used on silver, as they leave a yellowish tinge on the surface.

The third method is to brush the surface with a brush wheel of hard and soft hog bristles, or nylon fibers charged with Tripoli, as is normally used for buffing. This is particularly effective when contrasting metals are used in one article, because the different colors immediately become visible.

The fourth method is sand blasting with a small bench-top machine (see Fig. 249). The machine is operated by air pressure supplied by an air compressor, which maintains air pressure at 18 to 20 p.s.i. (pounds per square inch). The blasting mix is usually 85% sand blasting quartz (200 mesh) and 15% washed silica sand (100 mesh). Blasting sands are sold in various grits, depending upon the degree of satin finish desired. For a frosted surface a heavier mesh sand is used.

Burnishing

Surfaces can be brightened by burnishing with a tool made of either steel or agate. The tips

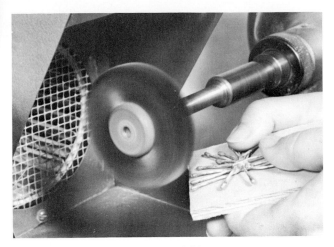

FIG. 248

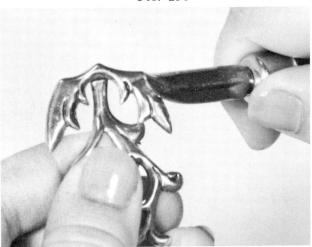

FIG. 249

FIG. 250

are round or flat types (see Fig. 250). The tool is rubbed on the surface of the metal with circular or back and forth strokes, with liquid soap mixed with water for a lubricant. The burnisher should "bite" into the metal but not scratch it. When the burnisher begins to slide over the surface without burnishing it, it must be honed on a strip of leather that has been impregnated with crocus dust. Buffing and polishing wears metal away, whereas burnishing pushes the metal down and over by a rolling pressure. The edges of an article can also be rolled over and burnished to a luster with this tool.

The burnished article is polished with a cake rouge, such as green rouge mixed with glycerine. Red rouge should not be used for polishing, because it is worked down into the metal by the burnisher, contaminating the metal surface. To prevent rusting, the metal burnishing tools should be coated with beeswax when not in use.

Matte finishing

A matte finish is a fine texture that can be effected on silver-plated articles by scratch brushing the surface with a nickel or monel wire wheel. Brass wheels are used on other metals. Soap dissolved with water to a thick cream or kerosene are used as lubricants on the wire wheels, which are operated between 800 and 1200 s.f.p.m. (see Appendix).

Matting tools have various design imprints, which leave different textures and designs on metal surfaces. They can be purchased separately, or in sets of twenty-five. If desired, they can be constructed in the workshop by heating a flat strip of steel to a bright cherry-red and pressing the end against a textured surface such as a steel file, holding it for a few seconds until an imprint is made as the steel strip cools. It is then quenched in water or lightweight oil for tempering. The fire scale is removed by sanding, and the tool is held in the alcohol-lamp flame until a light-straw color is evident. It is then quenched in water to harden the metal.

Matte surfaces on metals, in addition to being produced by tools and by scratch brushing, can be obtained by heating the article to produce the cuprous oxide that forms on the surface. It is then dipped in the strong pickling solution for 2 or 3 seconds only, to dissolve the alloy in the metal that has come to the surface in the form of oxides. The article is then rinsed in running water. This leaves a bright pure metal color. The thin layer of color is easily lost if buffed or polished. It can be thickened by burnishing the surface with a wire brush, scrubbing the surface clean, reheating the article, dipping it in the pickling solution again, rinsing in clear water, followed by brush burnishing. The steps are repeated until the article has gone through the process three or four times.

Coloring metals by oxidation

Bright-dips are used to clean pickled metals before oxidizing. Articles are suspended on a twisted brass or copper wire and are immersed for a maximum of 30 seconds in a cold solution (1 part sulfuric acid mixed with 1 part nitric acid, or, for a weaker solution, 1 part each acid with 2 parts water). They are then rinsed in clear water. Dipping-wires of other metals should not be used. Because of the fumes from the acids, the solution should be used out of doors or in a well-ventilated room.

Silver is oxidized by dipping the article in a solution of potassium sulfide (liver of sulfur). A paintbrush can be used to apply the solution if only a portion of the article is to be oxidized. Brushes used for painting different coloring solutions on metals should not be interchanged; a brush for each different solution should be used and marked for easy identification. The solution is formulated by combining 1 ounce each of potassium sulfide and ammonia with a quart of water. The article is continuously painted or left in the heated solution until the desired shade of dark gray is obtained; then, to halt the action, the casting is rinsed in running water. The coloring will chip off if the solution is overheated. If chipping should occur, the metal must be heated, pickled, and bright-dipped before the coloring process is attempted again.

Gold can be oxidized with the same solution as that just given for silver oxidation; but, in the case of gold, both the metal and the solution must be heated before the solution is used. Gold is oxidized best when commercial solutions are used; however, 1 gram of ammonium sulfide added to 8 ounces of water will do the job. The solution is warmed before being ap-

plied. The casting is heated with a torch, and the solution applied with a brush; then the article is rinsed in running water.

Copper is oxidized or colored in the same solution as that used for silver coloration. It can be colored brown by being dipped in a hot solution of 4 ounces of copper sulfate mixed with 8 ounces of water. For black color on copper, the article is dipped in a hot solution of 1 gram of ammonium sulfide in 7 ounces of water. Brass is colored or oxidized by being coated with butter of antimony (antimony chloride solution) and set aside to dry.

A blue-black color on copper, brass, and nickel silver is made of 4 ounces of lead acetate (sugar of lead) dissolved in 8 ounces of sodium thiosulfate (antichlor). The object, suspended on a copper or brass wire, is immersed when the solution reaches the boiling point, remaining there until the desired color is attained. It is then rinsed in running water.

A blue, green, and black combination of colors is produced on copper, brass, or bronze by dipping the article in acetic acid for 2 to 3 minutes. The article is then placed in a closed container in which an uncovered dish of ammonia has been placed. The exposure to the ammonia fumes for several hours will produce the three-toned color.

Metal surfaces with discolored areas that have been caused by oxidizing or by other surface coloring methods can be cleaned by being rubbed with a paste made of whiting and alcohol. The paste is rubbed on the surface with the finger or with a small cotton-tipped stick. This is followed by a gentle scrubbing in warm detergent suds with a soft nylon-bristle brush.

Gold-colored silver

Silver can be given a "gold" coating by immersion in a solution of iron oxide (micronized umber) and diluted sulfuric acid. When the desired color is reached, the article is rinsed in running water.

Copper patina

To color copper, bronze, and brass with a green patina, brush the metal with a solution of 1 gram each of copper nitrate, ammonia chloride, and calcium chloride and 1 ounce of water. The article after being coated with the solution is

FIG. 251

FIG. 252

allowed to dry. Another way of bringing out the green patina on copper and brass is to pour a hot solution of 1½ grams of copper nitrate and 6 ounces of water onto a clean metal casting and allow it to dry. To obtain a natural metal color on bronze, heat the metal, apply a coat of thin oil, and rub the surface with a soft cloth.

Bring out highlights in the colored metal surfaces by rubbing the areas with a fine paste of pumice and thin lubricating oil.

Chasing tools

Chasing tools are primarily used for metal embossing or repoussé (see Figs. 251 and 252). Their use in surface finishing techniques is primarily to define an outline or retrace, regroove, or re-emphasize areas that were sharp in the wax model but became less clearly defined during the casting process. Lines, either faint or obscured, can be brought out more distinctly if painted with Chinese white, Aero white (both watercolors in dry block or concentrated form) or with white showcard poster paint. These are applied to the casting surface in a thin opaque coating and allowed to dry before the surface is tooled.

The tools, usually sold in sets of twelve to twenty-five assorted shapes are classed variously as liners, tracers, groovers, raisers, sinkers, planishers, and matte texturing tools. The liners appear to be sharp and chisel-like although the tips are rounded and polished so that the tool makes a line or groove in the metal without showing any tool marks. Matting tools produce a series of ridges and depressions, or a mosaic of these textures. The remaining tool groups are used in hand-wrought metal work.

Holding the metal for chasing

The casting is usually held in a pitch bowl or block for support (see Fig. 253). The pitch is heated and the casting coated with Vaseline to ensure easy removal of the pitch. The coated casting is then pressed lightly into the surface of the softened pitch. The pitch remains soft to fingernail pressure while the chasing is being done.

If the chasing step must be halted for any length of time, the metal must be removed from the pitch bowl. The torch is passed over the metal, which is lifted out with tweezers and placed on the asbestos sheet. The metal is heated almost to annealing temperature and plunged quickly into a pickling solution to remove the adhering pitch. Pitch hardens after 3 to 4 hours, making it difficult to remove the metal from the compound. Sandbags can also be used to hold the casting while surface details are chased.

Using the tools

The chasing tool is held with the fingers widely spaced down the shank of the tool and the thumb placed centrally between the second and third fingers. The little finger acts as a guide for the tool, which, when tapped with light, even blows of the chasing hammer, glides along the surface of the metal. The tool always moves toward the operator with the top of the tool tilting backward (see Fig. 253).

FIG. 253

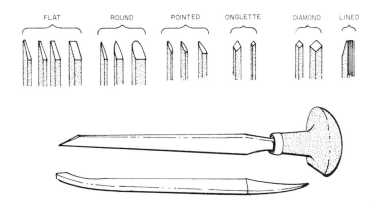

FIG. 254

Gravers

Gravers, plain or lined, come in various shapes and sizes. Round points and flat points are used for large cuts or the removal of metal (see Fig. 254). Diamond (or square) and onglette points are used for intricate details, fine lines, and shading. Tapered lozenge and tapered square gravers with angular faces turn a curve easier than those with faces parallel with the tool shaft.

Line gravers are available in fourteen sizes with two to twelve lines on the cutting surface. The most popular ones are sizes 8 to 16 with four to twelve lines. These tools are used for the "Florentine" finishing texture on metals. Attractive wriggled effects (see Fig. 255) are produced by increasing the angle between the metal and the graver face and "walking" and "rocking" the sharp edge of the tool from corner to corner. Flat gravers can also be used for a

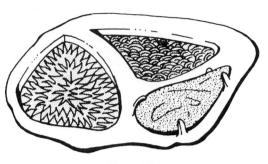

FIG. 255

wriggled final finish and used, like line gravers, to produce a texture under transparent enameled sections.

The gravers should be used in different ways to get the maximum benefit from them. Although their primary use has been mentioned, other uses prove invaluable, such as removing solder from hard-to-get-to areas, from those areas too small for the hollow scraper, or for reaming out a shoulder or bearing for a gemstone support.

Sharpening the tools

Gravers should be kept so sharp that they cut the moment they touch the metal. Whenever considerable pressure is necessary to cut a line, remove metal, shade an area, or produce a texture, they should be resharpened.

When purchased, gravers usually are not sharp. Sharpening must be done by the craftsman before he uses them. To sharpen, grind the face of the tool on an oil-saturated carborundum or India stone. Any fine grade of lubricant, such as that used for fine machinery or shotguns, etc., can be applied to the stone. The face of the tool should always remain parallel with the surface of the grinding stone as it is sharpened. When the graver face has been ground flat or angular, according to its use, it is ground on an Arkansas stone to remove the rough carborundum stone markings. When completely smooth, the graver is polished with 4/0 emery paper placed on a smooth, hard surface, and the tool is always pulled (never pushed) with the face of the point trailing.

Mechanical sharpeners

Mechanical graver sharpeners, which are small jigs designed to hold the tool at the proper angle for grinding, provide the greatest degree of accuracy on graver faces (see Fig. 256). Because their design varies with manufacturers, the operation of the small sharpener should be according to the specific instructions packed with the tool. When not in use, the gravers should be coated with a film of light oil as a rust preventive.

Holding the metal

The casting is held in a ring clamp fastened in a bench vise; (see Fig. 257), in a bench vise covered with copper jaw protectors, in a jeweler's engraving block (see Fig. 258), or in a pitch bowl or block (see Fig. 253). The work may also be held by temporarily attaching it to a piece of wood placed in a bench vise. Dopping wax, used by lapidaries to hold stones on polishing mandrels, is used to secure the casting to the wood.

Jewelers' sandbags are also used to hold the metal for texturing or decorating with the graving tools. Two holes are drilled into the work bench about 6" apart, the sandbag is then placed between the holes and the webbing straps are threaded through the holes to hold the metal in place on the sandbag. The straps are cinched from under the bench, or at one side of the sandbag on the bench-top (see Fig. 259).

FIG. 256

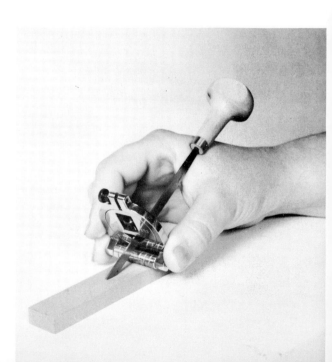

Use of the graver

The graver is inserted into wooden graver handles in any one of the various shapes available, such as round, pear, mushroom, oval, or half-head. The half-head handles are preferred, as the handle can be gripped more easily and securely (see Fig. 254). The graver is held in one hand, as if holding a short screwdriver, with the thumb extended down toward the point for steadiness. The other hand is positioned tentlike over the work and around the engraving block, with the thumb extending and contacting the other thumb tip for support as the tool is guided over the surface of the metal (see Fig. 258). This hand, while helping to steady and support the graver, turns the work, which is held in a movable base, such as the pitch bowl or engravers' block.

The gravers are held so that the face is tilted at a 45° angle (see Fig. 260). If the face is raised so that the angle is greater than 45° between the graver face and the worked metal surface, a deep cut is made by the tool. With a face angle less than 45° between these two points, a shallow cut is made and the point of the tool often breaks, except when used on softer metals such as pewter and lead.

FIG. 259

Bent gravers

Gravers can be curved up slightly at the ends if the tip is heated while being held with slight pressure against an asbestos sheet (see Fig. 254). When the tool is heated sufficiently (indicated by a cherry-red color), it will bend. The tool is then quenched in water or oil to harden the metal. The curve on the graver should be slight, so that the tool does not have to be held at a high angle. All gravers, except line and round, can also be ground at the point so that the graver belly will not scratch the casting surface as the tool cuts the design or texture.

After quenching, the fire scale is removed from the tool with a metal brush. The tool is then heated in the flame of an alcohol lamp or Bunsen burner until a pale straw color is visible, after which it is quenched in water to temper the metal.

FIG. 257

FIG. 258

FIG. 260

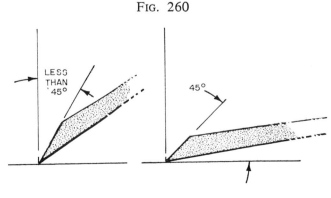

LESS THAN 45°

45°

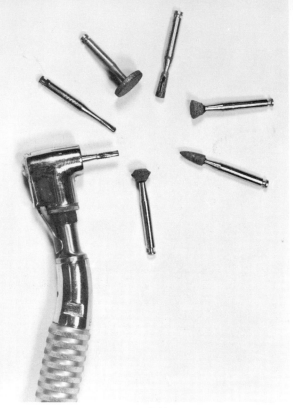

Other uses of gravers

The regular gravers can be used to enlarge openings, especially where a gemstone will be mounted, because they often fit into areas inaccessible to the hollow scraper. They are also used to clean up the casting in general. Small carbide dental burs or rotary files used with the power-driven handpieces have even greater value than the regular gravers in detailed and hard-to-get-at areas of the casting (see Fig. 261).

Some practice will be required to use the gravers, especially when tracing a scribed line of a design or when re-emphasizing groovings or lines made in the original wax model.

FIG. 261

CHAPTER 17

Gemstone Mountings and Findings

GEMSTONE MOUNTINGS

Gemstones, added after all the other finishing steps have been completed, can be selected from opaque, translucent, and almost transparent gemstone material of varying degrees of hardness and cut into various shapes, as follows (see Figs. 10, 11, 12, 13, and 262–263).

Gem types and shapes

1. Two-dimensional flats (in any regular geometric outline or free form—no equal sides)
2. Spheres
3. Carvings
4. Tumbled "baroque" nuggets
5. Single natural crystals
6. Crystal clusters
7. Small crystal-lined geodes (sliced to reveal their hidden beauty)
8. Faceted stones in various shapes and forms
9. Cabochons with polished convex surfaces, which can be round, square, oval, cushion, octagonal, flat-slabbed, heart-shaped, triangular, cross, kite, teardrop, rectangular. The surfaces can be high, low, medium, or equally convex (lentil-shaped), or laminated shapes of two-layers (doublets) or three layers (triplets) of material.

In addition to being cut into definite shapes as listed, the gem material can be inlaid with other gem materials or inlaid in cloissons of metal (see photos of finished items, transparencies or black/white). The material can also be reduced to a gravel or fine powder for other applications.

Baroque stones must be hand-picked from gem stock to obtain similar sizes and shapes for a specific design.

The widest part of a faceted stone is called the girdle, and the widest part of a cabochon is called the bezel (see Figs. 262 and 263). Some types of metal mountings, such as boxed, circular, and oval vertical frames, are also called bezels. Cabochons are set into metal bezels so that the bezel of the stone is either near the bottom of the frame or resting on an inner shoulder of the metal, called a bearing.

Mountings

Mounting devices for holding gemstones are as varied as the objects they will hold in place. Many of the mountings or attachments for holding stones were developed when standard mountings such as bezels or prong wires were impossible to construct to fit an irregular stone outline. Often they were either impossible to attach as desired on castings, or they were not subordinate enough to the gemstones, which

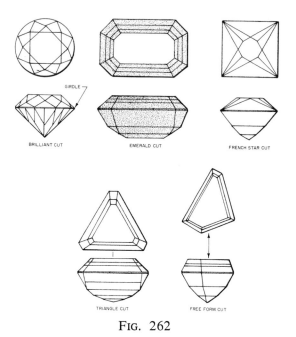

GIRDLE

BRILLIANT CUT   EMERALD CUT   FRENCH STAR CUT

TRIANGLE CUT   FREE FORM CUT

FIG. 262

must always be the focal point of interest when they are used.

The mountings are usually added before the final buffing and polishing steps, except when constructed of wax and cast centrifugally with the model. Tumbled stones, which are always in baroque or nugget shapes, are usually set in metal castings with wire prongs to hold the stone securely in place (see Fig. 264). A stone requires only those prongs necessary to hold it firmly in the casting, unless special effect is desired, such as many tiny prongs which give a radiating effect of light through the stone facets out to the metal itself. Bezels with irregular outlines are also used.

Mountings such as bezels, pronged boxes or baskets, delicate wire prongs or coronets, and twisted filigree wire cages are used to hold the stones in position. Other types of mountings include domed settings, tension or pressure mounts, slotted or V-grooves, burnished feather edges, stones diamond-drilled and attached with jump-rings, and stone inlay on a flat or slightly convex surface.

"Spider" mounts

Wires can emerge from a single base and flare out to encompass a stone, whether it be symmetrical, free-form, or irregular in shape (see Fig. 265). The strands of wire are inserted in a hole drilled in the casting and soldered into place. The wires are then bent parallel with the surface of the casting, the stone placed on the wire "bed," and wires bent up and around the stone so that the stone cannot be lifted out vertically or sidled out. The wires are cut to length and lifted to allow removal of the stone temporarily while the wire ends are filed to blunt rounded points and buffed and polished. The stone is then replaced, and the prongs burnished down over it with a flat or curved burnisher. Any marks on the metal made by the burnisher are removed with light buffing and polishing. The wire prongs, either part of the casting or soldered on after casting, are filed to the correct length and to a dull rounded point. The gemstone is positioned on the casting in a predetermined spot, and the prongs burnished over the stone with a flat or curved

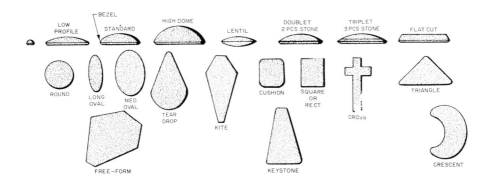

FIG. 263

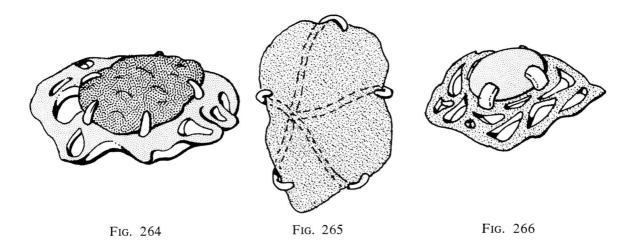

FIG. 264   FIG. 265   FIG. 266

burnisher. The prongs are then buffed and polished.

Wider prongs of half-round wire or flat short sections of metal are soldered into position, filed to a long taper, and buffed and polished (see Fig. 266). The stone is placed inside the prongs, and the prongs are bent down over the stone lightly, the end prongs set first and then the sides. This is followed by setting the remaining prongs. Additional pressure is put upon the prongs in the same order as when first bent, so that the stone seats correctly in its mounting. If the prongs are bent down consecutively over the stone in a clockwise or counterclockwise motion, it will be almost impossible to level or seat the stone properly.

Cast prongs

Prongs that are part of the casting are notched with a square file. To determine where the notch will be on the inside of the prong, the stone is placed inside the mounting and leveled (see Fig. 267). The stone when set should not protrude through the underside of the mounting. If the casting is a ring, it can be held on a ring mandrel that has been wrapped with a strip of wet-or-dry sanding paper or crocus cloth sanding paper, which prevents the ring from slipping sideways. The prongs are marked with a scribe at the point of contact with the girdle of the stone. The stone is removed, and another mark is made on the prong just below the first mark (approximately $\frac{1}{32}''$). A notch

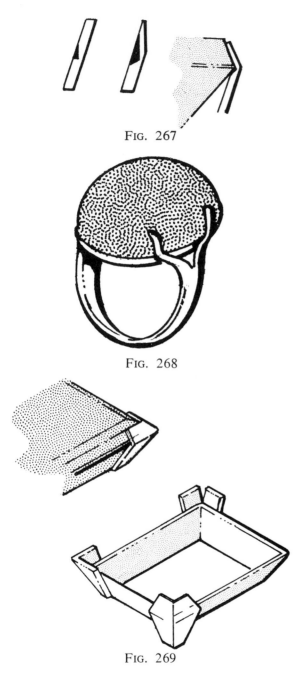

FIG. 267

FIG. 268

FIG. 269

over the stone is to place a small flat-ended wedge-shaped tool (which is highly polished) on them and gently tap them down over the stone with a small hammer. The prongs can be split down the center with the jewelers' saw to three-fourths of the distance between the prong point and the gemstone notch and spread to make a double prong on each side of the stone (see Fig. 268). Square-cornered prongs and corner prongs are split centrally down to the filed notch with the saw. The tops of the prongs are filed on an angle so that the edges meet when the prongs are burnished or set over the stone (see Fig. 269). The wedge-shaped setting tool can also be used here.

Collet mounts

A prong mounting called a collet can be made from a strip of metal curved into a ring and soldered together (see Fig. 270). It is shaped on the round ring mandrel or oval mandrel to a slight taper. Smaller collets can be shaped on a short section of drill rod placed in a bench vise. The prongs or coronets are spaced as desired and sawed or filed down to a depth of three quarters of the distance between the top and the bottom of the collet (see Appendix—Construction of Tapered Cone).

This type of mounting can be made from a curved strip of metal, which will form a tapered "ring" when soldered. The stone is placed in the mounting and a line scribed where the girdle meets the metal, as previously mentioned (see Fig. 270). The prong or coronet is filed away on the inside so that a fine taper remains. The collet mounting is placed on the casting and soldered into position. After pickling, rinsing, buffing, and polishing, the stone is inserted and the prongs burnished down over it. The section of the prong that is bent over the stone should not be less than $\frac{1}{32}$″ and can be increased according to stone size and its surface angle or curvature.

Star mountings are formed from a sawed and filed five- or six-point star (see Fig. 270). The star has a small hole drilled in the center just large enough for a fine jewelers' saw blade to enter, so that a slot can be made from the center out toward the star point to within about $\frac{1}{16}$″ from the end. The points are turned up into a basket (the slot makes the mounting shape possible); the edges are filed smooth,

is sawed with the jewelers' saw or filed with a square file to one-third of the prong thickness at that point. Then it is lengthened all the way or partially out to the end of the prong. The prongs are filed to the desired shape and buffed and polished.

The stone is placed in the mounting, seating itself in the notches just made. The prongs are bent over the stone with a burnisher and prong-setting pliers. Another way of fixing them down

FIG. 270

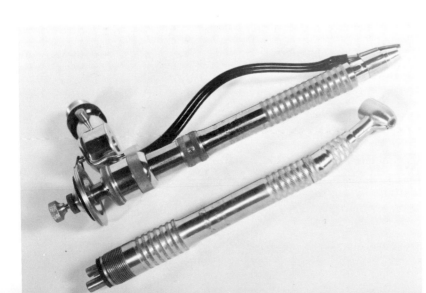

FIG. 271

FIG. 272

buffed and polished. The mounting can be soldered to a small disc the same diameter as the bottom star points, or it can be soldered directly to a casting. The mounting stands upright without support and can be soldered easily.

Pearl mounts

Predrilled pearls are available, or they can be partially drilled to permit placing them on small pins and posts. Undrilled pearls in prong- or cage-type mounts are also used. A small metal pin that just fits into the drilled hole in the pearl is soldered into place. The tip of the metal pin is split to permit the insertion of a thin metal wedge. A very small amount of pearl cement is put into the drilled hole, and the pearl is placed on the pin. As it is gently pressed into place, the pearl forces the wedge down into the split pin so that it remains secure (see Fig. 271). Smaller pearls can be attached securely by simply bending the wire into an S-shaped curve, which wedges the pearl tightly when filled with cement and pressed on the pin (see Fig. 271). Pearls are easily dislodged if placed on a straight peg.

Drilled stones

Other gemstones that can be drilled with air turbine handpieces are mounted in the same manner as is used for pearls. The stones are drilled with small diamond-charged burs or drills, such as those used in the dental profession (see Fig. 272). These diamond points should be operated at high speed with water used as a cooling agent and to wash away the grindings during drilling (see Fig. 273). The speeds used to rotate the diamond and the friction created will produce heat in the stone, so that the water must be used copiously to prevent fracturing, especially when translucent stones are drilled.

The points or burs are manufactured in multitudinous shapes, such as long cylinders, tapered cones and needles, inverted tapers, flatwheels, tapered wheels, and safe-sided discs, and in ball, bud, and hollow core shapes (see Figs. 212a and 261). A tiny indentation should be drilled first in the stone with a small ballshaped diamond point. This acts as a centerpunched hole to guide the large diamond point as it starts to drill.

Stones can be mounted by being drilled partially or all the way through and threaded onto a jump-ring or length of wire, which is then soldered into position (see Fig. 274). Extreme care must be used here to protect the stone from the heat of the torch. The stone is wrapped in dampened asbestos or embedded in a raw potato for protection during soldering. When soldering the findings or mountings to the main section, apply the heat to the metal instead of directly to the solder. If the solder is heated first, it balls and will not flow until the surrounding metal is raised to the same temperature. Solder also will roll up if it is not clean, or if the metal surfaces are not cleaned and properly fluxed.

Leaf mounts

Articles can be cast with filigree or small leaves around the gem-mounting area (see Fig. 275). The leaves are gently bent back to permit the seating of the stone down in the metal, and then brought back over the stone with a wooden stick or plastic rod tapped with a small hammer, or tapped lightly with a rawhide mallet. Metal setting-tools will dent or scar the detail in the leaves.

Tab prongs

Stones are set in the surface of metals by tabs or prongs soldered to the underside. These are bent up to permit an exact fitting. The angle of the contoured walls of the opening are filed

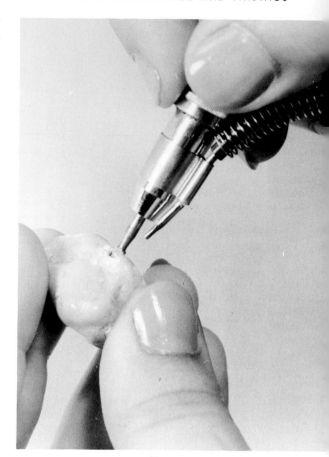

FIG. 273

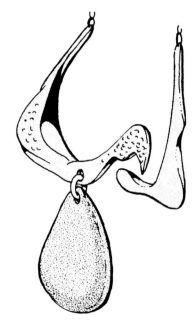

FIG. 274

to fit the curvature or angle of the stone perfectly when it is positioned (see Fig. 276). After buffing and polishing, the stone is placed in the opening from the underside, and the tabs or prongs burnished down over it.

Castings can be created with a partially attached extension which, when filed to a point or wedge during the finishing steps, will hold a small sphere of gem material or a pearl in position. The metal directly under the small sphere is usually ground to a cone shape with the stone-setting burs (see Fig. 277).

Half-dome settings

Half-domes of thin sheet metal made with the dapping-die block and punches make convex-curved tubs for gems. A wire ring is bent to fit inside the half-dome for the bearing or seat, and the lip above the ring becomes the bezel, which is burnished or sawed and filed into prongs, which are bent over the stone to hold it in place (see Fig. 278). The half-dome is soldered to the casting and buffed and polished afterwards. To make half-domes on the dapping-die block, cut circular discs and place them in hollow depressions that are larger than the disc. This avoids marks on the underside of the half-dome and, because the depression is a half-circle, the metal will be formed perfectly regardless of its position.

Half-domes of metal can be sawed and filed, or easily ground to produce three or more prongs, with small mounted grinding stones, which are used in the flexible shaft or dental handpiece.

Free-form mountings

Free-form faceted stones are frequently mounted in soldered partial bezels of V-grooved metal if the grooved section is not cast on the original wax pattern (see Fig. 279). These mountings need not encompass the stone completely, but they must surround it enough to

Fig. 275

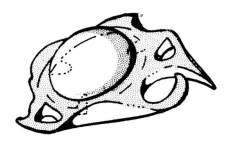

Fig. 276

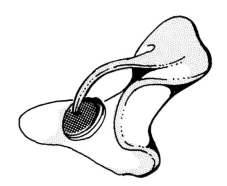

Fig. 277

Fig. 278

TUBING OR STRIP
BEZEL

HALF DOME
SETTING

TAPERED BOX
BEZEL

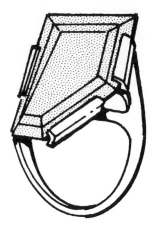

FIG. 279

FIG. 280

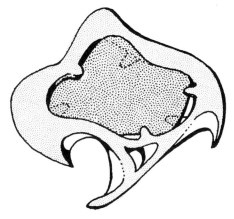

FIG. 281

prevent the stone from slipping out of the mounting in any direction. A V-groove mounting can be curved around one side of a stone, the other side secured with the prong that is an integral part of the casting. The prong is grooved to fit around the bezel or girdle of the stone, but is not burnished down over the stone, only held against it by tension.

Crystal mountings

Gemstones, or rough material such as crystal clusters, or tiny crystal coatings, called drusy crystals, which form on another mineral or a matrix (any natural material in which mineral crystals are imbedded) can be suspended in open areas of the metal as well as mounted on solid flat areas or impressions in the casting.

Small fork-like prongs are constructed in wax, becoming a portion of the original casting, or they may be placed on the edge of the opening or inserted in a slot made by the saw blade and then soldered securely. They are filed to fit the outline or curvature of the stone as closely as possible. When the stone is mounted one or two of these prongs are gently bent sideways and returned to the correct position after the stone has been inserted (see Fig. 280). The prongs can also be soldered parallel with the surface of the casting and bent up to allow insertion of the stone.

Supporting prongs can be soldered on the underside of the metal opening and aligned with the upper prong, or they can be spaced alternately so that one prong is on the viewing surface and the next projects from the undersurface of the metal (see Fig. 281). These prongs can be an integral part of the casting so that they are not readily distinguishable as mountings. The prong may also be an outside loop or yoke-type mounting, cast as a part of the article or soldered on during the finishing step. The ends can be flattened to enhance the design and, in addition, hold the stone so that it cannot rock or rotate in the mounting.

Tension mounting

Stones can be set into castings by pressure or tension if the inner surfaces of the mounting area are grooved with a small rotating disc. The groove serves as a bearing for the girdle of the stone. The metal is forced open just enough to permit entry of the stone, after which it springs back into place (see Fig. 282). The metal can also be grooved enough to fit the stone easily without being opened. After the stone is placed, the outer metal surface is tapped lightly with a small rawhide hammer to compress it around the stone. In both methods practice is necessary to avoid fracturing the stone either by the pressure of the springing metal or by setting the metal with a hammer.

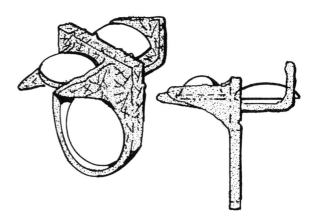

Beaded settings

Beads made by a round-pointed graver will hold small stones in place without prongs. The mounting surface and edge is flat, and the stone is placed down in the opening of the casting. The stone can be seated in a perfectly formed tapered cone by a stone-setting bur (see Figs. 283 and 284). These burs are mounted on ⅛″ shanks for use in the small electric hand drills and range in diameter from .81 mm. to 9.54 mm. Force the graver tool into the metal by cutting down toward the stone, raising a burr, which is rolled over by manipulating a beading tool from side to side to form a bead (see Fig. 285).

FIG. 282

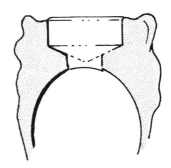

A simple beading tool can be made from a section of an old file. The section is sawed from a flat file where it is ¾″ to 1″ wide. Anneal it by heating it to a bright red and then setting it aside to cool without quenching. Notches are sawed ¹⁄₁₆″ apart and ⅛″ deep along one edge. These posts are sanded or filed into round beads. The tool is heated to a deep straw color to temper it or return it to its original hardness, then dipped quickly in cold water, dried, buffed, and polished to a fine smoothness (see Fig. 286). To use the tool, place it against the metal edge or bezel and tap it lightly with a chasing or small pein hammer, which leaves tiny round indentations in the metal where it meets the stone (see Fig. 286).

FIG. 283

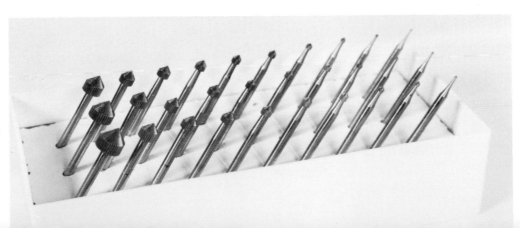

FIG. 284

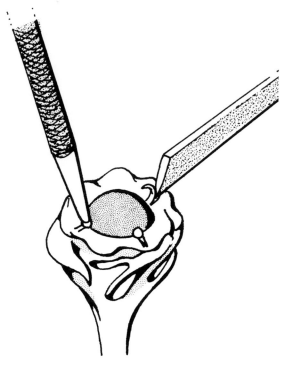

FIG. 285

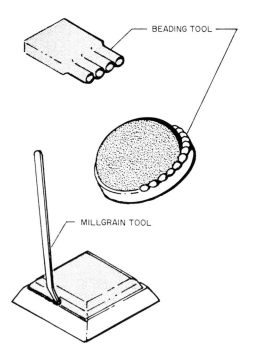

FIG. 286

Use of millgrain tools

To set a stone in metal with a thin wall rising in a crater-like edge, burnish the edge of the metal with a millgrain tool. This tool has a small wheel set in the end of a steel shank which follows the bezel or metal rim around the stone, making a beaded edge on the metal (see Fig. 287).

Tubing mountings

Prong mounts for very small stones can be made of short lengths of tubing held in the end of a section of dowel wood covered with sealing wax, stick shellac, or lapidary dopping wax. The prongs are sawed and filed while mounted on the stick, which otherwise would be too small to handle. Tubing is formed by pulling a narrow strip of metal through a wire draw-plate. The metal is snipped and filed to a tapered point at one end. The metal strip is placed over a groove in a swaging block, and a length of dowel wood the same size as the groove in the block is placed over it. The dowel wood is hammered to bend the metal strip partially as an aid in forming it before using the draw-plate (see Fig. 287). A swage block can be made by drilling holes of different sizes through the side of a block of wood. The block when sawed through the center of the drilled holes will produce two blocks with half-round grooves in the surfaces. The tapered end of the partially formed metal strip is inserted through the hole in the draw-plate and grasped with draw tongs. The strip is pulled through the plate and progressively through smaller holes to form the tube (see Fig. 288).

Thin-walled tubing can be bent without crimping if the tube length is filled with soft beeswax. When the bending is completed, the tubing is heated almost to the boiling stage to remove all of the wax.

Gypsy settings

To make gypsy settings, drill a tapered hole from the top of the casting surface and then cut a bearing or groove inside to seat the stone close to the surface. The stone is placed in the opening and the metal burnished down around it, after which the marks are removed with a Scotch stone and by buffing and polishing (see Fig. 289).

Bezel construction

Bezels are the most popular method of stone setting in the majority of contemporary pieces. They are constructed of flat wire or commercial bezel wire in karat golds, sterling, or fine silver —20 to 26 gauge. Bezels are not usually cast in metal. They are constructed of the same metal as the casting, but in a softer alloy, i.e., fine silver wire bezels are used on sterling or coin silver castings, and 18 to 24-karat gold wire is used on lower karat castings. Fine metal bezel wire is preferred because of its higher melting point.

The commercial wire comes in beaded and decorated surfaces. It is also available with a shoulder or bearing for the support of stones. The stone rests on the small inner bearing when it is exposed (see Fig. 278). This raises a shallow stone and permits the play of light through those that are translucent. Opaque stones do not require a bearing, as they are seated in bezels made from flat wire. To make a bezel, a round wire is wrapped around the stone at its girdle or bezel and twisted snugly. When removed, the wire is cut with the pliers and the two ends spread out to form a straight wire. By measuring the length of the wire, it can be determined how much flat wire or strip is needed to form the bezel for a specific stone. The width of the bezel wire should be kept to a minimum. It should only be high enough after forming to hold the stone in place, or else about one third of the height of the stone (see Appendix for determining bezel lengths).

The wire ends are filed absolutely flat for a good join, and the wire is bent into a round or circular shape. One should not be concerned with trying to form the bezel to the shape or outline of the stone, as this is usually done after it is soldered. The two ends are brought past each other so that when placed against each other they will hold their position by spring tension. The surfaces are fluxed, and the bezel is placed on a carbon ring-soldering mandrel, in the tweezers of a third hand soldering stand (see Figs. 242 and 243), or on an improvised soldering base. The bezel is placed on any one of these three implements with the joint down. Solder is placed inside the bezel on the joint, which is hard-soldered together. The bezel may be held together with iron binding wire, but it

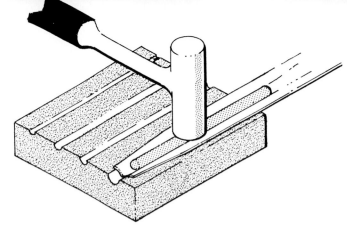

FIG. 287

FIG. 288

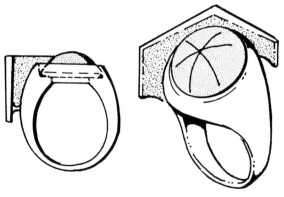

FIG. 289

must be removed before the soldered metal is dipped into the pickling solution.

A soldering stand is made of a length of steel drill rod flattened on one end and bent into a Z shape. The opposite end is placed in dental plaster or investment while the wire is held upright until the base sets up (see Fig. 290).

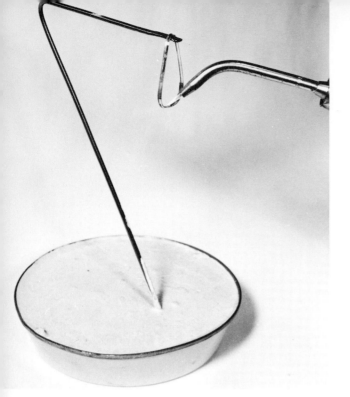

FIG. 290

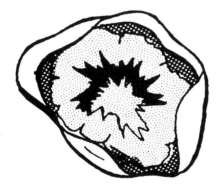

FIG. 291

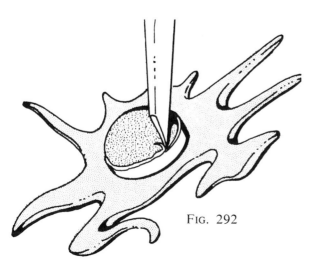

FIG. 292

The bezel itself can be soldered and attached to the casting in one soldering procedure, but this takes practice to be successful. After the bezel is soldered, the hollow scraper is used to remove excess solder from the inner surface and the bearing, if this type of bezel has been constructed. It is then shaped to fit the stone on the ring mandrel, on small oval mandrels, or on a small round bench stake.

If the bezel is too small to fit the stone, it can be stretched to fit by being tapped lightly on the outer surface when it is placed over one or another of these three instruments. If too large, it must be sawed apart, a section removed, and the ends resoldered. The bezel edges are filed so that they are parallel and uniform in height when soldered into position. The stone is placed in the bezel and the burnishing tool is pressed slightly against the bezel on one side and then the opposite side of the stone until the bezel is completely burnished (see Figs. 250 and 291). Another bezel burnisher is a rocker-type tool, which compresses the metal bezel around the stone gradually and eliminates crimping.

Burnished bezels often have a wavy uneven edge where the metal meets the stone because unequal pressure has been applied with the burnishing tool. The pointed graver, with its sharp cutting edge, is used to follow the edge of metal around the stone and level it (see Fig. 292). This is much more practical than buffing the metal edge, which often discolors the stone or "burns" the metal if excessive pressure is used.

When the bezel is being buffed and polished, care must be taken not to apply excessive pressure, in order to avoid the danger of cutting a groove in the metal at the edge of the bezel.

Tapered or mitered bezels

Bezels can be constructed of a strip of flat wire mitered to make square, rectangular, octagonal, hexagonal (the sides do not have to be equal), or free-form shapes of five or seven sides with a length of 24 gauge flat bezel wire. The sides are measured and small V-notches cut in the top edge of the wire down to the bearing, or halfway through the metal (see Fig. 293). The remaining metal below the notch is filed with a square file so that the metal, when bent to

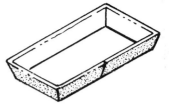

FIG. 293

shape around the girdle or bezel of the stone, will fit snugly at the corners. The ends of the bezel are cut to fit, filed smooth, and soldered together (see Appendix for bezel construction).

Picket bezels

Bezel boxes, after soldering, can be cut into slits $1/16''$ apart down to the bearing, or as deep as desired with the jewelers' saw blade. Careful use of the saw when making the slits eliminates sanding, which is almost impossible to do in the very fine cuts produced by the thin saw blade. The tiny slits, called "pickets," are easily burnished over the stone and buffed and polished (see Fig. 294).

Mitered prong bezels

Bezels constructed by mitering the corners of the wire can also be made from narrower bezel wire with wedge-shaped prongs soldered onto the outer surface to hold the stone (see Fig. 269). The frame, which becomes the bearing, is soldered to extensions on a ring or any other casting. The prongs are notched on the inner surface to fit the stone. The prongs can be extensions of the casting, and the bezel frame simply set evenly inside them and soldered into place. The bezels can be constructed with perpendicular or angular walls (see Fig. 269).

Bezel inserts

Stones can be mounted down in the metal casting itself if the opening in the casting is enlarged to fit a regularly constructed bezel. The bezel, shaped to fit the stone and held in position by tension of the wire ends or with iron binding wire, is inserted into the opening and soldered. The only protruding portion of metal is the bezel and, when it is burnished down and buffed and polished, the separation or seam between the bezel and casting is no longer visible. This is much easier to do than tapping the casting metal around a stone that is recessed in the casting (see Fig. 294).

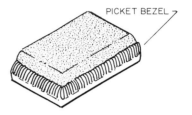

PICKET BEZEL

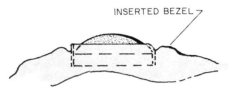

INSERTED BEZEL

FIG. 294

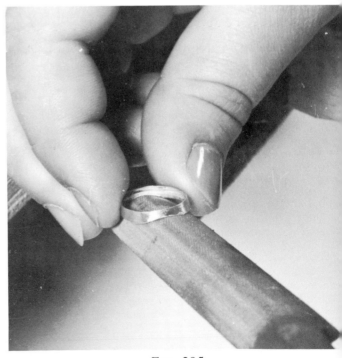

FIG. 295

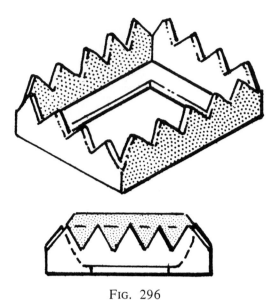

FIG. 296

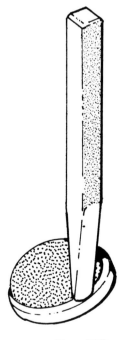

FIG. 297

Fitting bezels to curved surfaces

To fit bezel mountings to a curved ring or other casting surfaces, file the lower edge of the bezel with a half-round file (see Fig. 295). The bezel section must be tried on the casting many times as the work progresses to determine which areas need to be removed. This fitting process is quickened by the use of small rotary grinding stones.

A solid box with high thin walls cast as part of the mounting can be filed with triangular or flat files. The notches are spaced evenly around the perimeter of the mounting. The inner surfaces of the casting and prongs are scraped smooth with the hollow scraper so that the stone can be seated level without pressure. The prongs are filed and sanded, buffed, and polished. The stone is then set in place in the casting, and the wedge-shaped tool is used to push the prongs over the stone (see Fig. 296).

Bezel-setting punches

Bezels can also be set around stones with a setting punch instead of a burnisher, and a graver to clean out the bearing instead of a hollow scraper. The stone should always be checked to see that it fits in the bezel snugly without grabbing. Stones fitted too tightly or forced into undersized bezels will crack or chip when pressure is applied during the burnishing. Bearings filled with solder, or joints between the base of the bezel and the casting will also crack a stone, especially cabochons that have not been ground with a slight chamfer on the underside. The ring is fastened in a ring clamp during the cleaning out of the bearing and the setting of the stone. The setting punch is borrowed from the set of chasing tools; however, any tool with a fairly flat surface can be used. The tool is placed against the bezel and tapped gently with the chasing hammer, forcing the bezel down around the stone (see Fig. 297).

Cone bezels

Cone-shaped bezels can be made from tubing with parallel walls. The cone shape is obtained by a tapered wooden pin being tapped or forced through the short length of tubing. If the metal is placed in a tapered opening made in the work bench, the wooden pin can be forced as deep

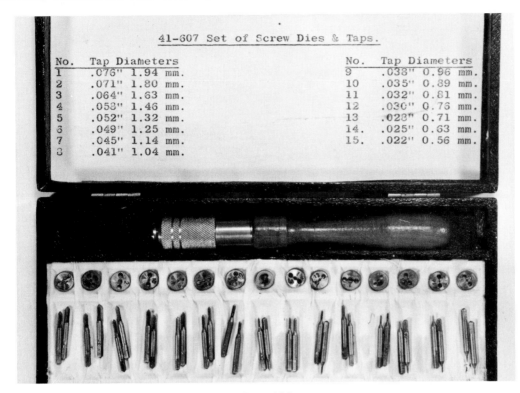

No.	Tap Diameters		No.	Tap Diameters	
1	.076"	1.94 mm.	9	.038"	0.96 mm.
2	.071"	1.80 mm.	10	.035"	0.89 mm.
3	.064"	1.63 mm.	11	.032"	0.81 mm.
4	.058"	1.46 mm.	12	.030"	0.76 mm.
5	.052"	1.32 mm.	13	.028"	0.71 mm.
6	.049"	1.25 mm.	14	.025"	0.63 mm.
7	.045"	1.14 mm.	15	.022"	0.56 mm.
8	.041"	1.04 mm.			

41-607 Set of Screw Dies & Taps.

FIG. 298

as desired through the tubing. The metal must be annealed before any attempt is made to form it, or it will crack and split. Tapered mountings can also be made from flat sheet metal, which is annealed before being bent (see Appendix for tapered cone bezel construction).

Small bezels with stems

Small metal parts, sections, domed, or star prong settings can be attached to threaded stems and inserted through drilled holes in the casting. A mating nut made from a small circle or square of metal is drilled and threaded with a tap to fit, after which it is fastened tightly to the post (see Figs. 298, 299a, and 299b). A drop of soft solder, applied after the excess threaded stem is cut off, will prevent the nut from loosening. Nuts can be as small as 3 mm. in diameter.

Gemstone inlay

Gemstone materials can be inlaid into the surface of a casting if a flat, shallow area is formed in the wax pattern (see photo of finished item "Bird" by Sharr Choate). The inner crevices

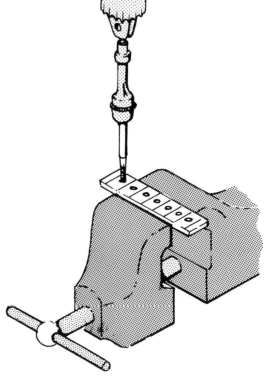

FIG. 299a

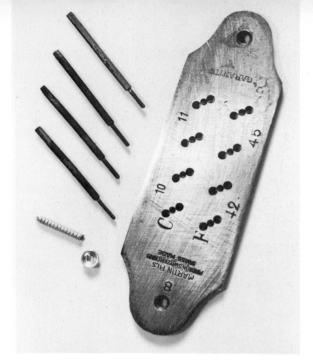

FIG. 299b Tap-and-die plate and sample of wire and nut. These small tools are used for threading fine earscrew wires and small nuts.

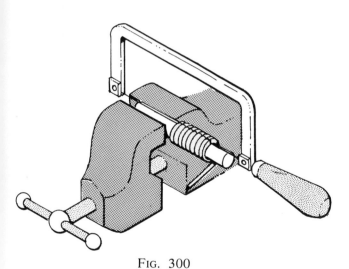

FIG. 300

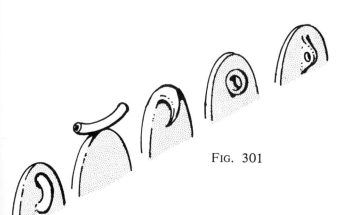

FIG. 301

and corners of the area are scraped with a graver or hollow scraper, and any roughness on the bottom surface is removed. Gemstone materials are slabbed (sliced) to the depth of the prepared space. This requires the use of lapidary equipment, such as a 8″ to 10″ trim saw, normally used to trim gem materials before they are shaped into cabochons by grinding. The material need not be in large pieces; small chunks are adequate.

The material is placed in a cardboard box or, preferably, in a collapsible frame (see Fig. 174) used for rubber molds, and the frame is filled with dental stone. Dental stone is a plaster used for making study models, which stands up under the sawing procedure much better than plaster of Paris. This stone is mixed with tap water to a thick paste consistency and poured over the gem material in the frame until the gemstones are covered. A small amount of table salt sprinkled over the surface will speed the setting time. The dental stone is usually hard enough for sawing in about 8 hours, but it is best to let it harden over night. After hardening, the frame is removed or, if used, the cardboard box is peeled off and scrubbed under running water to dissolve adhering paper.

The dental-stone block is placed in the slabbing-saw vice and slices are made to correspond to the depth of the area that has been prepared in the casting. After the block is sawed into slabs, the dental stone can easily be broken from the gem material with the slightest pressure. It should be thoroughly cleaned by a scrubbing in warm detergent suds and rinsing in running water. The gemstone is set aside to dry thoroughly, either in a warm spot or in the kitchen oven at 150°F. for several hours.

The gem material, usually slabbed to $\frac{1}{16}$″, can easily be sectioned into small pieces with a 4/0 blade in the jewelers' saw frame. It is no problem if the pieces break as they are sawed, because they can be used even if in odd shapes. If pieces without any breaks are desired, they should be ground to fit the area.

The largest pieces of gem material are placed in the prepared space. They are then cemented into place with a waterproof adhesive or with epoxy materials, which can be applied with a toothpick. The smaller crevices are filled with tiny bits of gem material, and the remaining area filled with a gem grout. Small bits of the gem material are ground to a fine powder in a mortar and pestle, or they can be hammered on a flat anvil or steel plate. Small cans with both top and bottom removed are effectively used as a dam to hold the material in a confined space as it is being powdered with the hammer. The small can must be shallow enough so that it does not impede the hammer action. The bits are ground to a powder as fine as common table salt and mixed into a paste with the same cement or epoxy resin that was used to cement the larger pieces of stone in place. A few drops of waterproof ink corresponding to the gemstone color can be added during mixing to deepen the color. The paste is pushed down into the crevices that separate the gem material and rammed firmly with the flat surface of the hammer face. It is then set aside to dry.

When hardened, all surface roughness is ground down with a small carborundum stone used under running water until it is level with the metal surface.

The stone can be left unpolished or, if desired, polished in the casting with a felt buff charged with tin oxide paste. After polishing, the compound is scrubbed off the completed piece with detergent suds, which is rinsed in running water, and dried.

Turquoise, opal, and other porous stones should not be dipped in any acid solutions. The solution absorbed under the surface of the gemstone material forms crystals, which grow and expand, forcing the gemmy material under the surface to crack or craze.

FINDINGS

Use of jump-rings

Jump-rings used to attach cast jewelry items to findings, to necklace chains, chains to clasps, and to larger rings used in bracelet or necklace construction are made by annealed wire wound around a mandrel of the desired ring size (see Fig. 300). Mandrels may be ordinary nails, knitting needles, wood doweling, drill rod, etc. To anneal wire, wind it into a coil and wrap it with a length of wire of the same metal. Smaller gauge wires are wrapped in smaller coils than heavier gauge wires. The wire wrap prevents protruding wire ends from melting as the heat is applied, and it can be left on the coil as it is dipped in the pickling solution, whereas iron binding wire must be removed before pickling. The annealed wire end is held against the mandrel as the wire is wound tightly around the mandrel, like a spring or coil, until the wire length is completely used or until it reaches the end of the mandrel. The wire coil, while still wrapped on the mandrel, is placed in a bench vise with smooth jaws or copper jaw-liners, and the coil is sawed down the center, parallel with the mandrel. Jump-rings are not opened by spreading, but by holding with a smooth-jawed, needle-nosed, or flat-nosed pliers so that the separated ends of the ring can be twisted in opposite directions. When the ring is to be closed, the ends are brought back to a closed position.

Mountings

Pendant loops, mountings, and bails by which pendants are strung can be constructed on the wax pattern or soldered on later (see Fig. 301). The bails can be either hidden from view, attached at the top of the pendant in a stationary position, or mounted so that they swivel. Wires can be bent, sheet metal drilled and filed to shape, and short lengths of small-diameter tubing cut to form a curved bail for soldering onto the pendant. The wax pattern can also be constructed so that a portion of metal is simply bent over into a loop.

Necklace construction

Necklaces can be formed by interlacing metal rings of identical size or assorted sizes and shapes. Bulkier rope-type chains need no soldering, as the method of intertwining the rings holds them together. Thinner or single-link necklaces usually require electric soldering to prevent the spreading of the wire rings and for better appearance (see Fig. 302).

To attach chain links made from silver or gold wire, divide the total number of links required. Half of the links are then hard-soldered as individual units and joined by a third link, which is medium-soldered. The hard-soldered links coated with anti-flux will prevent fire scale and solder flow, should the secondary soldering temperature be too hot (see Fig. 303).

A necklace can be made of short random lengths of small-diameter tubing filed, buffed, and polished, and strung on a fine necklace chain.

Soldering pin backs

Pin backs or brooches attached to jewelry articles should be soldered into position above the center of gravity or made to balance so that the pin will not "lop over" when worn (see Fig. 304). The pin portion of the clasp is not added until the swivel and clasp are soldered into position, because the thin wire melts readily during the soldering steps.

Pin-pendant conversion

Pins may be worn as pendants if a bail or loop is soldered to the back of the casting. An interchangeable pendant loop that will slide over the pin-back shaft is made of $\frac{1}{16}''$ diameter tubing cut to fit between the clasp hinge and the swivel (see Fig. 305). A small diamond-shaped section of 18 gauge metal is bent into a closed loop, and the two points are medium-soldered in the center of the tubing length.

Fig. 303

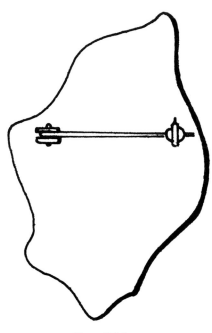

Fig. 304

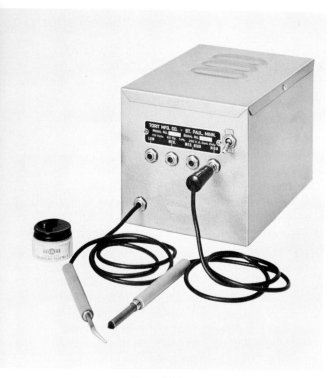

Fig. 302

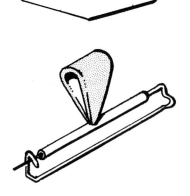

Fig. 305

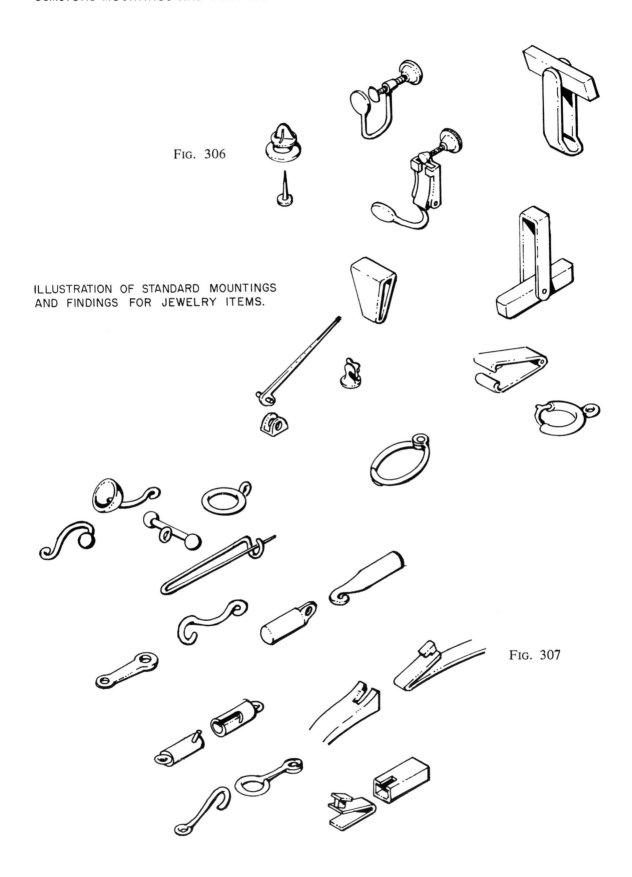

FIG. 306

ILLUSTRATION OF STANDARD MOUNTINGS
AND FINDINGS FOR JEWELRY ITEMS.

FIG. 307

CHAPTER 18

Electroplating

THE PURPOSE OF PLATING OR ELECTROPLATING is to decorate a metal in contrasting colors, to change the metal color completely, to protect it from wear or tarnish, or to improve it generally. Cold-plating or dipping does not have the enduring effect that is the result of electroplating. Deposits of metal on metal surfaces by electroplating can be as thin as one-millionth of an inch (0.000001″) up to two-thousandths of an inch (0.002″). Castings of sterling silver or coin silver can be plated with fine silver (pure silver without any alloy metals) to retard tarnishing, because fine silver does not darken as quickly. Gold can be plated in various colors, such as pink, red, green, and numerous shades of yellow, without alloying the casting metal to achieve the color.

Anodes

When an anode (a special strip of metal sold for plating) and a casting are suspended in a container of plating solution (electrolyte) and are activated with current from the electroplating machine, a thin transparent layer of metal (plating) is deposited on the casting, giving the desired color. The anode usually dissolves (in proportion to the deposit) onto the casting when plating solutions are correctly combined to maintain a constant balance.

Plating solutions

Specific metal coatings require correlated solutions and anodes. Unbalanced plating solutions and impure home-made anodes with incorrect metal content and grain structure will combine to produce an unsatisfactory plating. Anodes with a dense grain structure will not discharge fast enough. Plating solution containers should be Pyrex, glass, or rubber-coated. Enamel and metal tanks are never used.

Plating solutions are sold in concentrated liquids and are diluted to correct proportions with distilled water, never tap water. Minerals and other contaminants in ordinary water affect the plating process. When not in use, the solutions should be stored in tightly capped glass bottles to prevent evaporation. Water levels of solutions must be maintained according to directions supplied with them. Anodes after use should be removed from the solution, rinsed and dried, and stored in a clean, dustless container or wrap. Corroded copper anodes, caused by exposure to air, must be meticulously cleaned before being reused.

Capabilities of various metals and plating solutions

Metals can be plated with gold, silver, copper, nickel, and rhodium as follows:

1. Gold directly on copper, nickel and brass on karat golds to obtain different gold colors.
2. Gold on silver, other white metals, and those with soft solder, but the metal must be copper-coated first.
3. Rhodium directly on karat gold and platinum.
4. Rhodium on silver, but the silver must be gold-plated first.
5. Nickel on copper and brass. Used as an undercoat for rhodium, but a gold coating should follow the nickel coating before the article is rhodium-plated.

Gold colors available with properly formulated solutions are bright yellow 24-karat gold; rich, deep yellow 24-karat; 18 karat; light rose; dark rose; flesh color; pink; lavender; green; antique green; white.

Preparing the metal

The first step to successful electroplating is to have the metal surface prepared and finished (including buffing and polishing) to completion, just as though it were not intended to be plated (see Fig. 308). Scratches, discolorations, or other surface imperfections are not hidden by the plating. A chemically clean surface must be obtained on the metal so that no grease or fingerprints remain. Also, for successful results, a thorough preliminary cleaning and rinsing between immersions in the solutions are absolutely necessary. Polished surfaces will be free of oxides and discolorations, but like all other metal, surfaces must be steam-cleaned and "boiled out."

Fig. 308

FIG. 309

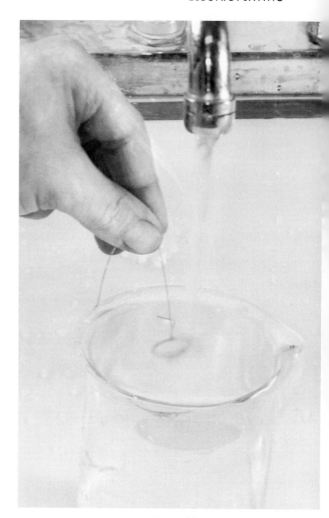

FIG. 311

A small jet cleaner placed over a gas burner and attached to the household water supply is used to clean the article after polishing (see Fig. 309). The article is attached to a copper wire dip-stick and suspended in a Pyrex beaker or a Pyrex saucepan containing a boil-out solution of 1 part of detergent (never use soap), 3 parts of water, and 2 tablespoons of household ammonia. The suspended article is left in the solution as the solution is brought to a boil and remains there for 5 to 10 minutes (see Fig. 310). After this point, it is not touched with the fingers. While the article is being boiled out, the small jet cleaner is prepared to produce a moist steam. The article is removed from the boil-out pan, transferred to self-locking tweezers, and held under the jet stream to remove all evidence of grease or dirt. It is then

FIG. 310   FIG. 313

returned to the copper wire and the boiling solution. The article should be frequently lifted out of the solution to check the surface. Dirt and grease will retain water in bubbles and droplets on the metal surfaces; a clean surface permits water to flow freely over it.

Electro-cleaning the metal

When it is evident that the article is clean, it is transferred, still held on the copper dipping-wire, to a running-water rinse (see Fig. 311). The article is attached to a copper wire with an alligator clip, and the other end of the wire connected to the negative pole on the plater. Another wire is attached in the same manner to a stainless steel anode and the other end attached to the positive pole on the machine. The anode is placed in the electro-cleaning solution, which is then heated to 180°F. (The voltage dial is set at 10 before the switch is turned on.) As soon as the solution has been heated to 180°F., the article is immersed in it and agitated for a maximum of 1 minute (see Fig. 312). It is then removed and rinsed under running water.

Various plating requirements

The plating procedure varies with the different plating solutions used. Copper- and rhodium-plating solutions are heated to 100°F. on an electric hotplate with a thermostatic control that will ascertain the correct temperature of the solution. Gold-plating solutions are heated to 140°F.; silver- and nickel-plating solutions are used at room temperature. Solutions should never be heated beyond the recommended temperatures. The plating procedure is identical to the electro-cleaning step, except that solutions, voltage, anodes, and immersion times vary (see Fig. 313).

FIG. 312

Plating solutions vary in that they have different immersion times, solution temperatures, and are used with different voltages, as follows:

Plating Color	Temp.	Voltage	Immersion Time
Copper plate	100°F.	6 volts	30 seconds or until completely colored
Gold (without base copper-plate)	140°F.	6 volts	30 seconds maximum
Rhodium (use gold or platinum dipping-wire)	100°F.	4 volts	20–30 seconds or until article is bright
Silver	Room temp.	2 volts	30 seconds or until colored
Nickel	Room temp.	2 volts	3–4 minutes or until covered with nickel

FIG. 314

Gold-plating on base copper-plate goes through the copper-plating process, followed by a rinse in running water, after which it is put through the regular gold-plating process.

Metals that are to be rhodium-plated are dipped (after electro-cleaning and rinsing) in an acid solution of 3 parts water to 1 part sulfuric acid. The acid dip is removed by another rinse in running water, and then the article is immersed in the rhodium-plating solution. Metals that are soluble in sulfuric acid should not be placed in rhodium- or chrome-plating baths that contain it. The metals must be plated with another metal before the finish plating is begun.

Finishing the plated article

When any of the solutions have been used for the required time and the color of the metal is satisfactory, the article is rinsed again in running water and placed in a box of hardwood sawdust so that it will dry without spotting. Gold-plated metals are rubbed with sodium bicar-

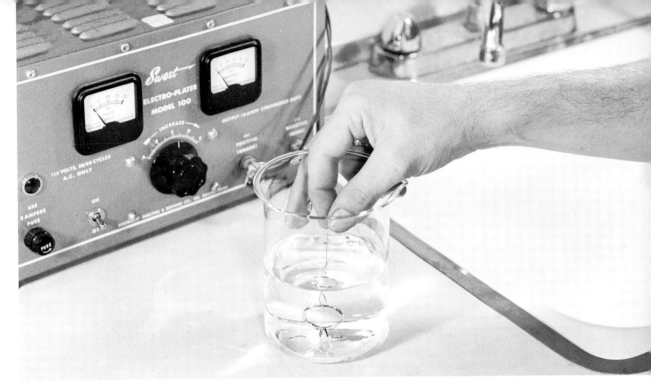

FIG. 315

FIG. 316

bonate (baking soda) and rinsed with running water (see Fig. 314). This neutralizes any acids remaining on the metal and adds luster to the finish. Rhodium-plated metals are rinsed after plating and dipped in isopropyl alcohol (common rubbing alcohol). Copper-plated articles must be thoroughly rinsed, or the subsequent plating will peel (see Fig. 315).

Two-color technique

If a two-color plating technique is used, or if only a portion of the original metal is to be plated, the rest of the casting, including those areas that are not visible when the article is worn, can be masked out with a lacquer to prevent those areas from being plated. After plating, the lacquer is removed with thinner or acetone (see Fig. 316).

Protecting exposed unplated areas

Design plating sections can be covered with a wax marking pencil or paraffin during plating to protect the surfaces from the cold solutions of another metal color.

CHAPTER 19

Enameling

ENAMELING AS AN ART HAS EXISTED SINCE 900 B.C. Fundamentally, the process used for this form of decoration has not changed since its discovery, except for improvements in equipment and materials. It should be studied and researched separately from other decorative processes in order to utilize the many different aspects of the technique to full advantage. Combining the many types of enamels with metal foils using various techniques opens an entirely new field to the craftsman, even to enabling him to combine cast and hand-wrought metal work with enamel decorative processes.

Metals for enameling

Enameling consists of fusing a colored glasslike material to clean metal surfaces. High-quality glass that is colored with various metal oxides shows an extraordinary capability of adhering to metal surfaces when properly applied.

Castings of gold, silver, and copper are used for enameling because their melting points are higher than the temperatures necessary to fuse the enamels on the surface of the metals. Sand and cuttlefish castings cannot be enameled satisfactorily, because they are much more porous than pressure- or centrifugal-type castings, and the porosity will cause pits and potholes in the enameled surface.

High-karat gold alloys cast into articles are softer, as they are close to their pure state, and difficult to enamel. The low-karat alloys, which are 50% pure gold combined with other alloying metals, can be successfully enameled. Articles can be made of copper or silver and, after enameling, the remaining exposed metal gold-plated. Silver castings to be decorated with enamels should be cast in fine silver instead of sterling. Sterling silver softens and becomes liquid at 1640°F. and is therefore limited to enamels that fuse at 1500°F or less. The fusing range of enamels is 1380°–1650°F. (Fine silver melts at 1762°F.) The copper alloy in sterling silver produces oxides, which discolor the metal and become visible through transparent enamels.

Soldered findings

Castings, preferably, should be one-piece items that require findings only. Findings are soft-soldered into position during the final finishing steps. Soldered joints that take higher temperatures would separate, because they have to be soldered at a lower degree of heat than is required for enameling.

Tests for fusing points

Enamels to be used on silver should be tested for their melting point on a small scrap of silver (prepared in the same manner as the casting) to ensure the maximum temperature requirement for fusing specific enamels safely.

The melting or fusing points of enamels to be used on all metals other than silver are checked by placing small dabs of enamel of different colors on a clean sheet of copper. The copper sheet is placed on a wire grid on a soldering stand, which is surrounded by a tin can with a side opening cut for observing the enamels as they are heated (see Fig. 317). A Bunsen burner (or torch flame) under the copper plate supplies the heat to melt the enamels. The enamels are observed continuously to note how much time is required for each color to melt.

The melting time for each color is noted on its container. In this way colors that are to be used in combination can be selected from those that have similar or relatively close melting points.

Enamel constituents and characteristics

Basically, enamels are glass or silica. Other components include potassium nitrate, arsenic, sodium carbonate, and metal oxides. Varying the proportions of the metal oxides creates several hundred different color hues in three types of enamels. Metal oxides, which provide the coloring, include selenium, antimony, iron, nickel, gold, silver, cobalt, copper, chromium, manganese, tin, and iridium. The combined ingredients are melted in a furnace at 2000°F. for approximately 15 hours, after which they are poured like pancake batter onto cold iron slabs. When cool, these slabs are broken into chunks and either reduced to fine powders by the manufacturer or sold as is to be ground by the individual craftsman.

Enamels are opaque, translucent, or transparent. The opaque materials allow no play of light or any visible evidence of metal through them; translucent materials permit some signs of metal and polishing details through the enamels; transparent enamels permit all areas and surfaces to be visible.

FIG. 317

Preparing the enamels

Enamels (or frit), if not purchased in powdered form, can be ground to suit in a steel, porcelain, or agate mortar with a porcelain pestle. Chunk enamel is ground to grains or fine powder from 80 to 200 mesh. The grain size of 80 mesh enamel is equal in size to table salt, whereas 200 mesh powder resembles flour. Enamels are washed with a solution of 1 to 2 drops of nitric or hydrochloric acid added to a pint of water. The solution is poured over the enamels and set aside to "decant." This first solution is poured off and fresh solution poured over the enamels. The second solution is then poured off after "decanting," or when the liquid no longer appears cloudy when stirred with a glass rod. The enamel is then washed several times in running water; the container is tilted at an angle so that the running water fills the container and siphons over the side (see Fig. 318).

Storing unused enamels

Enamels that are not used immediately after washing are stored in the same container and

FIG. 318

Use of colorless enamel on fine silver

Sterling silver should be fired first with a transparent flux that is a colorless enamel. The colors, which will appear more brightly and vividly than on copper, are added in subsequent firings.

Protecting exposed areas to prevent enameling

Exposed metal areas of the casting that are not to be enameled can be protected from fire scale by being painted with an anti-flux, yellow ochre, a boric acid, borax, and water solution, or a boric acid and alcohol solution.

Sections of the article that are not to be enameled can be masked off with tape during the enamel application and then gently stripped before the piece is placed in the kiln for firing. Protect soldered joints in a casting that is to be enameled by covering all areas of the metal with soldering investment so that only the surfaces that are to be enameled are exposed.

Applying enamel to metal surfaces

The metal surface should be sprayed with a thin coating of gum tragacanth; a thicker coating should be applied on curved, concave, or angular surfaces (see Fig. 319). The gum tragacanth, in powdered form purchased from a druggist, is mixed into a paste with wood alcohol (not isopropyl). The paste is mixed with

covered with distilled water to keep them clean and ready for use later on. Enamels to be stored for an indefinite time should be dried by being heated in an oven. They are then stored in sealed containers or tightly capped bottles.

Jewelry findings, if attached to the casting before the enameling step, must be soldered with solder having a higher melting point than any of the enamels used on the particular article. Soldered joints are visible through transparent enamels; therefore, it is best to use opaque enamels for such articles.

Metal decoration for transparent enamels

The metal surface, which is visible through transparent enamels, can be decorated with gravers, matte tools, etc., to give added luster to the thin enamel. One method is to insert a short section of wood doweling into a handpiece and dip it in oil, then in fine carborundum grit (see Fig. 255). The flat rotating end of the wooden stick polishes the metal surface in little round circles often seen on fancy watch cases.

FIG. 319

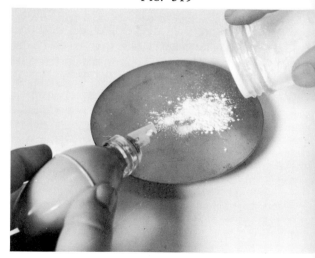

1 quart of distilled water and allowed to "de-cant" for 12 to 16 hours. The thin solution on top is used for spray (ordinary atomizers work nicely) and the thicker substance at the bottom used for the curved surfaces, etc.

Enamels are applied to the metal surface in several different ways. Damp enamel is applied with a small spatula and pushed into small areas with a scribelike pointer. It is then smoothed out to an even layer with a small diameter pin, which is bent at an angle. Old discarded dental tools, such as spatulas and curved scalers or explorers, make excellent tools for this step. Enamel is applied in a paste made by the finely ground colors mixed with pine or lavender oil thinned with a drop or two of turpentine if too thick. This tacky substance is applied to the metal surface with a small spatula (see Fig. 320). The colors can also be added dry. Sift them through fine 100 mesh screen baskets. The clean washed enamel is dried on a sheet of stainless steel either over a flame or on the open door of the heated kiln or furnace. The dried enamel is transferred to a sheet of paper (which is rolled into a funnel shape) and trans-ferred to its container. (Small sifting tops can be improvised from 100 mesh screen for trans-ferring the enamel onto the metal surface.) A small amount of enamel is put into the screen basket and is sifted onto the metal.

Different effects can be achieved by an initial firing of one color in damp or paste form and subsequently firings of contrasting colors with sifted enamels. The enamels should be pre-tested for melting or fusing points before this multiple firing process is attempted so that the enamel with the highest melting point is always applied to the surface first. Silver articles should be restricted to two firings.

As the enamel is added to the metal surface, either damp on an artist's spatula, or dry from a shaker, the metal must be continually sprayed or coated with the gum tragacanth to control the enamel and hold it in place. The coating does not affect the enamel; it is used simply as a control. The enamel should not be more than $\frac{1}{32}$" thick. This usually amounts to twice as much enamel as needed, but is necessary, as the enamel reduces to 50% of volume during fusing. Excess moisture is removed from the metal by a blotter touched to the edge. Enamels

FIG. 320

should be placed out to the very edge of the desired area, because they tend to recede during firing. The coated metal is placed on the open door of the preheated furnace to dry thoroughly. It is left there until the steam that rises from the surface is no longer visible.

Preparing the furnace

Protect the furnace from the enamel glaze by placing thin lengths of firebrick on the bot-tom and bridging them with a piece of asbestos. Small ceramic stilts or trivets, or stainless steel supports are placed on the asbestos to separate it from the coated metal (see Fig. 321). The casting is placed on the stilts with a kitchen spatula, crucible tongs, or wire tongs (see Fig. 321).

Fusing the enamel

When the enamel is fused, it becomes a shiny dull red to a cherry-red color, according to its own melting point. The fusing time can be from a few seconds to 3 or 4 minutes. During this time, the article should be observed by quick glances so as not to over-fuse the enamel. If the instrument used to place the article in the kiln is kept shiny, its reflection in the shiny surface of the enamel will show that the fusing is complete.

The article is removed from the kiln and placed on the open door. Check the fused enamel surface for incomplete areas or for those that have receded too much. These areas are

FIG. 321

scraped to a bright appearance with a sharp tool or a glass fiber brush. The surface is coated with gum tragacanth, and additional enamel is added. The stilts or steel support in the kiln should be red-hot before the enameled metal article is replaced on them for the second and subsequent firings. When the fusing is complete, with or without subsequent firings, the heat is turned off and the article is allowed to cool in the furnace or in a protected area of the workshop out of any draft. Enamels should be allowed to cool normally. They are never quenched in water or pickling baths while warm.

Surface finishing

When the enamel and metal are cooled (enamel cools much more quickly than metal), the fused surface is ground smooth with a carborundum stone under running water. The enamel is smoothed down as close as possible to the metal surface. The surface, smooth but unpolished, can be repolished by being returned to a heated furnace or buffed on a machine. If the article is to be placed back in the furnace for surface polishing by fusing, the surface

should first be washed with hydrofluoric acid. The acid attacks minute grains of the grinding stone, which may be adhering to the enameled surface even though the surface has been washed several times to remove grinding residue. If the machine-buffing method is used, a hard felt wheel charged with pumice works best, but care must be taken, because the metal is softer than the enamel and persistent buffing will remove it faster.

Removal of metal oxides

Remove visible metal oxides by bright pickling or dipping the article after the enamel has been smoothed by grinding or additional fusing. Copper is immersed in a pickling solution consisting of 1 part nitric acid to 5 parts water. Gold is immersed in the same solution and scratch-brushed after rinsing. Silver is immersed in a solution of 1 part sulfuric acid to 10 parts water. Buffing and polishing the metal follows. The enamel, after buffing, can be given a high polish on another hard felt wheel charged with tin oxide (a polishing powder used on fine gemstones).

Removal of enamel from metal surfaces

To remove excess enamel or unsatisfactorily fused enamel from the cool metal, flake out the enamel with a ball burnisher (no longer used for its original purpose). Hydrofluoric acid is used to loosen and eat away any stubborn enamel that remains. The article is then rinsed several times in running water, and the metal is recleaned, the coating and enamel added, and the fusing steps as given followed through to completion.

Frosted surfaces

To obtain a frosted translucent surface on the enamel, coat the surface with hydrofluoric acid and quickly wash away the acid by holding the article under running water. The article is held with wooden tongs obtained from a photo supply store. If desired, some areas may be left unfrosted for contrast. These areas are coated with paraffin before the acid is applied. The paraffin is removed in near-boiling water after the acid has been washed away with running water.

Appendix

COMPARATIVE WEIGHTS AND MEASURES

Avoirdupois weight

Drams	Ounces	Metric Grams	Pounds	Troy Grains	Troy Ounces
1	.0625 (1/16)	1.7719	.0039		
16	1	28.35	.0625	437.5	.91146
256	16	453.60	1	7,000	14.58
	34.20	1,000.00 (1 kilogram)	2.20		

Troy weight (used for precious metal weights)

1 dram = 1/18 Troy ounce.

Grams (Gm.)	Grains (Gr.)	Pennyweights (dwt.)	Ounces (oz.)	Pounds (lb.)	Metric Grams
15.43	1	.0416	.0020	.00017	.0648
	24	1	.05	.00416	1.5551
	480	20	1	.08333	31.10
	5,760	240	12	1 (13.17 ounce avoirdupois)	273.24

Only the Troy ounce, divided decimally, is used for a standard.

Apothecary weight

Grains	Scruples	Drachms	Ounces	Metric
1	.05	.01666	.00208	.0648
20	1	.3333	.04166	1.296
60	3	1	.125	3.888
480	24	8 (1 fluid ounce)	1	31.1035
20 fluid ounces (1 pint)				

The apothecary pound is obsolete.

Linear measure

1 inch	= 25.4 millimeters (mm.) = 2.54 centimeters (cm.)
1 foot	= 30.48 centimeters
1 micron	= .001 millimeter = .039 inch (appoximately 3/64 inch)
1 millimeter	= 1 centimeter = .393 inch
10 centimeters	= 1 decimeter = 3.937 inches
10 decimeters	= 1 meter = 39.37 inches = 1.0936 yards

Fluid measure

1 cubic centimeter (cc.)	= 16.23 miniums
1 ounce	= 29.57 cubic centimeters
1 dram	= 1/16 ounce = 1.85 cubic centimeters
16 ounces	= 1 pint
32 ounces	= 2 pints = 1 quart = 1/4 gallon
128 ounces	= 4 quarts = 1 gallon

1 cubic centimeter of water weighs 1 gram.

Carat weight

1 carat	= 200 milligrams = 1/5 gram = 3.086 grains = .007 ounce = 100 points
1/2 carat	= .50 point
1/4 carat	= .25 point
5 carats	= 1 gram
1 Troy ounce	= 155.54 carats
1 pennyweight	= 7.777 carats
1 avoirdupois ounce	= 141.76 carats

Carat weight for stones is based on the metric carat of 200 milligrams.

To convert Troy to avoirdupois ounces, multiply the Troy ounce by 1.0971.

To convert avoirdupois to Troy ounces, multiply the avoirdupois ounce by 0.9115.

To convert avoirdupois pounds to kilograms, multiply the pounds by 0.4535.

To convert kilograms to avoirdupois pounds, multiply the kilogram by 2.2046.

DETERMINING SPEEDS OF ROTATING WHEELS

Polishing speed (sfpm) should be 5000 or better for effective polishing; and for buffing the speed should produce at least 8000 sfpm. As the wheels wear down to a smaller diameter, the surface feet per minute speed also is reduced.

The motor pulley should always be the larger of the two pulleys if wheel rpm is to be increased. Pulleys of identical size, even as large as 5″ in diameter each, will still produce the basic engine speed.

A motor that rotates at 1725 rpm with a 2″ pulley attached to the shaft will produce the same motor speed if a 2″ pulley is used on the arbor shaft. With a 2″ pulley on the arbor, the speed of the wheel will increase approximately 280 rpm for each 1″ increase in motor pulley diameter. A 5″ motor pulley will turn an arbor with a 2″ pulley at 5040 rpm (using a 1725 rpm motor).

Surface feet per minute is determined by multiplying the circumference of the buffing or polishing wheel by the rpm of the motor (see motor and arbor pulley chart). Circumferences can be either measured or calculated by multiplying the diameter of the wheel by π (3.1416). For example, a motor with a pulley 2¾″ in diameter used with an arbor pulley of 2″ will produce 2550 rpm. The circumference of an 8″ muslin polishing wheel is 25⅛″ or 25.125″. This is multiplied by the 2550 rpm of the motor. The product is in inches, which must be divided by 12 to obtain the number of surface feet per minute, which in this case is 5339 sfpm.

Motor and arbor pulley combinations to obtain at least 8000 sfpm

Wheel	Motor Pulley	Arbor Pulley	Rpm	Sfpm
6″	5″	2″	4455	8665
8″	4″	2″	3850	8006
10″	3½″	2″	3100	8116
12″	4″	2¾″	2600	8168

Motor and arbor pulley combinations to obtain at least 5000 sfpm

Wheel	Motor Pulley	Arbor Pulley	Rpm	Sfpm
6″	3½″	2″	3200	5026
8″	3½″	2½″	2480	5195
10″	2½″	2¼″	1900	5000
12″	2″	2″	1600	5027

Two-speed motors will produce the higher speeds necessary without any pulley change. The rpm is doubled if the motor runs at 3400 rpm.

DETERMINING BEZEL METAL LENGTHS

Bezel lengths for round or oval cabochon gemstones are cut to match the circumference of the stone. To find the circumference of a round stone, multiply the diameter of the stone by π (3.1416) to obtain the length of the bezel wire. To determine oval gemstones' circumferences, add the longest diameter and the narrowest diameter of the stone. The sum of the two dimensions is divided and half of this amount is multiplied by π (3.1416) to get the circumference of the stone. The decimal inches are converted to fractional measurements for easy marking on the bezel material (see Fig. 322).

25.125 × 2550 = 64,068.750
64,068.750 ÷ 12 = 5339.06 sfpm
4″ diameter wheel at 1725 rpm produces only 1805 sfpm.
6″ diameter wheel at 1725 rpm produces only 2710 sfpm.
8″ diameter wheel at 1725 rpm produces only 3612 sfpm.
10″ diameter wheel at 1725 rpm produces only 4516 sfpm.
12″ diameter wheel at 1725 rpm produces only 5420 sfpm.

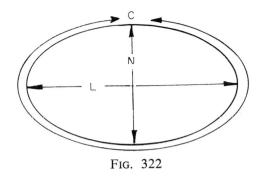

FIG. 322

Example: A round circle with a 1″ diameter x 3.1416=3.1416 (3⁹⁄₆₄″) circumference. An oval or elliptical shape with a long dimension of 1″ and a narrow dimension of ½″ (1″ + ½″) = 1½″ divided in half = ¾″ diameter. The diameter when multiplied by π (3.1416) = 2-²³⁄₆₄″ circumference.

Measure square, rectangular, and free-form shapes along the sides to determine the outside measurement for bezel matching.

Diameters of circles and corresponding circumferences

Diameter	Circumference
¹⁄₁₆″	¹³⁄₆₄″
⅛″	²⁵⁄₆₄″
³⁄₁₆″	¹⁹⁄₃₂″
¼″	1²⁵⁄₃₂″
⁵⁄₁₆″	1⁶³⁄₆₄″
⅜″	1¹¹⁄₆₄″
⁷⁄₁₆″	1⅜″
½″	1³⁷⁄₆₄″
⁹⁄₁₆″	1⁴⁹⁄₆₄″
⅝″	1³¹⁄₃₂″
¹¹⁄₁₆″	2⁵⁄₃₂″
¾″	2²³⁄₆₄″
¹³⁄₁₆″	2³⁵⁄₆₄″
⅞″	2¾″
¹⁵⁄₁₆″	2¹⁵⁄₁₆″
1″	3⁹⁄₆₄″
1⅛″	3½″
1¼″	3⅞″
1⅜″	4⁵⁄₁₆″
1½″	4¹¹⁄₁₆″
1⅝″	5¹⁄₁₆″
1¾″	5⁷⁄₁₆″
1⅞″	5⅞″
2″	6¼″
2⅛″	6⅝″
2¼″	7″
2⅜″	7⁷⁄₁₆″
2½″	7¹³⁄₁₆″
2⅝″	8³⁄₁₆″
2¾″	8⅝″
2⅞″	9″
3″	9⅜″

Decimal equivalents of fractions of an inch

¹⁄₆₄	.0156	³³⁄₆₄	.5156
¹⁄₃₂	.0313	¹⁷⁄₃₂	.5312
³⁄₆₄	.0469	³⁵⁄₆₄	.5469
¹⁄₁₆	.0625	⁹⁄₁₆	.5625
⁵⁄₆₄	.0781	³⁷⁄₆₄	.5781
³⁄₃₂	.0937	¹⁹⁄₃₂	.5937
⁷⁄₆₄	.1093	³⁹⁄₆₄	.6094
⅛	.1250	⅝	.6250
⁹⁄₆₄	.1406	⁴¹⁄₆₄	.6406
⁵⁄₃₂	.1562	²¹⁄₃₂	.6562
¹¹⁄₆₄	.1719	⁴³⁄₆₄	.6719
³⁄₁₆	.1875	¹¹⁄₁₆	.6875
¹³⁄₆₄	.2031	⁴⁵⁄₆₄	.7031
⁷⁄₃₂	.2187	²³⁄₃₂	.7187
¹⁵⁄₆₄	.2344	⁴⁷⁄₆₄	.7344
¼	.2500	¾	.7500
¹⁷⁄₆₄	.2656	⁴⁹⁄₆₄	.7656
⁹⁄₃₂	.2812	²⁵⁄₃₂	.7812
¹⁹⁄₆₄	.2968	⁵¹⁄₆₄	.7969
⁵⁄₁₆	.3125	¹³⁄₁₆	.8125
²¹⁄₆₄	.3281	⁵³⁄₆₄	.8281
¹¹⁄₃₂	.3437	²⁷⁄₃₂	.8437
²³⁄₆₄	.3594	⁵⁵⁄₆₄	.8594
⅜	.3750	⅞	.8750
²⁵⁄₆₄	.3906	⁵⁷⁄₆₄	.8906
¹³⁄₃₂	.4062	²⁹⁄₃₂	.9062
²⁷⁄₆₄	.4219	⁵⁹⁄₆₄	.9219
⁷⁄₁₆	.4375	¹⁵⁄₁₆	.9375
²⁹⁄₆₄	.4531	⁶¹⁄₆₄	.9531
¹⁵⁄₃₂	.4687	³¹⁄₃₂	.9687
³¹⁄₆₄	.4843	⁶³⁄₆₄	.9844
½	.5000	1	1.0000

To determine the approximate fractional dimensions of gemstones, convert the millimeters to decimal equivalents and then to fractions. There are no millimeter dimensions (in round figures) that match simple fractional or decimal dimensions. For comparison, a few fractional, decimal, and millimeter dimensions are given here:

Fraction	Decimal	Millimeters
¹⁄₁₆	0.0625	1.5875
⅛	0.1250	3.1850
³⁄₁₆	0.1875	4.7624
¼	0.2500	6.3499
⁵⁄₁₆	0.3125	7.9374
⅜	0.3750	9.5249
⁷⁄₁₆	0.4375	11.1124
½	0.5000	12.6999

Faceted stones are cut to millimeter dimensions. Standard brilliants are cut as small as 1 mm. up to 12 mm. Large brilliants and other faceted shapes are also available, but the stone should be either cut or purchased before the casting is made. The angle of the pavillion or bottom portion of standard faceted stones varies from 39° to 45°, and the depth of this portion is approximately two thirds of the complete depth of the stone.

Fractional inch measurements with millimeter equivalents

Inch	Millimeters	Inch	Millimeters
1	25.4	$\frac{1}{4}$	6.3499
$\frac{7}{8}$	22.225	$\frac{1}{8}$	3.185
$\frac{3}{4}$	19.050	$\frac{1}{16}$	1.587
$\frac{5}{8}$	15.875	$\frac{3}{64}$	1.190
$\frac{1}{2}$	12.699	$\frac{1}{32}$	.793
$\frac{3}{8}$	9.524	$\frac{1}{64}$	.396

RING SIZES

Ring sizes match calibrations on the ring mandrel. The size is the inner diameter of the ring shank. Sizes are listed according to specific numbers, and the diameter increases $\frac{32}{1000}''$ (0.032″) for each full ring size.

Ring Size	Diameter Inches	Ring Size	Diameter Inches
0	0.458	6½	.666
¼	.466	7	.682
½	.474	7½	.698
¾	.482	8	.714
1	.490	8½	.730
1½	.506	9	.746
2	.522	9½	.762
2½	.538	10	.778
3	.554	10½	.794
3½	.570	11	.810
4	.586	11½	.826
4½	.602	12	.842
5	.618	12½	.858
5½	.634	13	.874
6	.650	13½	.890

GEMSTONE SIZES

Gemstones purchased commercially are cut to specific sizes calculated in millimeters. 1 mm. = 0.0394″ (1″ = 25.3998 mm.) Oval stones are cut to fit commercial mountings in the following popular sizes:

Millimeters	Millimeters	Millimeters
2 × 3	10 × 14	15 × 25
3 × 4	10 × 18	15 × 30

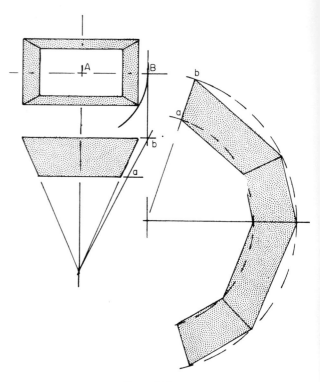

Fig. 323

4 × 5	10 × 20	15 × 32
5 × 7	10 × 22	18 × 25
5 × 20	10 × 24	18 × 35
6 × 8	10 × 28	18 × 40
6 × 20	12 × 14	19 × 25
7 × 9	12 × 16	20 × 30
8 × 10	12 × 18	22 × 34
8 × 14	12 × 20	24 × 30
8 × 16	12 × 26	25 × 38
8 × 22	13 × 18	25 × 50
8 × 28	13 × 24	27 × 38
9 × 11	13 × 35	30 × 40
9 × 14	14 × 16	30 × 45
9 × 16	14 × 20	32 × 60
9 × 18	14 × 24	35 × 50
10 × 12	15 × 20	50 × 80

Rectangular or cushion-shaped gemstones are available commercially in the following common sizes:

Millimeters	Millimeters	Millimeters
6 × 8	10 × 12	12 × 16
8 × 12	10 × 14	13 × 18
8 × 13	11 × 15	14 × 16
8 × 16	12 × 14	

When lapidary equipment is available, the

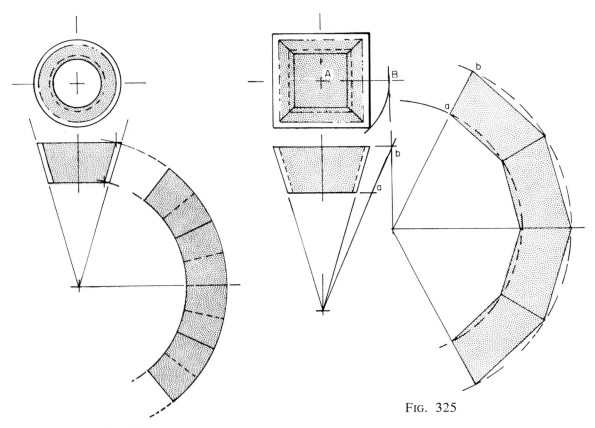

FIG. 324

FIG. 325

stones can be cut to any dimension called for in the design.

CONSTRUCTION OF FRUSTRUM OF A PYRAMID AND TAPERED CONE FOR BEZEL PATTERNS

The construction of a frustrum of a pyramid (used for a square tapered bezel), a rectangular tapered bezel, and a tapered cone is shown in the illustrations (see Figs. 323, 324, and 325).

The distances between AB and ab as indicated on the side view of each example are correct for the width of the bezel material. (Measuring the bezel height from the side view never gives the correct width.)

BRIGHT-DIP SOLUTIONS

Always use bright-dips cold and with plenty of ventilation. They should not be heated at any time.

hydrofluoric acid	1 pint
water	3 pints
hydrofluoric acid	1 pint
nitric acid	½ pint
water	5 pints

sulfuric acid	1 pint
nitric acid or	1 pint
sulfuric acid	2 pints
nitric acid	1 pint
hydrofluoric acid	1 quart
nitric acid	1½ pints
table salt	2 tablespoons

sulfuric acid 70 ounces
nitric acid 12 ounces
hydrochloric acid ½ ounce
water to make one gallon of solution

Hydrofluoric acid dipping solution which has been used considerably can be re-activated by the addition of 3 ounces of sulfuric acid to every gallon of old solution.

ADDITIONAL METAL-COLORING SOLUTIONS

To color bronze:

Antique:	ammonium chloride	½ ounce
	copper sulfate	3 ounces
	water	1 quart

Warm the metal and apply with a brush.

Rinse in cold running water, then hot water, and dry thoroughly.

Yellow-green: ammonium chloride   15 ounces
                copper acetate   8 ounces
                water   1 quart

Heat the solution to 212°F. and apply to the casting with a brush.

To color copper:

Deep blue-black: ammonium sulfate   2 ounces
                 water   1 quart

Apply cold with a brush to the casting.

Apple green: ammonia   4 fluid
                                   ounces
                sodium chloride   5 ounces
                ammonium chloride 5 ounces
                acetic acid   1 quart

Dab the casting surface until dry.

Brown: barium sulfide   1 ounce
                potassium sulfide ¼ ounce
                ammonia   2 ounces
                water   3–5 quarts
                    or
hydrosulfide of potash 10 grams   water   1 pint

Blue patina: ammonium chloride   4 parts
                ammonium carbonate 12 parts
                water   100 parts

Dissolve and mix constituents and paint onto the casting.

To color soft solder gold:

          water   3 ounces
          copper sulfate 2 teaspoons
          zinc sulfate   1 teaspoon

After 24 hours add 1 drop of sulfuric acid. Solution is brushed on solder and rubbed with a piece of zinc. Article is then flushed with water, dried, and lacquered.

TESTING GOLD FOR KARAT CONTENT

A set of needles can be purchased for testing gold for karat content or for testing gold-seeming metals to determine any gold content. The assorted needles are made of various karats of gold. Only gold above 10 karat can be tested with the needles.

The metal to be identified is rubbed on the testing stone (supplied with the kit) to transfer a small amount of the metal to the stone. A needle close to the supposed karat is also rubbed on the testing stone next to the first mark. Aqua regia (any combination of hydrochloric acid and nitric acid) is applied to the two scratch marks. If the reaction is simultaneous on the two scratch marks, the karats match and the karat content has been quickly ascertained. If the needle scratch reacts first, a new scratch must be made with a needle of a higher karat, and the solution applied to the mark. This procedure is continued until simultaneous reaction is arrived at.

Metals of 10 karats or less may also be tested by a notch filed in the metal deep enough to penetrate any plating and applying nitric acid to the file mark. If the gold is only a plating over a base metal, the reaction will be green color. If the gold is over silver, the reaction will be pink frothy cream color. On 10-karat-gold articles there is no reaction at all.

TESTING METAL TO DETERMINE PRESENCE OF SILVER

A notch is filed in the metal and nitric acid is applied to the notch with a glass rod. A plated base metal will turn to a green color, coin silver to a black foam, nickel silver to a green foam, silver to a cloudy cream color.

METALS AND THEIR ALLOY CONTENTS

Metals are made up of thousands of microscopic single crystals combined to make a mass. Each of these tiny crystals (mentioned previously in the casting and alloying references) is called a grain. The grains are visible if an etched surface of a highly polished metal is observed under a microscope. The single crystals grow in various sizes individually, but when they touch another crystal the growth stops. These single crystals cluster and remain as units (rather than homogenizing into a larger crystal), which indicates a definite grain structure.

There are ninety-six elements or elementary metals and metaloids. Elementary metals include such familiar names as gold, silver, copper, etc.; metaloids are elements that either in appearance or in general properties resemble metal, such as arsenic, bismuth, etc.

Alloys are substances composed of two or more metals intimately united, usually by being melted into a molten mass. Alloys composed of metal and metaloids in various compounds are numerous, but only a few are used for casting. Each alloy has individual characteristics—properties, color, hardness, ductility—and requires different heat treatment methods. Generally alloys are harder than their individual constituents, and often they are heavier, more dense, or both combined.

Alloys that are lighter than either of their constituents are gold with silver, copper, or nickel; silver with copper or nickel; tin with antimony or lead.

Alloys that are harder than any of their constituents individually are gold with antimony, tin, or zinc; silver with antimony, bismuth, or zinc; copper with bismuth or zinc.

The melting range varies in some alloys. One constituent may be in a molten stage at one temperature while others are still solid, so that an upper and lower melting range is usually necessary. For this reason metals are usually heated from one hundred to two hundred degrees hotter than the temperature noted when the metal appears molten, so that all constituents, including those not visible, will be molten. Graphite rods are used for stirring metals during the alloying steps.

Melting points of various metals

pewter	425°–440°F.	18 kt. red gold	1655°F.
tin	450°F.	18 kt. green gold	1810°F.
cadmium	610°F.	18 kt. yellow gold	1700°F.
lead	621°F.	18 kt. white gold	1730°F.
zinc	787°F.	14 kt. red gold	1715°F.
aluminum	1218°F.	14 kt. green gold	1765°F.
brass	930°F.	14 kt. yellow gold	1615°F.
copper	2000°F.	14 kt. white gold	1825°F.
bronze	1825°F.	10 kt. red gold	1760°F.
coin silver	1615°F.	10 kt. green gold	1580°F.
sterling silver	1640°F.	10 kt. yellow gold	1665°F.
fine silver	1760°F.	10 kt. white gold	1975°F.
platinum	3223°F.	nickel	2651°F.
24 kt. gold	1945°F.	palladium	2820°F.

Boiling points of several metals

24 kt. gold	4914°F.	nickel	5251°F.
platinum	8186°F.	tin	4182°F.
silver	3542°F.	zinc	5270°F.
copper	4237°F.	palladium	3992°F.

Color hues of metals at various degrees of temperature

barely visible	900°F.	cherry-red	1660°F.
visible	977°F.	orange	2100°F.
dull red	1175°F.	white	2210°F.
dark red	1280°F.	white-bright	2740°F.
bright red	1545°F.		

Melting points of some commonly alloyed metals

Constituents				Melting Point
copper	70%	+ aluminum	30%	1390°F.
copper	80%	+ zinc	20%	1822°F.

copper	70%	+	tin	30%	1390°F.
silver	90%	+	copper	10%	1615°F.
silver	92½%	+	copper	7½%	1640°F.
silver	70%	+	copper	30%	1450°F.
silver	66⅔%	+	platinum	33⅓%	2246°F.
silver	50%	+	gold	50%	1910°F.
silver	90%	+	gold	10%	1795°F.
silver	72%	+	copper	28%	1600°F.
gold	90%	+	copper	10%	1665°F.
gold	90%	+	platinum	10%	2030°F.
gold	80%	+	silver	20%	1920°F.
gold	80%	+	copper	20%	1635°F.

Common low-fusing (any metal that melts under 350°F.) alloys

	Constituents							Melting Point
Mellotte's metal:	bismuth	50%	+	tin	31%	+	lead	19%	211°F.
Newton metal:	bismuth	50%	+	lead	32%	+	tin	18%	208°F.
onion metal:	bismuth	50%	+	lead	30%	+	tin	20%	197°F.
rose metal:	bismuth	50%	+	lead	26%	+	tin	24%	200°F.

Alloys of various metals suggested for casting

red gold 18 kt.	fine gold	75%	+	copper	25%					
green gold 18 kt.	fine gold	75%	+	silver	25%					
Argentine (used in good-quality toys)	tin	85½%	+	antimony	14½%					
Bath brass (used for hotel sugar and creamers, usually heavily silver-plated)	copper	55%	+	zinc	45%					
beryllium gold (harder and tougher than 24 kt. gold)	fine gold	98%	+	beryllium	1%	+	nickel	1%		
beryllium copper	copper	97½%	+	beryllium	2¼%	+	nickel	¼%		
beryllium silver (harder than fine silver—does not tarnish)	silver	99%	+	beryllium	1%					
brass	copper	80%	+	zinc	18%	+	lead	2%		
statuary bronze	copper	88%	+	tin	10%	+	silver	13%		
Chinese silver (called nickel-silver)	copper	65%	+	tin	20%	+	silver	2%	+ nickel	13%
Colorado silver (also called nickel-silver)	copper	57%	+	nickel	25%	+	silver	18%		
pewter U.S.	tin	94%	+	copper	4½%	+	silver	1½%		
pewter English	tin	80%	+	lead	20%					
pewter French	tin	82%	+	lead	18%					
Fahlun's diamond metal (when cast looks like gemstones)	tin	60%	+	lead	40%					
jeweler's brass	copper	86%	+	zinc	12%	+	tin	2%		
pseudo-platinum	copper	44%	+	zinc	57%	+	tin	1%		
pseudo-silver	aluminum	83%	+	tin	10%	+	copper	6½%	+ phosphorous	½%
platino	gold	89%	+	platinum	11%					
Roman brass	copper	60%	+	zinc	39%	+	tin	1%		
Roman bronze	copper	60%	+	zinc	33%	+	lead	6%	+ tin 1%	

CONSTITUENTS OF VARIOUS GOLD ALLOYS

Gold quality is denoted by karat amounts. Pure gold is 24 karats, 18 kt. gold is 18 parts pure gold and 6 parts alloy metal, 14 kt. is 14 parts pure gold and 10 parts other metals.

Gold, silver, and platinum are weighed using Troy measurements. With other metals the more common avoirdupois system is used for determining weight.

White gold in any of the alloys is mostly gold with nickel, copper, and zinc in various percentages. Yellow gold contains the same metals in different percentages. Green gold contains the same metals, but the silver percentage is greater than the copper content in the basic yellow gold alloy. Red gold contains the same metals, but with the copper percentage greater than the silver content of yellow gold.

Fine gold must be 99.9% pure gold.
Fine silver must be 99.9% pure silver.
Fine soft solder must be 64% tin and 36% lead.
18 kt. gold must have 75% fine gold.
16 kt. gold must have 67% fine gold.
14 kt. gold must have 58½% fine gold.
12 kt. gold must have 50% fine gold.
10 kt. gold must have 41.7% fine gold (not usually labeled as karat gold).

22 kt.	fine gold 92%	+ copper	4%	+ 4% silver	
18 kt. red	fine gold 75%	+ copper	25%		
18 kt. green	fine gold 75%	+ silver	25%		
18 kt. yellow	fine gold 75%	+ copper	15½%	+ silver 9½%	
18 kt. white	fine gold 75%	+ nickel	10%	+ palladium 10%	+ zinc 5%
18 kt. brown	fine gold 75%	+ palladium	18¾%	+ silver 6¼%	
18 kt. purple	fine gold 75%	+ aluminum	23%	+ thorium 1½%	+ tin ½%
14 kt.	fine gold 58½%	+ other metals 41½% (29% copper + 12½% silver)			

Other metals used in alloying gold for various colors and percentages include nickel, white iron, cadmium, and cobalt. In lower-carat alloys, zinc and cadmium in amounts less than 1% and ½% respectively of the volumes are added to lower the melting point, but only when the balance of the metal is at the molten stage. *They are not added in the crucible with the other metals and brought up to white heat together.*

VARYING THE KARAT CONTENT OF GOLD ALLOYS

In gold alloys karats indicate the quality of the alloy. Remelted scrap gold must have new metal to change the quality (reducing or increasing the karat designation) to a different karat alloy. Calculation for changing the alloy to different karat designations is important should a certain karat gold be needed and not immediately available. All metals must be free of impurities before being combined or alloyed with pure gold.

In order to make correct calculations, it is necessary to understand the weights used. The numeral 20 is used because 1 ounce of gold (Troy weight) is divided into 20 pennyweights (dwts.).

To increase 1 ounce of 14 kt. gold to 18 kt., the following method of calibrating the additional pure gold required to raise the quality of the alloy to the higher karat is used:

20 dwt. × 18 kt. = 360
20 dwt. × 14 kt. = 280
360 − 280 = 80
80 ÷ 6 = 13.33 dwt., or 13 dwt., 7 grains of pure gold required

The divisor 6 (24 kt.-18 kt.) is determined by subtracting the karat gold desired from 24 kt. The dwt. requirement 13.33 (13⅓ dwt.) is reduced to grains by determining what percentage the .33 dwt. is of 20 dwt.

To increase 12 kt. gold (1 ounce) to 14 kt. gold, use the following example:

20 dwt. × 14 = 280
20 dwt. × 12 = 240
280 − 240 = 60
24 kt. − 14 kt. = 10
60 ÷ 10 = 6 dwt. pure gold to raise the 12 kt. gold to 14 kt. quality

The divisor, used when reducing high-karat gold alloys to those of lesser gold content, is the karat number of the karat gold that is to be the end product of the alloying step.

To lower 1 ounce Troy 24 kt. to 18 kt. quality, use the following example:

20 dwt. × 24 = 480
20 dwt. × 18 = 360
480 − 360 = 120
120 ÷ 18 = 6.6 dwt. of other metal(s) needed to reduce the 24 kt. gold to 18 kt. quality. The 6.66 dwt. is reduced to a common measurement of 6.66 dwt. = 6 dwt., 14 grains.

To lower 24 kt. to 14 kt.:

20 dwt. × 18 kt. = 360
20 dwt. × 14 kt. = 280
360 − 280 = 80
80 ÷ 14 = 5.71 dwt. or 5 dwt., 14 grains

Metals vary in weight so that the addition of alloying metals to pure gold to lower the karat will result in a different weight for each alloy; therefore, gold alloyed with increasing amounts of copper will result in less weight than higher karat gold with a smaller percentage of copper in the alloy. Combining gold with percentages of platinum, palladium, or iridium will result in a heavier metal alloy.

22 kt. gold = 22 parts pure gold + 2 parts of other metals (1 part silver, 1 part copper, both by weight)

18 kt. gold = 18 parts pure gold, 3 parts copper, 3 parts silver, both by weight

14 kt. gold = 14 parts pure gold, 7 parts copper, 3 parts silver, both by weight

12 kt. gold = 12 parts pure gold, 6 parts copper, 6 parts silver, both by weight

10 kt. gold = less than half being pure gold, it is not called 10 kt. gold

CONSTITUENTS OF SILVER

Silver quality is reckoned in the percentage of fine (pure silver) combined with other metals. The standard indication of Sterling silver usually listed is 92½% (.925) or 925 parts of fine silver per thousand. Coin silver with 90% silver is usually called .900 silver.

CONSTITUENTS OF PLATINUM

Platinum contains a total of six elements which are isolated in this natural metal. These are iridium, osmium, rhodium, palladium, and ruthenium. Platinum is usually alloyed with 3 parts of copper to make it more workable.

PICKLING SOLUTIONS FOR PRECIOUS METALS

Platinum is pickled in a solution of 9 parts hydrochloric acid to 2 parts nitric acid (aqua regia). All other casting metals, such as copper, brass, bronze, silver, gold, and nickel-silver are pickled in a solution of sulfuric acid and water, usually 6 to 10 parts of water to 1 part acid, according to the strength of the solution desired. Rhodium is pickled in hot sulfuric acid. Gold and platinum can be completely dissolved in aqua regia (any mixture of nitric and hydrochloric acids) and silver, palladium, copper, brass, and bronze are soluble in nitric acid.

Solder alloy constituents

Solder	Flux	Solder Melting Point	Metal Melting Point	Constituents
aluminum:	Stearin or stainless steel	650°F.	1218°F.	tin 94%, zinc 2%, aluminum 4%
platable soft	commercial	484°F.		tin 94%, cadmium 6%
fine soft	commercial	358°F.		tin 64%, lead 36%
soft	commercial	340°F.	(used with pewter)	tin 60%, lead 40%
soft	commercial	450°F.		tin 50%, lead 50%
soft	commercial	460°F.		tin 40%, lead 60%
silver: (easy-flow)	borax and boric acid	1325°F.	fine 1760°F. sterling 1640°F.	silver 65%, copper 20%, zinc 15%
medium	boric acid	1390°F.		silver 70%, copper 20%, zinc 10%
hard no. 1	boric acid	1425°F.		silver 80, copper 16%, zinc 4%
hard	boric acid	1460°F.		silver 50%, copper 34%, zinc 16%
gold: 10 kt. yellow	boric acid	1340°F.	1450°F.	gold 41%, silver 37%, copper 21.7%, zinc 0.3%
14 kt. yellow	boric acid	1441°F.	1563°F.	gold 50%, silver 33%, copper 17%
18 kt.	boric acid	1517°F.	1650°F.	gold 75%, silver 15%, copper 10%
22 kt.	boric acid	1610°F.	1832°F.	gold 92%, silver 4.9%, copper 3.1%

Condensed step chart of investment procedures (manufacturers' recommendations)

Investment: Description of Step:	Kerr Cristobalite Low-burn-out technique cristobalite only	Ransom and Randolph Gray Double-mix technique for intricate jewelry and flower reproductions	Single-mix technique for simple castings	Whip-Mix Beauty-Cast Single-mix technique for simple castings
Preparation of Ring or Flask:	Line with single thickness of asbestos, lapped and ⅛″ short on both ends—moisten thoroughly	Requires a liner	Line with wet asbestos loosely placed in ring, lapped ½ of ring	Line with single thickness asbestos ⅛″ short at both ends to provide an investment seal, then wet asbestos
Water Temperature:	Room	Room	Room	Room
Mixing Ratio Water to Powder:	15–17 cc. water to 40 grams powder—when mixing add investment to water	For first mix, 7 cc. water to 25 grams investment *	14 cc. water to 50 grams investment	15 cc. water to 50 grams investment—no change when using vacuum equipment
Mixing Technique:	Hand spatulate—vibrate bowl 30 seconds then mechanical mixer for 30 seconds	Spatulate for 1 minute with a mechanical mixer	Spatulate for 1 minute with a mechanical mixer	Add powder to water, hand spatulate to wet, then 50 turns with mechanical mixer—if vacuum equipment is used follow manufacturer's own instructions
Investing Pattern:	Paint carefully with camel's hair brush—this painting may be blown off and pattern then repainted —do not dust with dry investment	Paint pattern, then dust with dry investment and vibrate gently till powder is absorbed—repeat 3–4 times—allow to set for 5–10 minutes	Paint carefully with fine brush then vibrate gently to eliminate any trapped air	Paint with brush and vibrate with serrated instrument on the crucible former
Filling Ring or Flask:	Fill ring with same mix and insert painted pattern with a slight wavy motion	Fill ring or flask with second mix of 16 cc. water to 50 grams investment—immerse painted pattern nomentarily in water and insert in ring or flask	Pour investment into ring and carefully vibrate painted pattern into ring or flask	Place ring around painted pattern and fill slowly, using a spatula, vibrate to place
Setting Time:	Allow to set 30 minutes or longer	Allow to set for 10–15 minutes	Allow to set for 10–15 minutes	Allow to set for at least 30 minutes under water **

(*Continued*)

* This w/p ratio will produce a very thick mix which contradicts normal painting procedures specifying a creamy mix.
** No setting time prior to immersion in water is indicated by the manufacturer. Allow at least 10 minutes' setting time as a precaution.

Wax Elimination and Burn-out:	Place flask or ring in furnace preheated to 850°–900°F., with sprue hole down —cast in approximately 1 hour and after the discolored investment has regained a white color	Heat invested ring until sprue hole shows dull red color (1200°–1300°F.) —cast immediately	Heat invested ring until sprue hole shows a dull red color (1200°–1300° F.)—cast immediately	Place ring or flask in furnace and bring to 900°F. for at least 40 minutes—cast any time thereafter —if a good grade of inlay or casting wax is used, it is not necessary to eliminate wax with boiling water or any other method before burn-out

CONVERTING CENTIGRADE TO FAHRENHEIT

To convert Centigrate temperatures to Fahrenheit temperatures, the Centigrade figure is multiplied by 9, the product is divided by 5, and 32 is added to the quotient. The result is degrees Fahrenheit.

Example:
$50°C. \times 9 = 450 \div 5 = 90 + 32 = 122°F.$

CONVERTING FAHRENHEIT TO CENTIGRADE

To convert Fahrenheit temperatures to Centigrade temperatures, subtract 32 from the Fahrenheit number, multiply the remainer by 5, and divide the product by 9. The quotient is degrees Centigrade.

Example:
$212°F. - 32 = 180 \times 5 = 900 \div 9 = 100°C.$

GEMSTONE HARDNESS CHART

for determining stones of sufficient hardness to be invested and cast in the metal mold

The Mohs scale of hardness is the standard for determining the hardness of gem material:

1	talc	6	feldspar
2	rock salt or gypsum	7	quartz
3	calcite	8	topaz
4	fluorite	9	corundum
5	apatite	10	diamond

Some of the more common gemstones that can be used for inclusion in the mold during the casting steps. Sample tests should always be made:

8	emerald	9	corundum
	spinel		sapphire
	topaz		titanium
8½	chrysoberyl	10	diamond

Although the stone should have a hardness of at least 8 on the Mohs scale, some gemstones with hardnesses between 6-7½ may stand up without damage during casting, such as:

6	zircon (low type), rutile, turquoise, feldspar, sodalite, lapis lazuli, prehnite, zoisite (thulite)
6½	nephrite, pyrite, epidote, idocrase, andradite garnet, olivine, hematite, benitoite, amazonite, marcasite
7	agate, amethyst, quartz, spodumene, chalcedony, jadeite, tourmaline, bloodstone
7¼	zircon (high type), pyrope and spessartite garnet
7	andalusite, almandine garnet, beryl, staurolite

SPECIFIC GRAVITY OF METALS

for determining metal requirements for castings

Specific gravity of substances is normally calculated by determining how much heavier a substance is when it replaces its volume in water. A metal with a specific gravity of 10½ indicates that it is 10½ times heavier than the same volume of water.

Because it is impossible for the individual craftsman to determine these numbers accurately, some of the numbers for commonly used casting metals are given.

The gram weight of the model with sprues and vents that is to be used for the casting is multiplied by the s.g. (specific gravity) number on the particular metal to be used for the casting. The product determined by multiplication is the weight of the metal that will be required to replace the original model with metal.

silver:	fine	10.50
	sterling	10.46

gold:	24 kt.	19.36
	22 kt.	17.7
	18 kt.	15.5
	14 kt.	13.4
	10 kt.	11.57
	9 kt.	11.3
copper		8.9
brass		8.5
bronze		9.0
aluminum		2.7
platinum		21.43
palladium		12.16

rhodium	12.44
iridium	22.41
nickel	8.85
tin	7.30
lead	11.3
zinc	7.14
bismuth	
low-fusing alloys for rubber mold molds	2.83–11.3

Bibliography

ABBEY, STATON. *The Goldsmith's and Silversmith's Manual*, 1952.

AMERICAN DENTAL ASSOCIATION. *Guide to Dental Materials*, 1962–63.

AUERBACH, ARNOLD. *Modelled Sculpture and Plaster Casting*, 1961.

BAERWALD, MARCUS, and MAHONEY, TOM. *The Story of Jewelry*, 1960.

BATES, KENNETH F. *Enameling*, 1951.

BAXTER, WILLIAM T. *Jewelry, Gem Cutting and Metalcraft*, 1950.

BORSIG, TED. *Designs in Nature*, 1962.

BOVIN, MURRAY. *Jewelry Making*, 1952 and 1964.

BOWMAN, JOHN J. *The Jewelry Engraver's Manual*, 1954.

BOWMAN, JOHN J., and HARDY, R. ALLEN. *Jewelry Repair Manual*, 1956.

CAL-RESIN COMPANY. *Plasti-flex Technical Manual*, 1963.

Craft Horizon Magazine, 1959–63.

DOUGLAS AND SURGESS COMPANY *Plastic Technical Bulletins*, 1949.

DOW CORNING CORPORATION. *Silicone, RTV and Silastic Technical Bulletins and Books*, 1963–64.

DOWNER, MARION. *The Story of Design*, 1963.

ELISCU, FRANK. *Sculpture Techniques in Clay, Wax, Slate*, 1959.

EMERSON, A. R. *Handmade Jewelry*, 1953.

FRANKE, LOIS. *Handwrought Jewelry*, 1962.

GENERAL ELECTRIC COMPANY. *Silicones, Technical Data Bulletins*, 1960–65.

GRISWOLD, LESTER. *Handicraft* (8th edition), 1948.

HARDY, R. ALLEN, and BOWMAN, JOHN J. *Jewelry Repair Manual*, 1956.

HATTON, RICHARD G. *Design*, 1925.

HEY, MAY H. *Chemical Index of Minerals*, 1962 and 1963.

HORNUNG, CLARENCE. *Designs and Devices*, 1946.

HYSOL CORPORATION. *RTV Technical Data Sheets*, 1962–65.

JELENKO, J. F.: *Crown and Bridge Construction*, 1956.
        Partial Dentures, 1953.

KERR COMPANY. *Lost Wax, The New Modern Craft*, 1948.

LINICK, LESLIE. *Jeweler's Workshop Practices*, 1948.

LYNCH, JOHN. *Metal Sculpture*, 1957.

MAHONEY, TOM, and BAERWALD, MARCUS. *The Story of Jewelry*, 1960.

MARTIN, CHARLES J. *Making Modern Jewelry*, 1960.

MARYON, HERBERT. *Metalwork and Enameling* (4th edition), 1959.

MILLER, JOHN G. *Metal Art Crafts*, 1948.

NEUMANN, ROBERT VON. *The Design and Creation of Jewelry*, 1961.

NEWMAN, THELMA R. *Plastics as an Art Form*, 1964.

NEY, J. M. COMPANY. *Bridge and Inlay Book,* 1958.

    Planned Partials, 1959.

OSBRUN, BURL N., and WILBER, GORDON O. *Pewter, Spun, Wrought, Cast,* 1938.

OSTIER, MARIANNE. *Jewels and the Woman,* 1962.

PARLANTI, E. J. *Casting a Torso in Bronze,* 1953.

PERCY, HUGH MONTAGU. *New Materials in Sculpture,* 1962.

PERMA-FLEX MOLD COMPANY. Technical Bulletins, 1960–63.

PFAFFENBARGER, GEORGE, and SOUDER, WILLIAM. *Physical Properties of Dental Materials,* 1942.

RANSOM AND RANDOLPH COMPANY. Technical Bulletins, 1963.

REEVES, RUTH. *Cire Perdue Casting in India,* 1962.

ROTTGER, ERNEST. *Creative Paper Design,* 1961.

ROYDHOUSE, R. D. *Materials in Dentistry,* 1962.

SAUNDERS, ALEXANDER COMPANY. *Fine Jewelry, Casting Equipment and Supplies,* 1961.

SCHOENFELT, JOSEPH F. *Designing and Making Handwrought Jewelry,* 1960.

SINKANKAS, JOHN. *Gem Cutting,* 1955.

SKINNER, DR. EUGENE. *The Science of Dental Materials,* 1960.

SOUDER, WILLIAM, and PFAFFENBARGER, GEORGE. *Physical Properties of Dental Materials,* 1942.

SOUTHWEST SMELTING AND REFINING. *Plating for Profit and Ease,* 1964.

STEEL, GERALD L. *Fiberglass Projects and Practices,* 1962.

STORY, MICKEY. *Centrifugal Casting as a Jewelry Process,* 1963.

THOMAS, RICHARD. *Metalsmithing,* 1960.

U.S. NAVY. *Dental Technician's Handbook,* 1962.

WAGER, VICTOR H. *Plastic Casting for the Student Sculptor,* 1952.

WEINER, LOUIS. *Handmade Jewelry* (2nd edition), 1960.

WILBER, GORDON D., and OSBRUN, BURL N. *Pewter, Spun, Wrought, Cast,* 1938.

WINEBRENNER, KENNETH. *Jewelry Making,* 1955.

WINTER, EDWARD. *Enamel Art on Metals,* 1958.

Index